what did you eat yesterday? 1
fumi yoshinaga

VERTICAL.

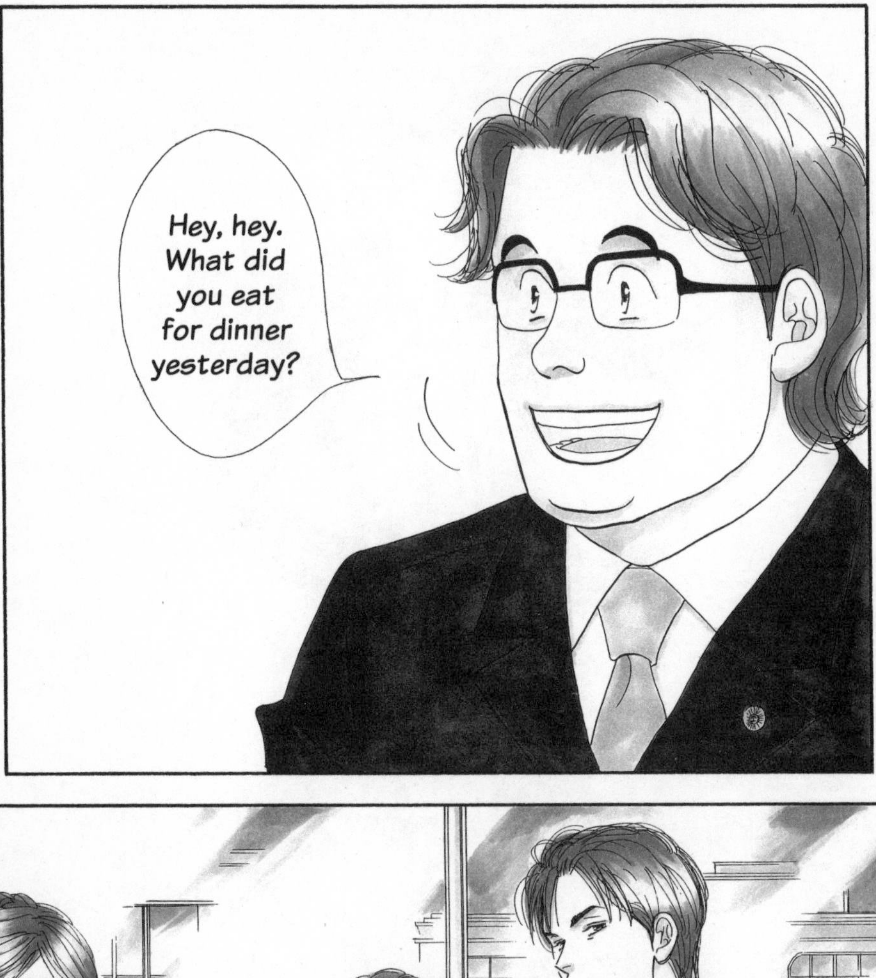
Hey, hey. What did you eat for dinner yesterday?
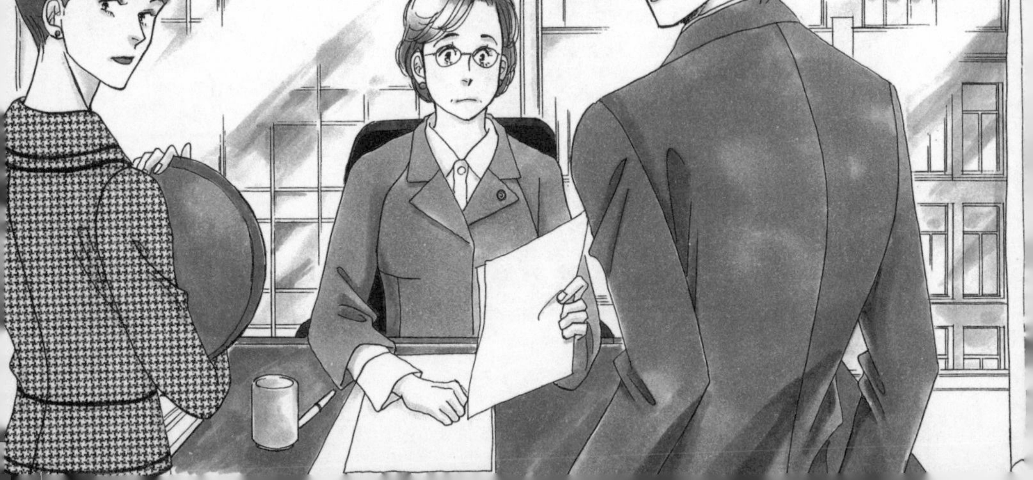

\#1

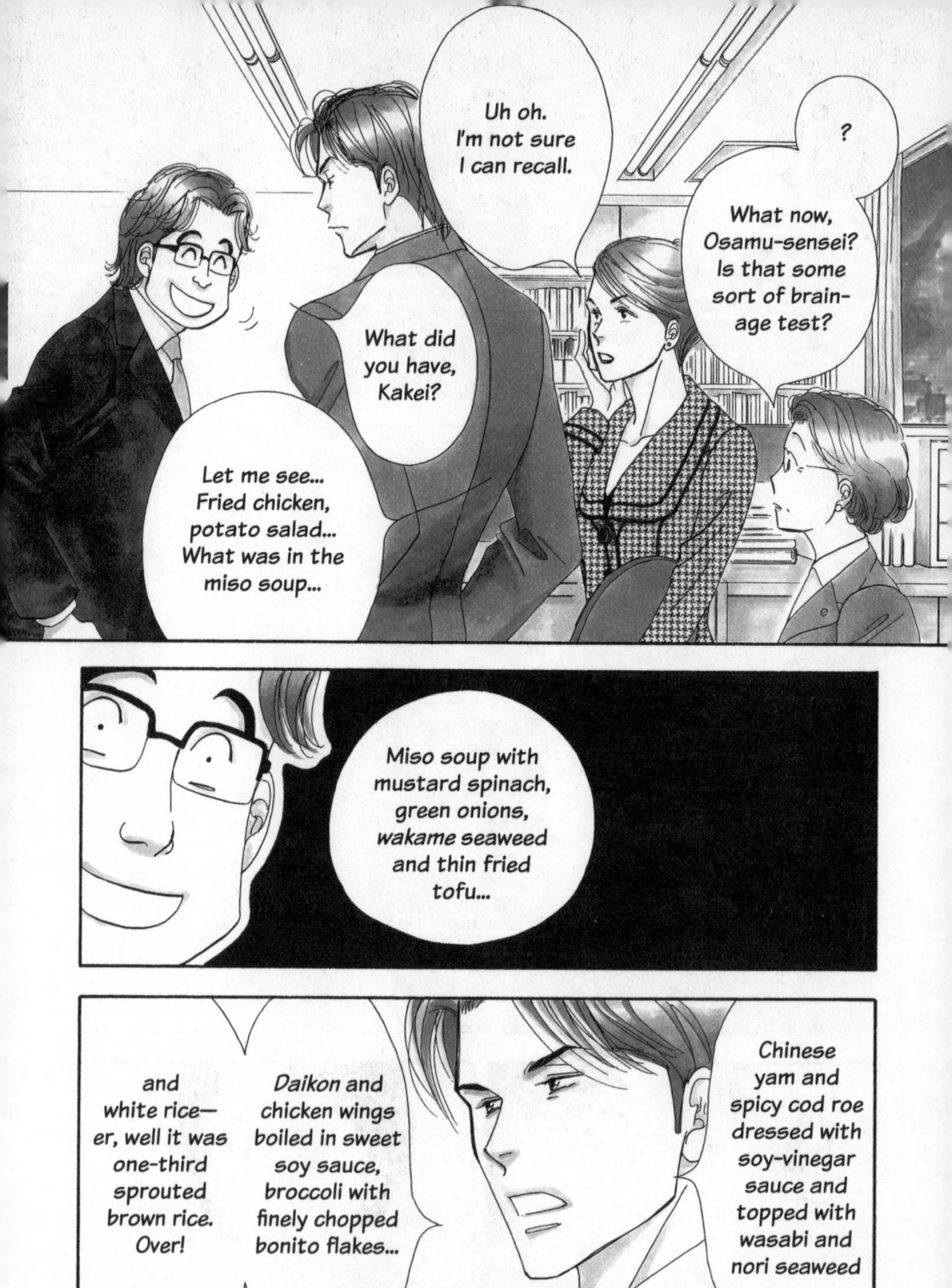
?
What now, Osamu-sensei? Is that some sort of brain-age test?
Uh oh. I'm not sure I can recall.
What did you have, Kakei?
Let me see... Fried chicken, potato salad... What was in the miso soup...
Miso soup with mustard spinach, green onions, *wakame* seaweed and thin fried tofu...
Chinese yam and spicy cod roe dressed with soy-vinegar sauce and topped with wasabi and nori seaweed ...
Daikon and chicken wings boiled in sweet soy sauce, broccoli with finely chopped bonito flakes...
and white rice— er, well it was one-third sprouted brown rice. Over!

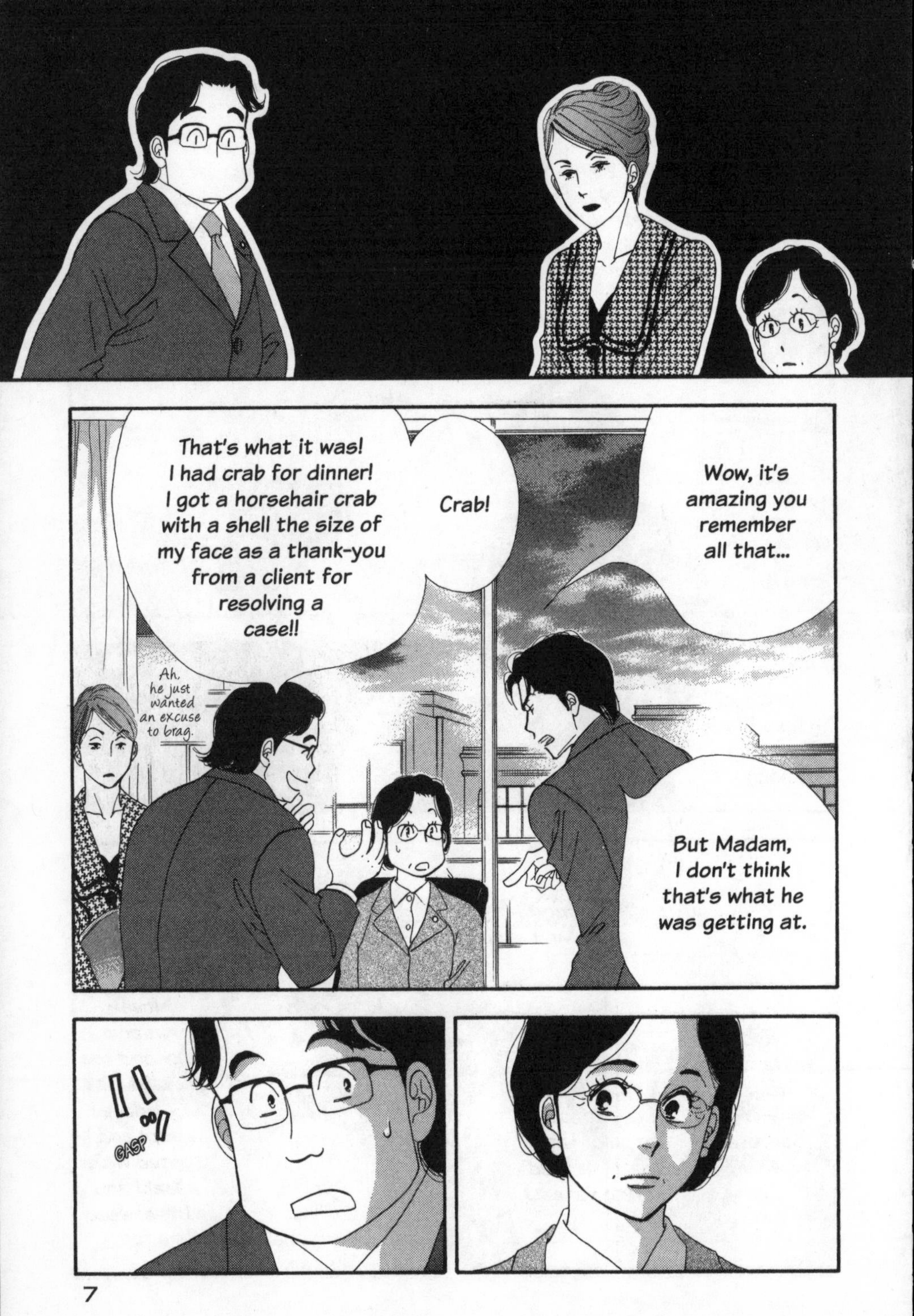
Wow, it's amazing you remember all that...
Crab!
That's what it was! I had crab for dinner! I got a horsehair crab with a shell the size of my face as a thank-you from a client for resolving a case!!
But Madam, I don't think that's what he was getting at.
Ah, he just wanted an excuse to brag.
GASP

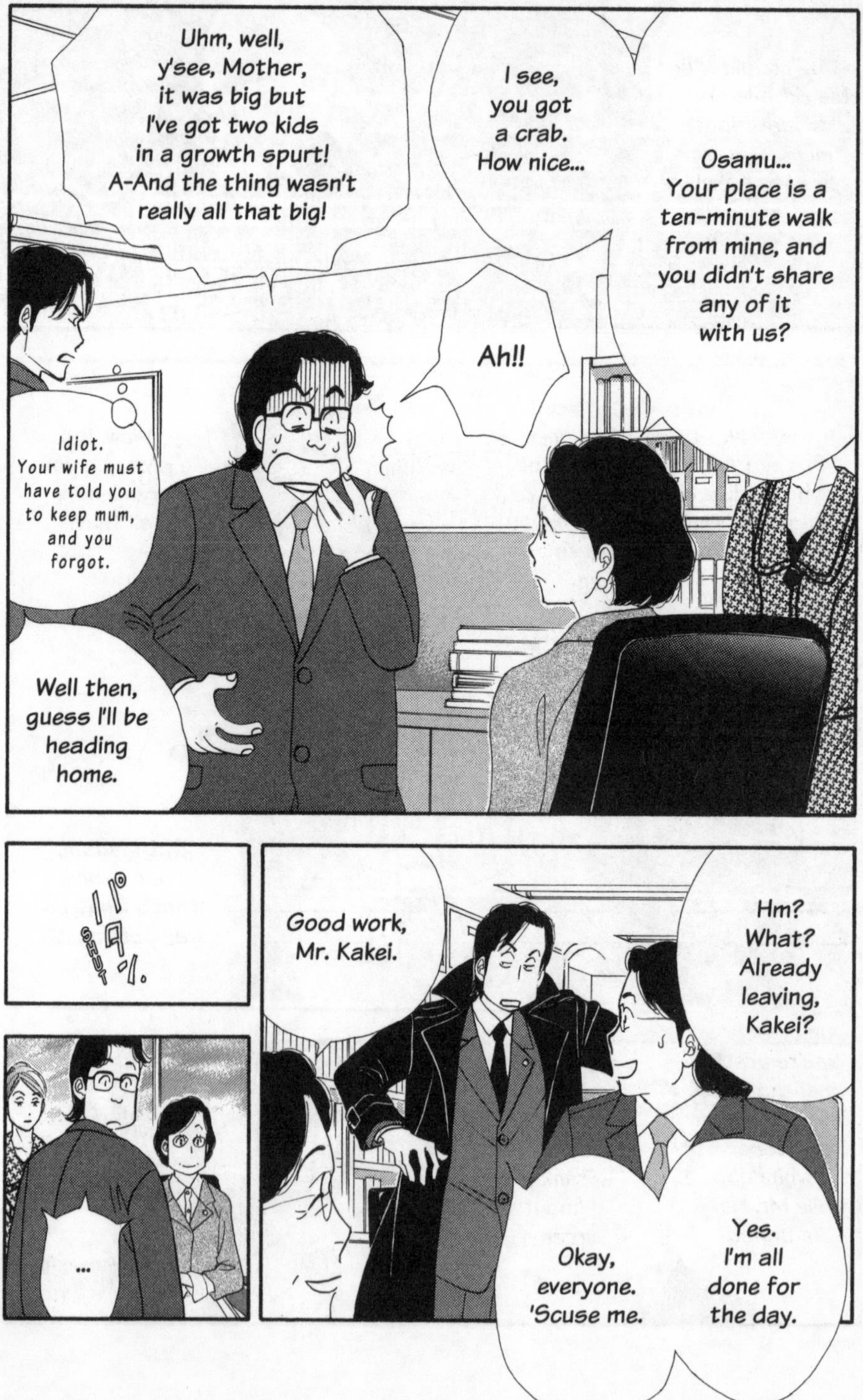
Osamu... Your place is a ten-minute walk from mine, and you didn't share any of it with us?
I see, you got a crab. How nice...
Ah!!
Uhm, well, y'see, Mother, it was big but I've got two kids in a growth spurt! A-And the thing wasn't really all that big!
Idiot. Your wife must have told you to keep mum, and you forgot.
Well then, guess I'll be heading home.
Hm? What? Already leaving, Kakei?
Good work, Mr. Kakei.
Yes. I'm all done for the day.
Okay, everyone. 'Scuse me.
パタン。
SHUT
...

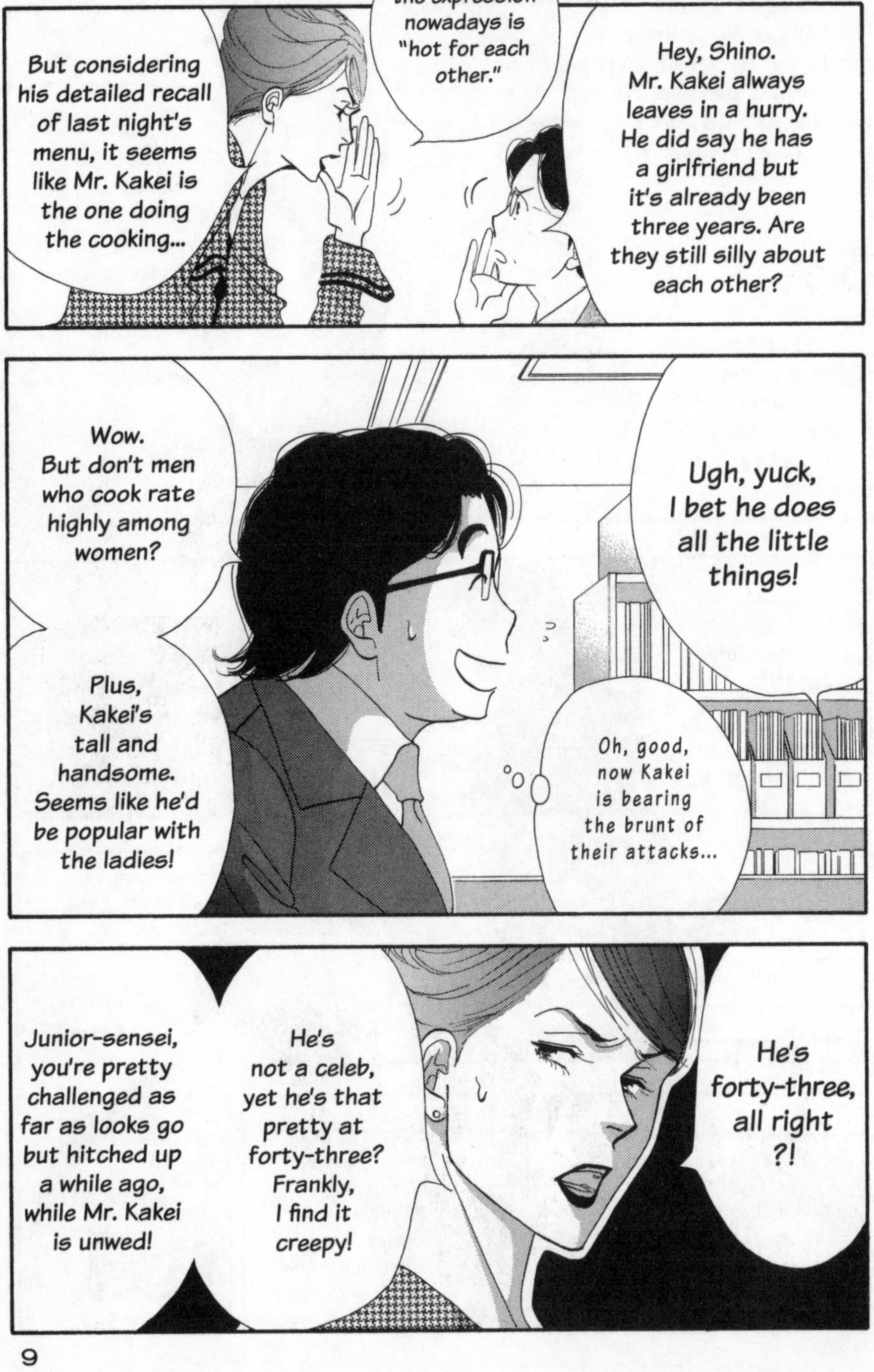
Hey, Shino. Mr. Kakei always leaves in a hurry. He did say he has a girlfriend but it's already been three years. Are they still silly about each other?
Madam, the expression nowadays is "hot for each other."
But considering his detailed recall of last night's menu, it seems like Mr. Kakei is the one doing the cooking...
Ugh, yuck, I bet he does all the little things!
Oh, good, now Kakei is bearing the brunt of their attacks...
Wow. But don't men who cook rate highly among women?
Plus, Kakei's tall and handsome. Seems like he'd be popular with the ladies!
He's forty-three, all right ?!
He's not a celeb, yet he's that pretty at forty-three? Frankly, I find it creepy!
Junior-sensei, you're pretty challenged as far as looks go but hitched up a while ago, while Mr. Kakei is unwed!

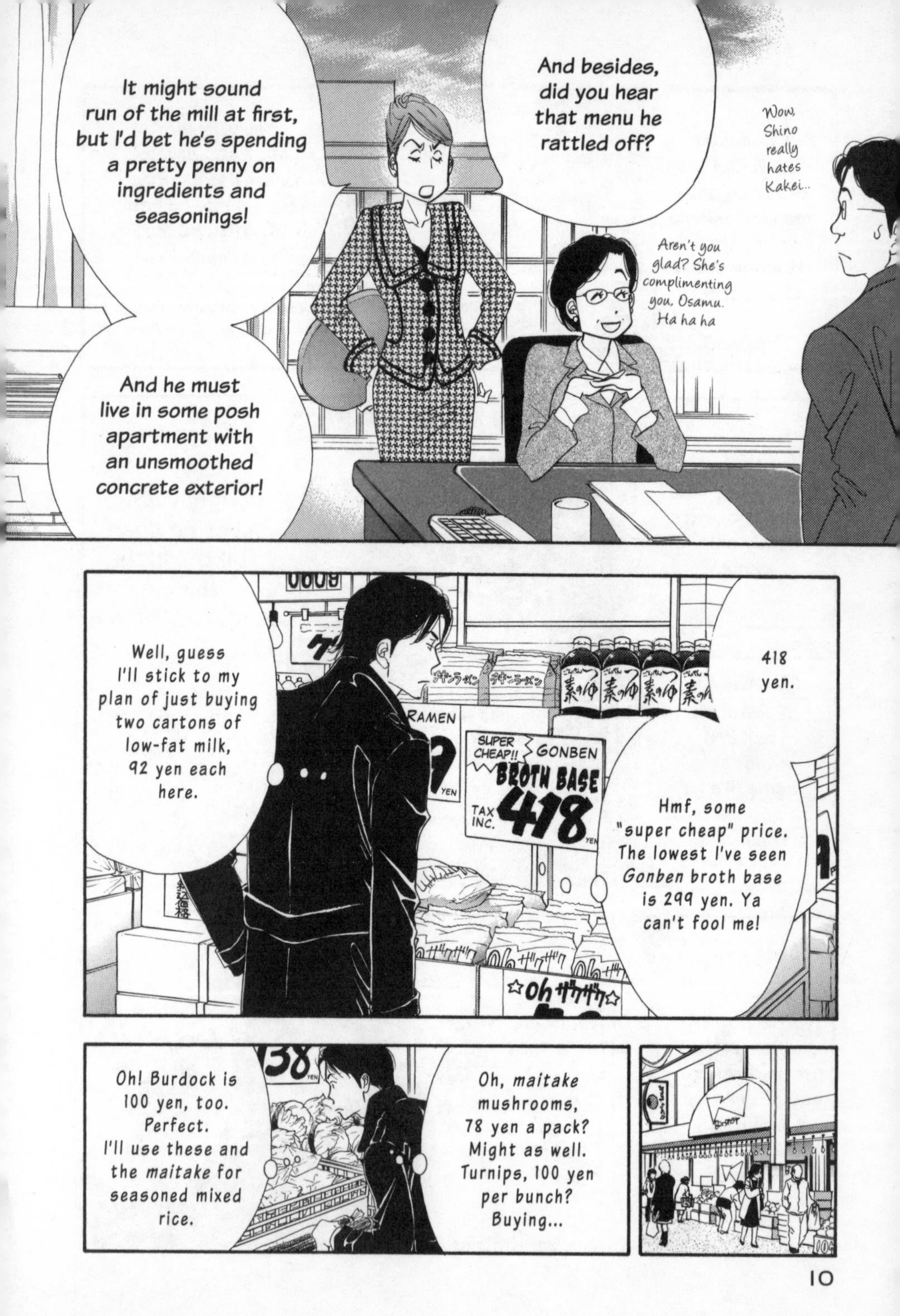

And besides, did you hear that menu he rattled off?
Wow, Shino really hates Kakei...
It might sound run of the mill at first, but I'd bet he's spending a pretty penny on ingredients and seasonings!
Aren't you glad? She's complimenting you, Osamu. Ha ha ha
And he must live in some posh apartment with an unsmoothed concrete exterior!
418 yen.
SUPER CHEAP!! GONBEN BROTH BASE TAX INC. 418 YEN
RAMEN
Hmf, some "super cheap" price. The lowest I've seen *Gonben* broth base is 299 yen. Ya can't fool me!
Well, guess I'll stick to my plan of just buying two cartons of low-fat milk, 92 yen each here.
Oh, *maitake* mushrooms, 78 yen a pack? Might as well. Turnips, 100 yen per bunch? Buying...
Oh! Burdock is 100 yen, too. Perfect. I'll use these and the *maitake* for seasoned mixed rice.

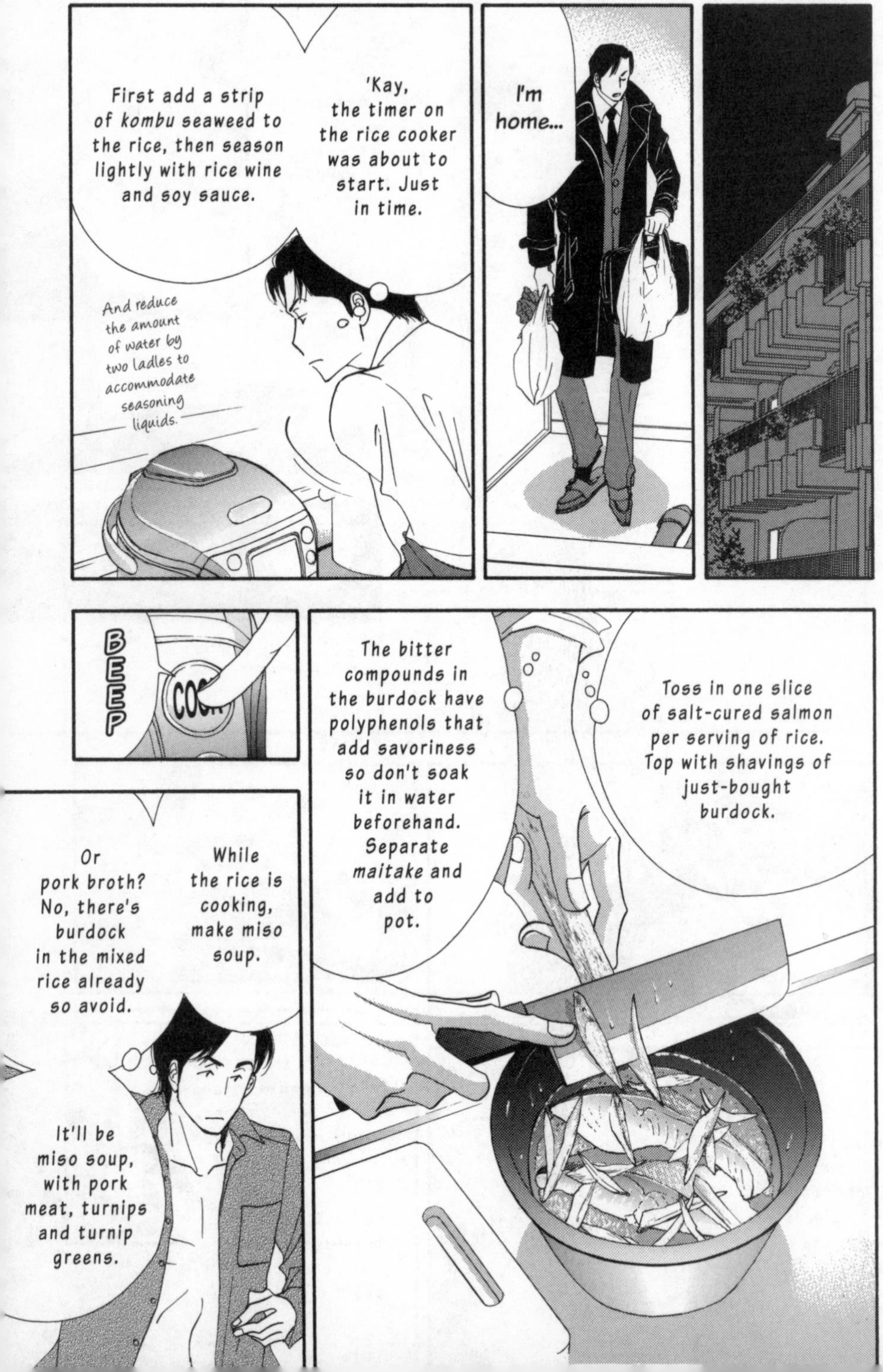
I'm home...
'Kay, the timer on the rice cooker was about to start. Just in time.
First add a strip of *kombu* seaweed to the rice, then season lightly with rice wine and soy sauce.
And reduce the amount of water by two ladles to accommodate seasoning liquids.
Toss in one slice of salt-cured salmon per serving of rice. Top with shavings of just-bought burdock.
The bitter compounds in the burdock have polyphenols that add savoriness so don't soak it in water beforehand. Separate *maitake* and add to pot.
BEEP
COOK
While the rice is cooking, make miso soup.
Or pork broth? No, there's burdock in the mixed rice already so avoid.
It'll be miso soup, with pork meat, turnips and turnip greens.

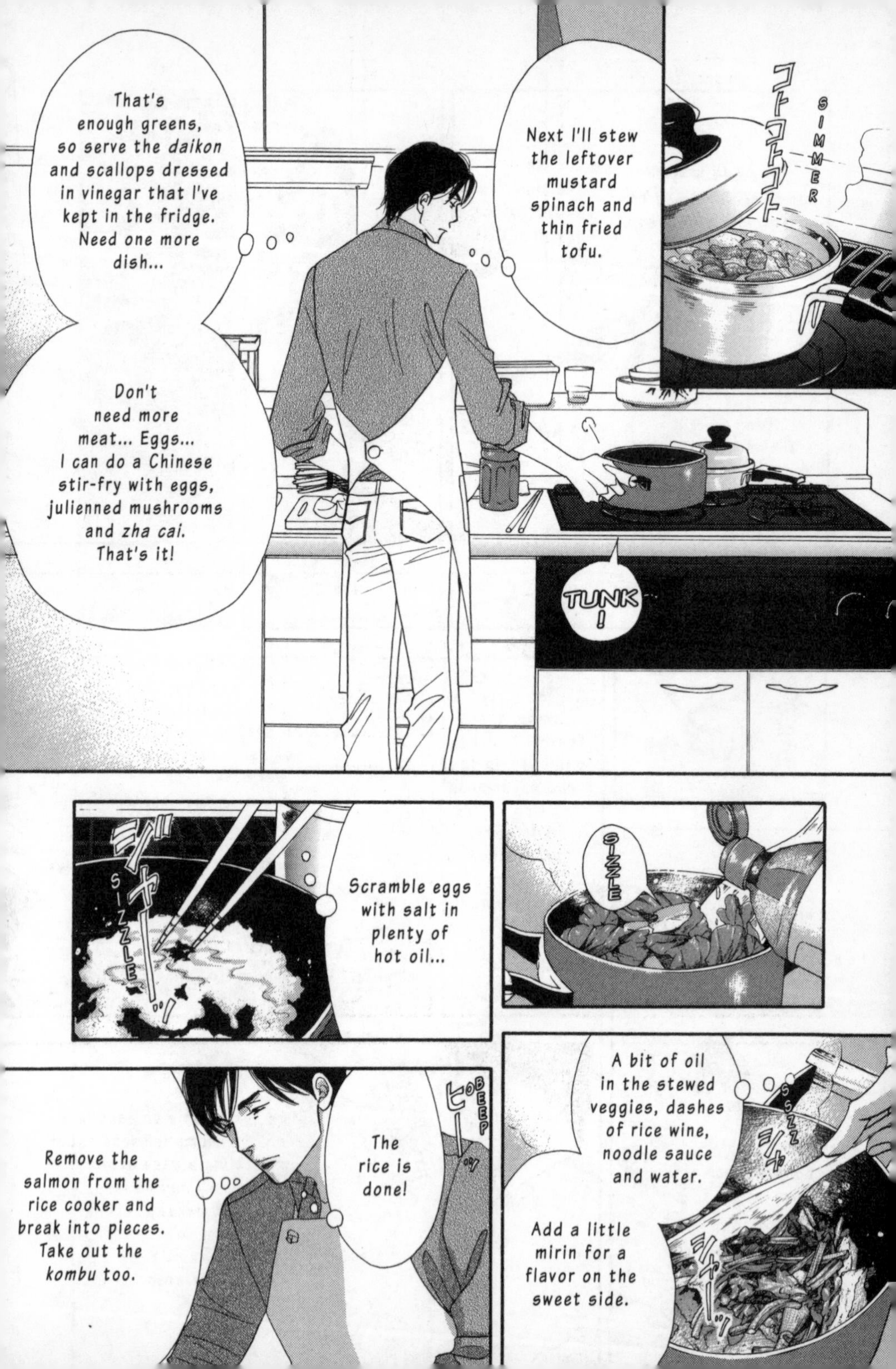
SIMMER
Next I'll stew the leftover mustard spinach and thin fried tofu.
That's enough greens, so serve the *daikon* and scallops dressed in vinegar that I've kept in the fridge. Need one more dish...
Don't need more meat... Eggs... I can do a Chinese stir-fry with eggs, julienned mushrooms and *zha cai*. That's it!
TUNK!
SIZZLE
Scramble eggs with salt in plenty of hot oil...
SIZZLE
A bit of oil in the stewed veggies, dashes of rice wine, noodle sauce and water.
SSZZ
Add a little mirin for a flavor on the sweet side.
BEEP
The rice is done!
Remove the salmon from the rice cooker and break into pieces. Take out the *kombu* too.

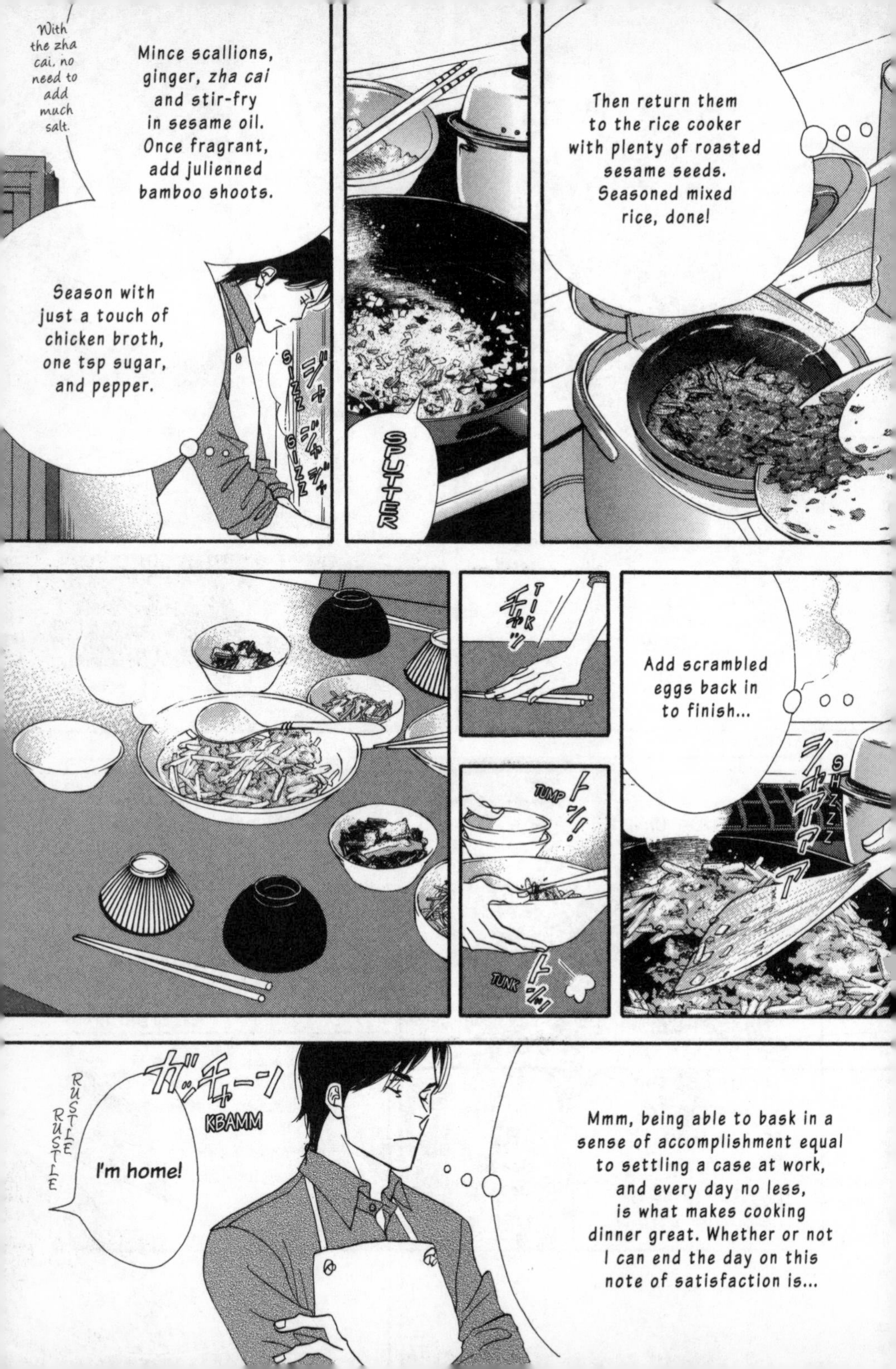

Then return them to the rice cooker with plenty of roasted sesame seeds. Seasoned mixed rice, done!
SPUTTER
Mince scallions, ginger, *zha cai* and stir-fry in sesame oil. Once fragrant, add julienned bamboo shoots.
With the zha cai, no need to add much salt.
Season with just a touch of chicken broth, one tsp sugar, and pepper.
SIZZ
SIZZ
Add scrambled eggs back in to finish...
SHZZZ
TIK
TUMP
TUNK
Mmm, being able to bask in a sense of accomplishment equal to settling a case at work, and every day no less, is what makes cooking dinner great. Whether or not I can end the day on this note of satisfaction is...
KBAMM
I'm home!
RUSTLE
RUSTLE

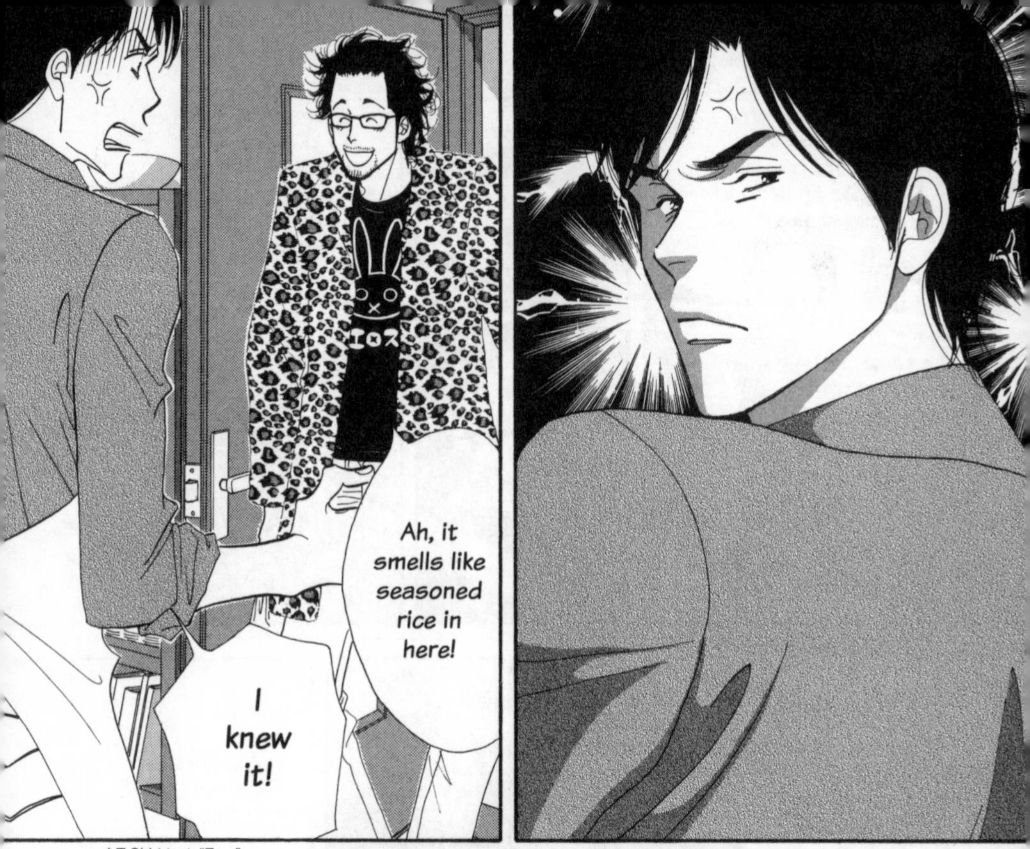
Ah, it smells like seasoned rice in here!
I knew it!

* T-Shirt text: "Eros"

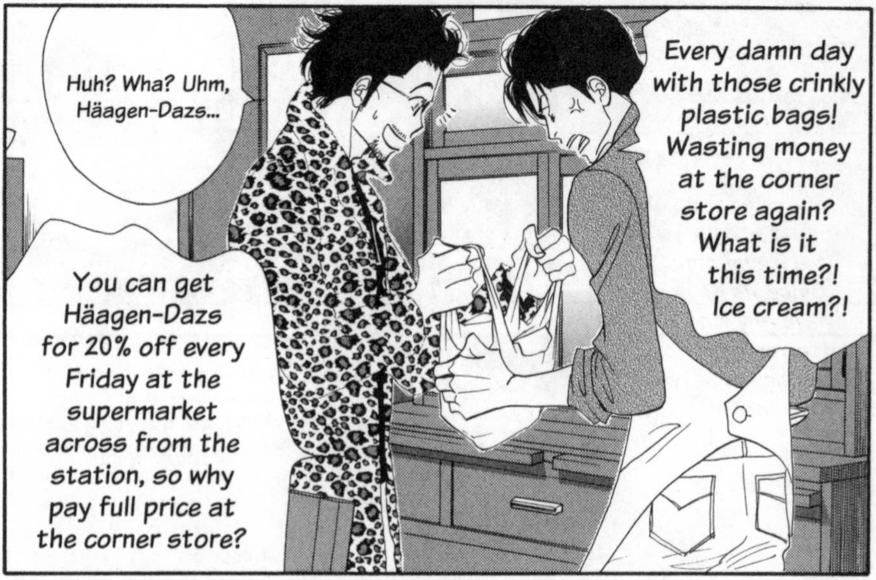
Every damn day with those crinkly plastic bags! Wasting money at the corner store again? What is it this time?! Ice cream?!
Huh? Wha? Uhm, Häagen-Dazs...
You can get Häagen-Dazs for 20% off every Friday at the supermarket across from the station, so why pay full price at the corner store?

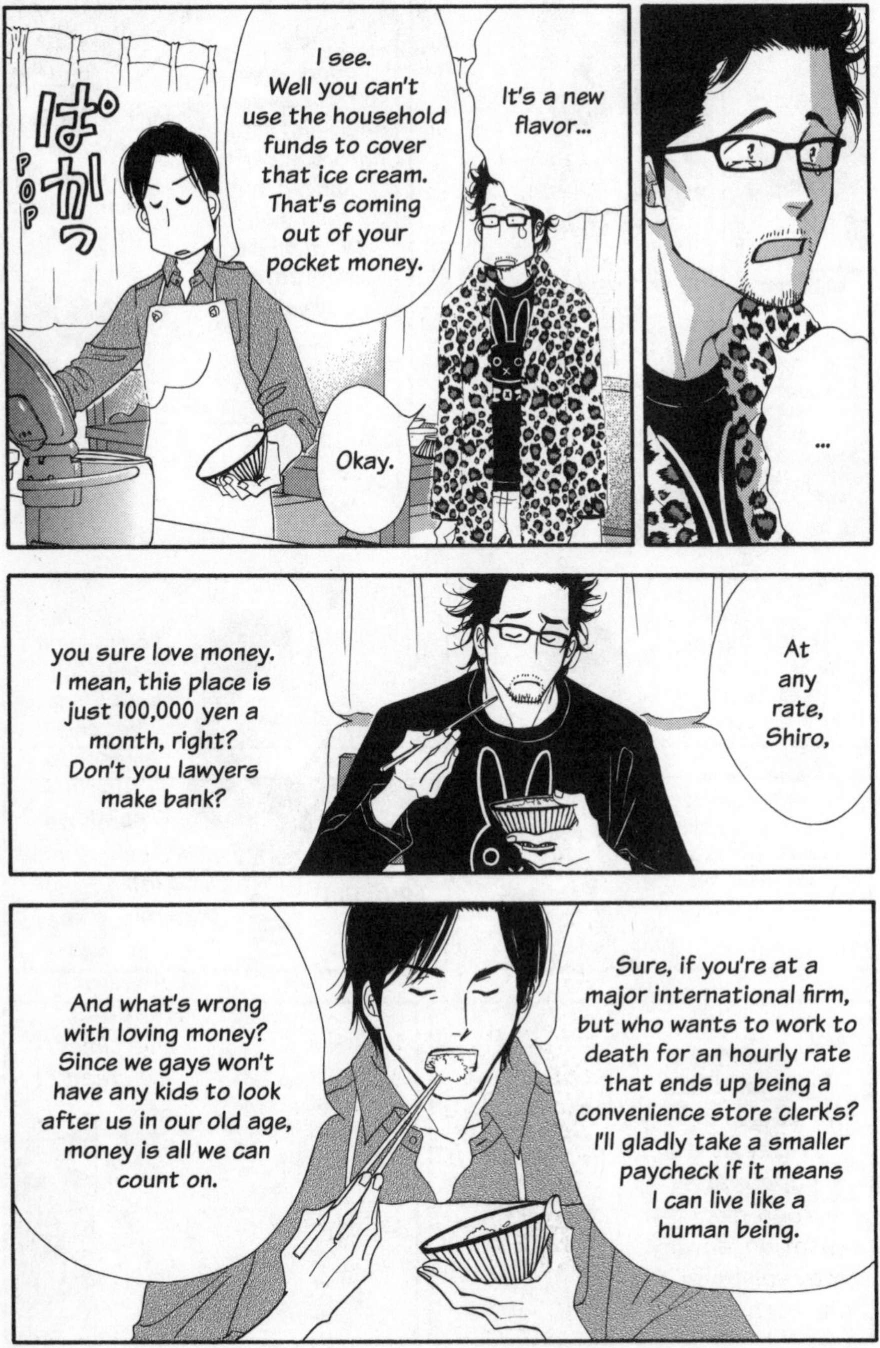
...
It's a new flavor...
I see. Well you can't use the household funds to cover that ice cream. That's coming out of your pocket money.
ぱかっ
POP
Okay.
At any rate, Shiro,
you sure love money. I mean, this place is just 100,000 yen a month, right? Don't you lawyers make bank?
Sure, if you're at a major international firm, but who wants to work to death for an hourly rate that ends up being a convenience store clerk's? I'll gladly take a smaller paycheck if it means I can live like a human being.
And what's wrong with loving money? Since we gays won't have any kids to look after us in our old age, money is all we can count on.

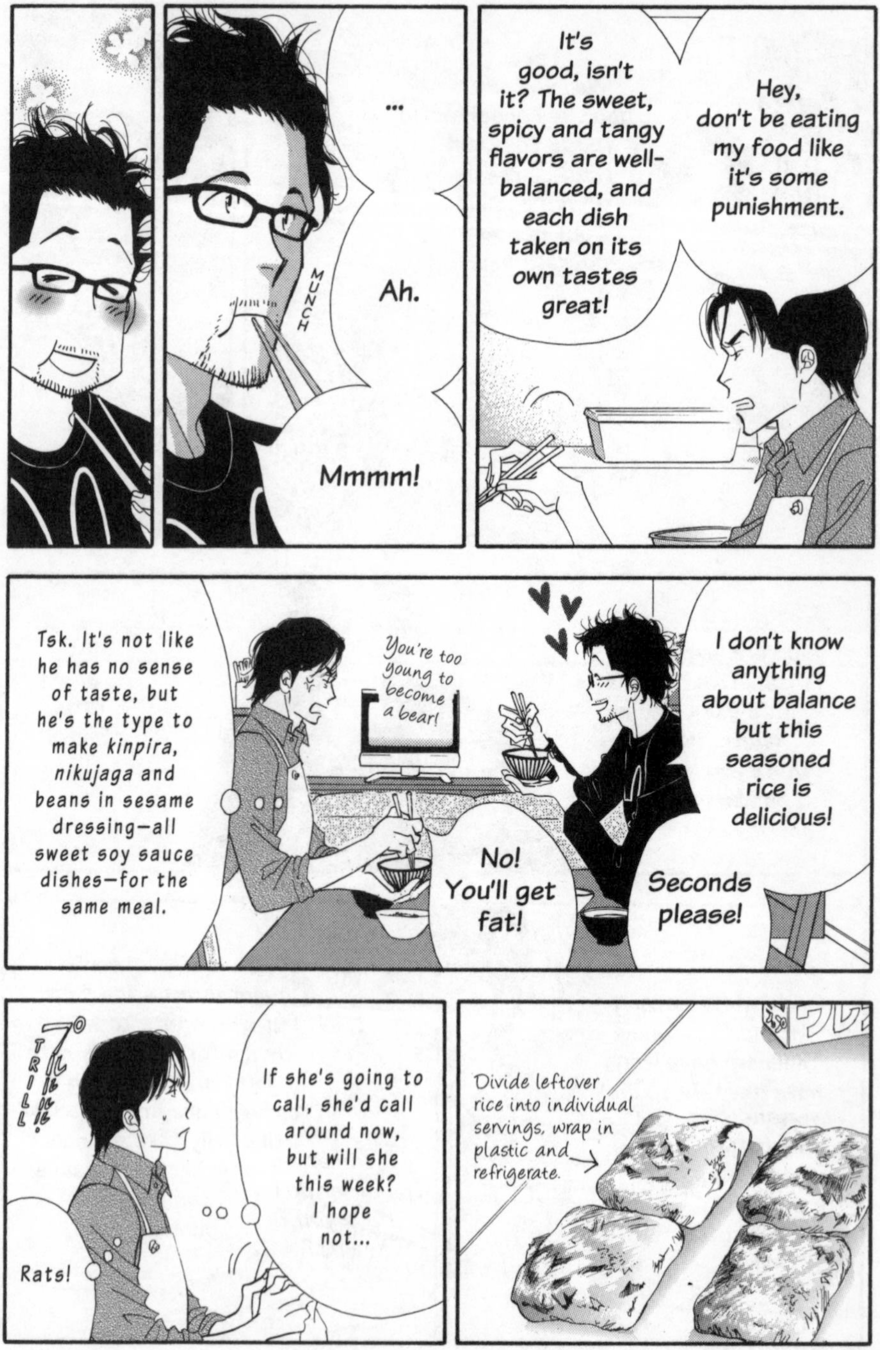
Hey, don't be eating my food like it's some punishment.
It's good, isn't it? The sweet, spicy and tangy flavors are well-balanced, and each dish taken on its own tastes great!
...
MUNCH
Ah.
Mmmm!
I don't know anything about balance but this seasoned rice is delicious!
Seconds please!
No! You'll get fat!
You're too young to become a bear!
Tsk. It's not like he has no sense of taste, but he's the type to make *kinpira*, *nikujaga* and beans in sesame dressing—all sweet soy sauce dishes—for the same meal.
Divide leftover rice into individual servings, wrap in plastic and refrigerate.
TRILL
If she's going to call, she'd call around now, but will she this week? I hope not...
Rats!

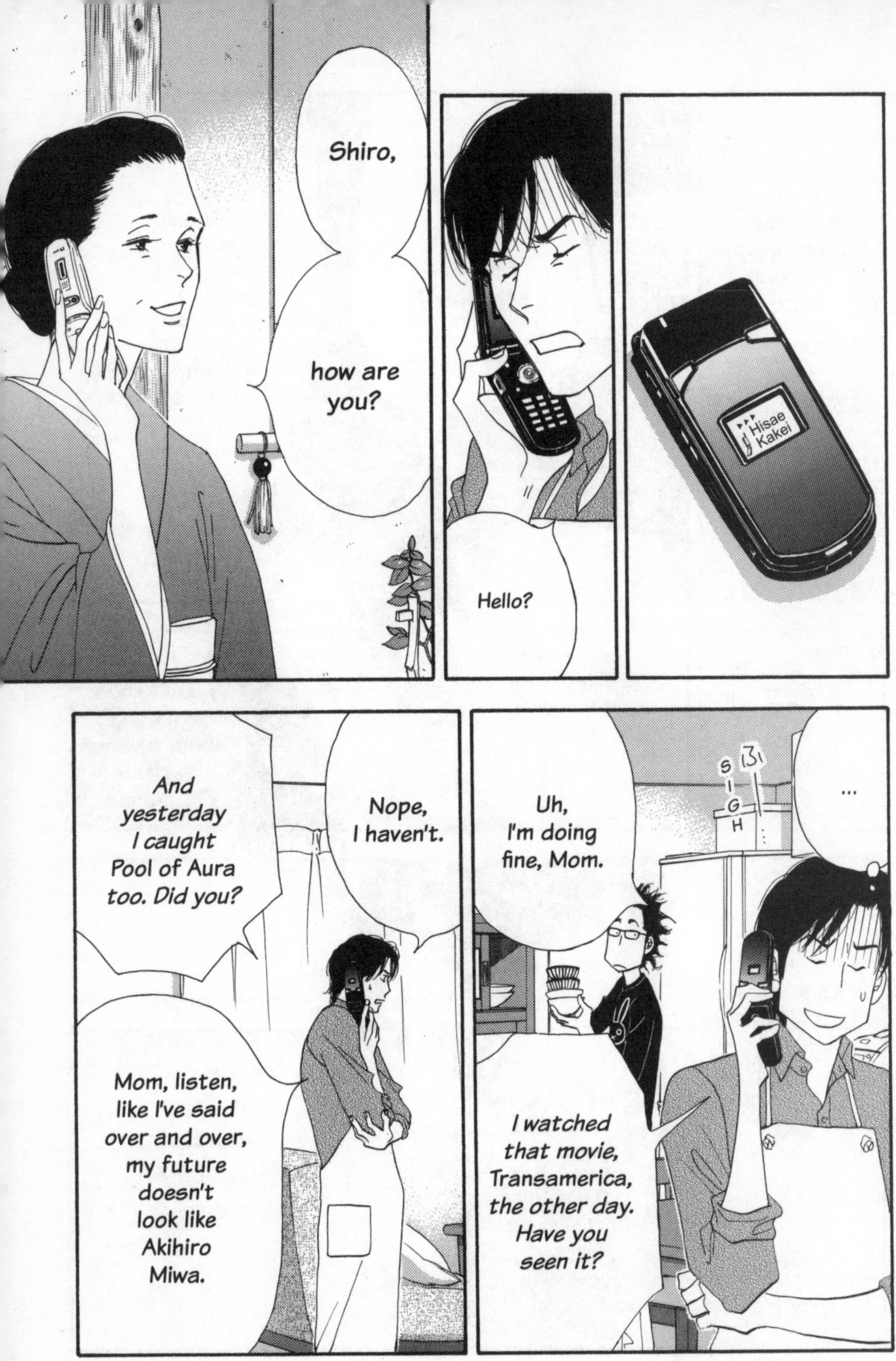
Hisae Kakei
Hello?
Shiro,
how are you?
...
S I G H
ふぃ
Uh, I'm doing fine, Mom.
I watched that movie, Transamerica, the other day. Have you seen it?
Nope, I haven't.
And yesterday I caught Pool of Aura too. Did you?
Mom, listen, like I've said over and over, my future doesn't look like Akihiro Miwa.

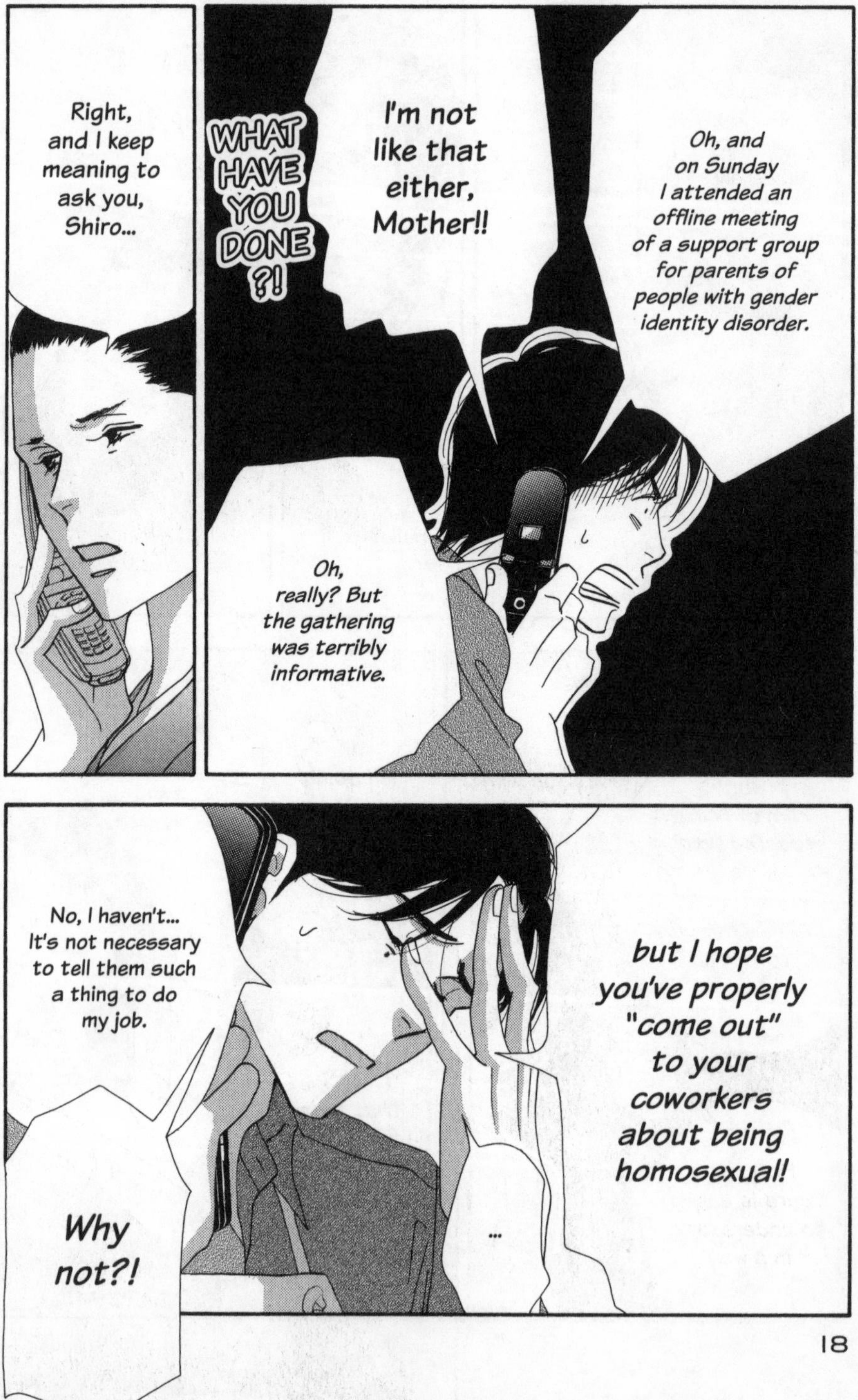
Oh, and on Sunday I attended an offline meeting of a support group for parents of people with gender identity disorder.
I'm not like that either, Mother!!
WHAT HAVE YOU DONE?!
Oh, really? But the gathering was terribly informative.
Right, and I keep meaning to ask you, Shiro...
but I hope you've properly "come out" to your coworkers about being homosexual!
No, I haven't... It's not necessary to tell them such a thing to do my job.
...
Why not?!

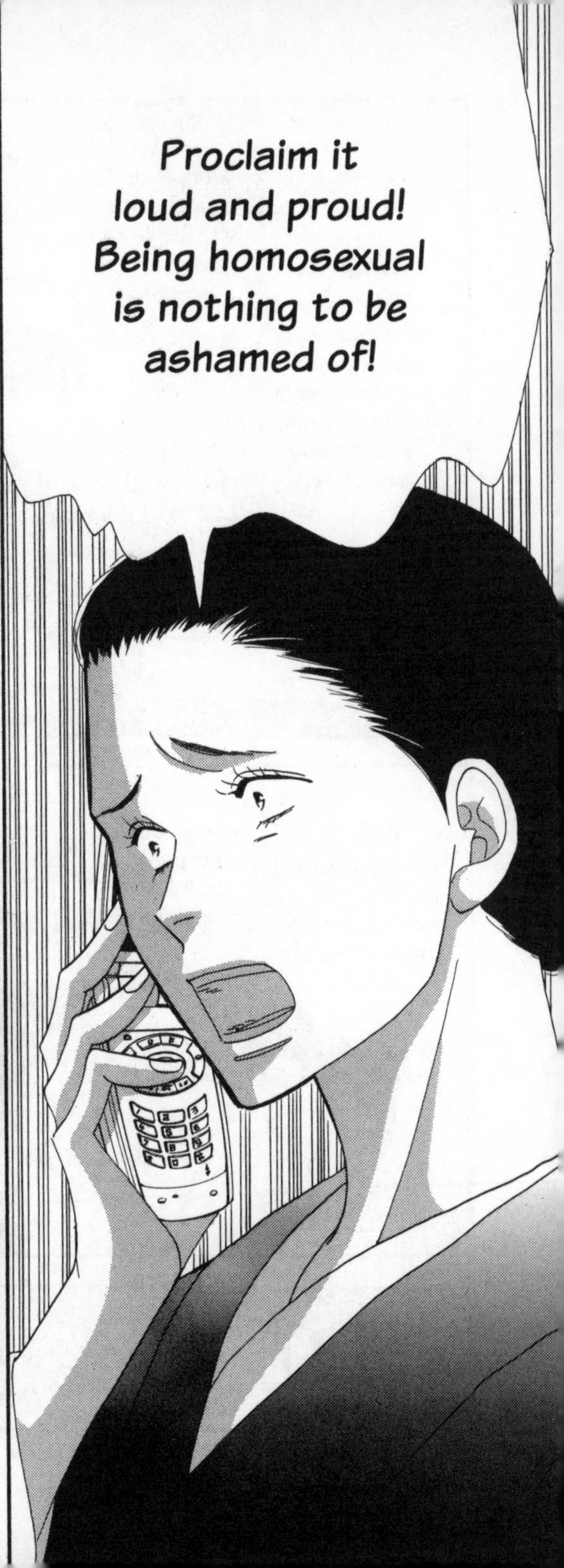
Proclaim it loud and proud! Being homosexual is nothing to be ashamed of!

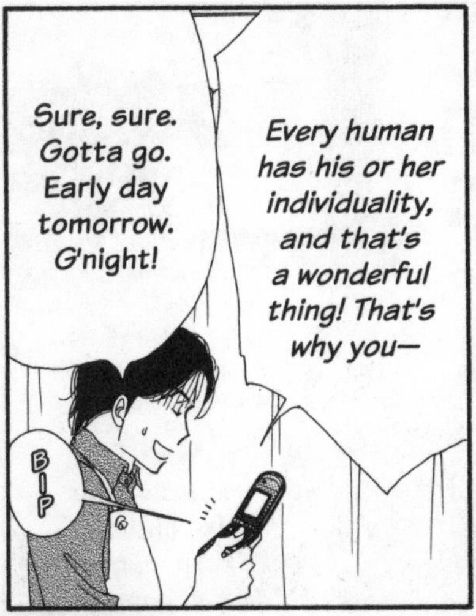
Every human has his or her individuality, and that's a wonderful thing! That's why you—
Sure, sure. Gotta go. Early day tomorrow. G'night!
BIP

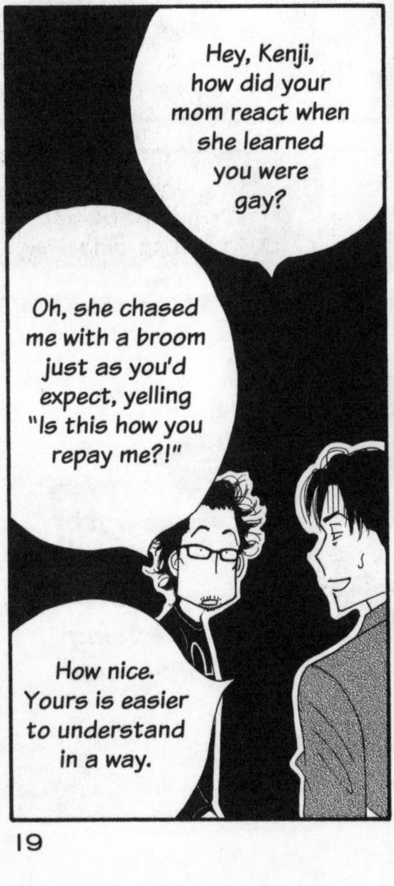
Hey, Kenji, how did your mom react when she learned you were gay?
Oh, she chased me with a broom just as you'd expect, yelling "Is this how you repay me?!"
How nice. Yours is easier to understand in a way.

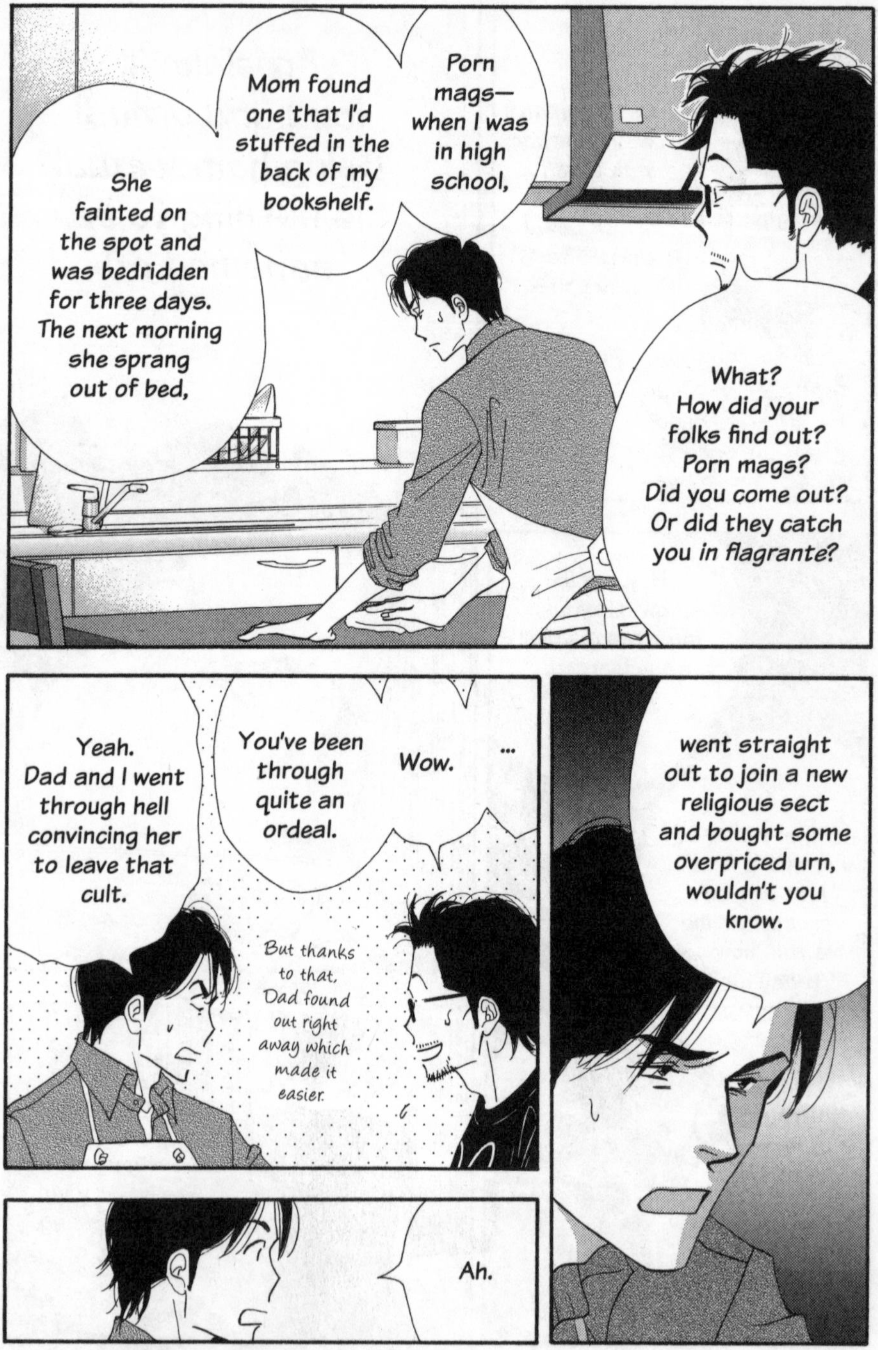
What? How did your folks find out? Porn mags? Did you come out? Or did they catch you in flagrante?
Porn mags— when I was in high school,
Mom found one that I'd stuffed in the back of my bookshelf.
She fainted on the spot and was bedridden for three days. The next morning she sprang out of bed,
went straight out to join a new religious sect and bought some overpriced urn, wouldn't you know.
...
Wow.
You've been through quite an ordeal.
Yeah. Dad and I went through hell convincing her to leave that cult.
But thanks to that, Dad found out right away which made it easier.
Ah.

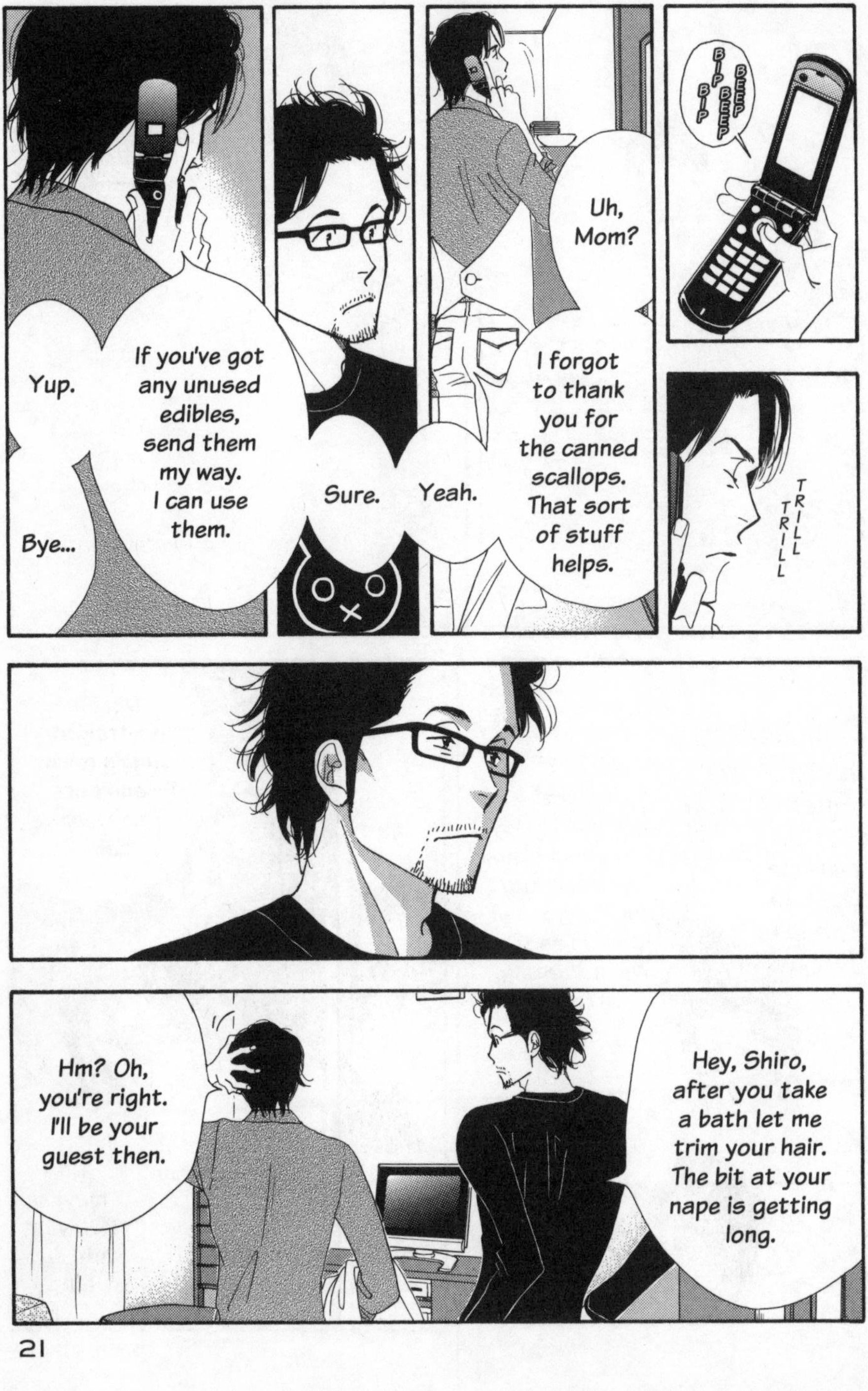
BIP BIP BEEP BEEP
TRILL TRILL
Uh, Mom?
I forgot to thank you for the canned scallops. That sort of stuff helps.
Yeah.
Sure.
If you've got any unused edibles, send them my way. I can use them.
Yup.
Bye...
Hey, Shiro, after you take a bath let me trim your hair. The bit at your nape is getting long.
Hm? Oh, you're right. I'll be your guest then.

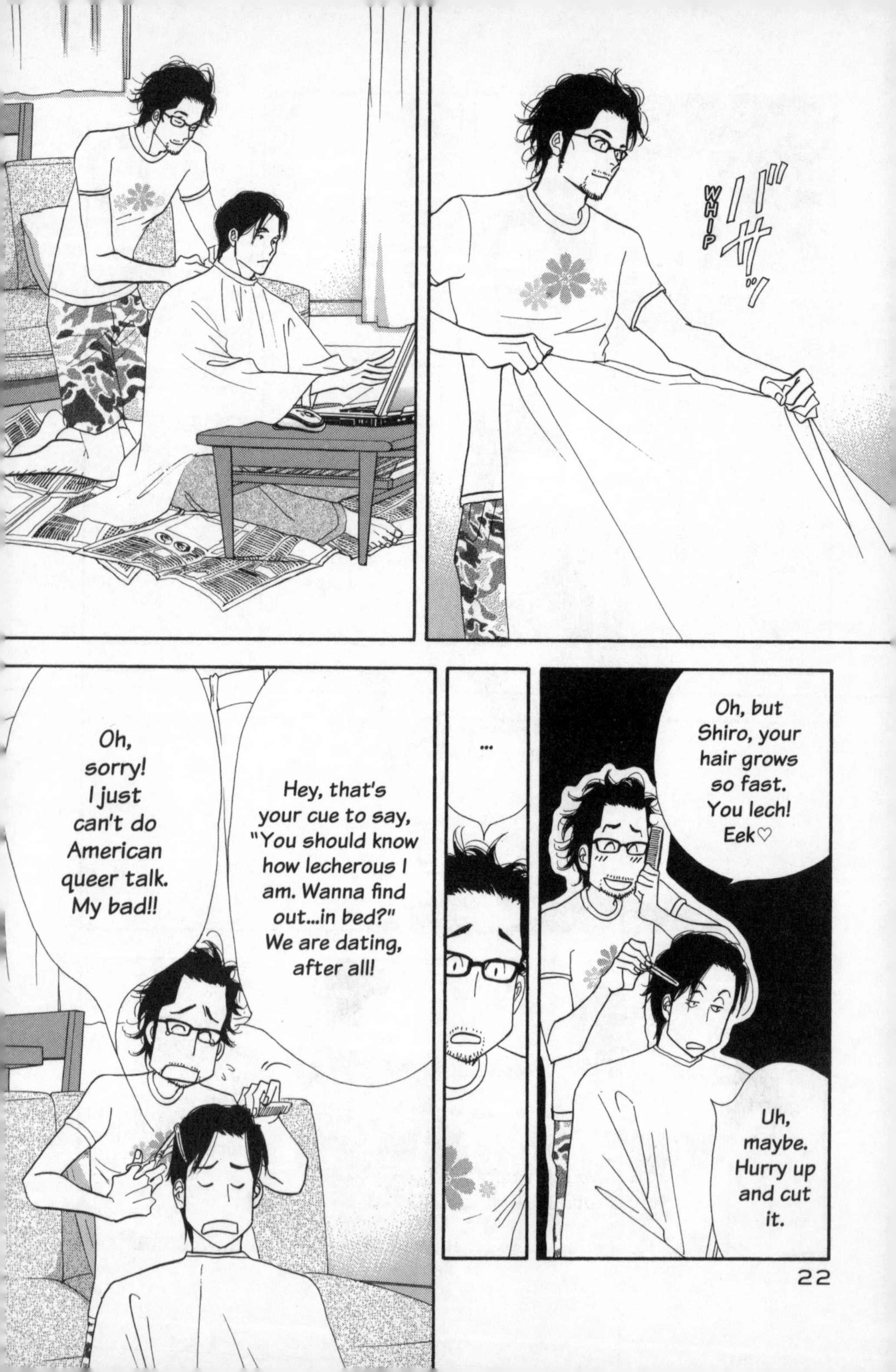

WHIP
バサッ
Oh, but Shiro, your hair grows so fast. You lech! Eek♡
Uh, maybe. Hurry up and cut it.
...
Hey, that's your cue to say, "You should know how lecherous I am. Wanna find out...in bed?" We are dating, after all!
Oh, sorry! I just can't do American queer talk. My bad!!

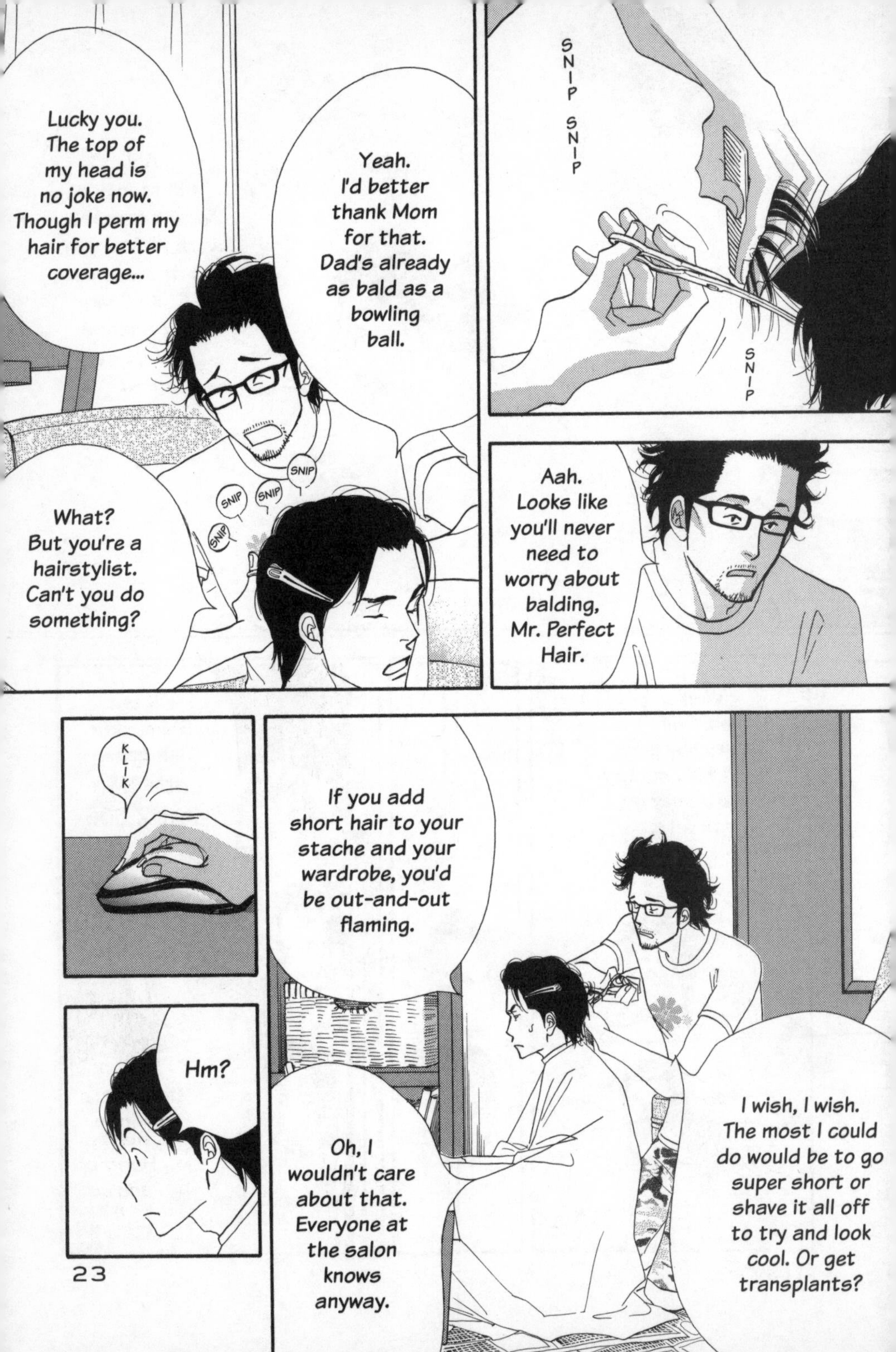
SNIP SNIP
SNIP
Aah. Looks like you'll never need to worry about balding, Mr. Perfect Hair.
Yeah. I'd better thank Mom for that. Dad's already as bald as a bowling ball.
Lucky you. The top of my head is no joke now. Though I perm my hair for better coverage...
SNIP
SNIP
SNIP
SNIP
What? But you're a hairstylist. Can't you do something?
I wish, I wish. The most I could do would be to go super short or shave it all off to try and look cool. Or get transplants?
If you add short hair to your stache and your wardrobe, you'd be out-and-out flaming.
Oh, I wouldn't care about that. Everyone at the salon knows anyway.
KLIK
Hm?

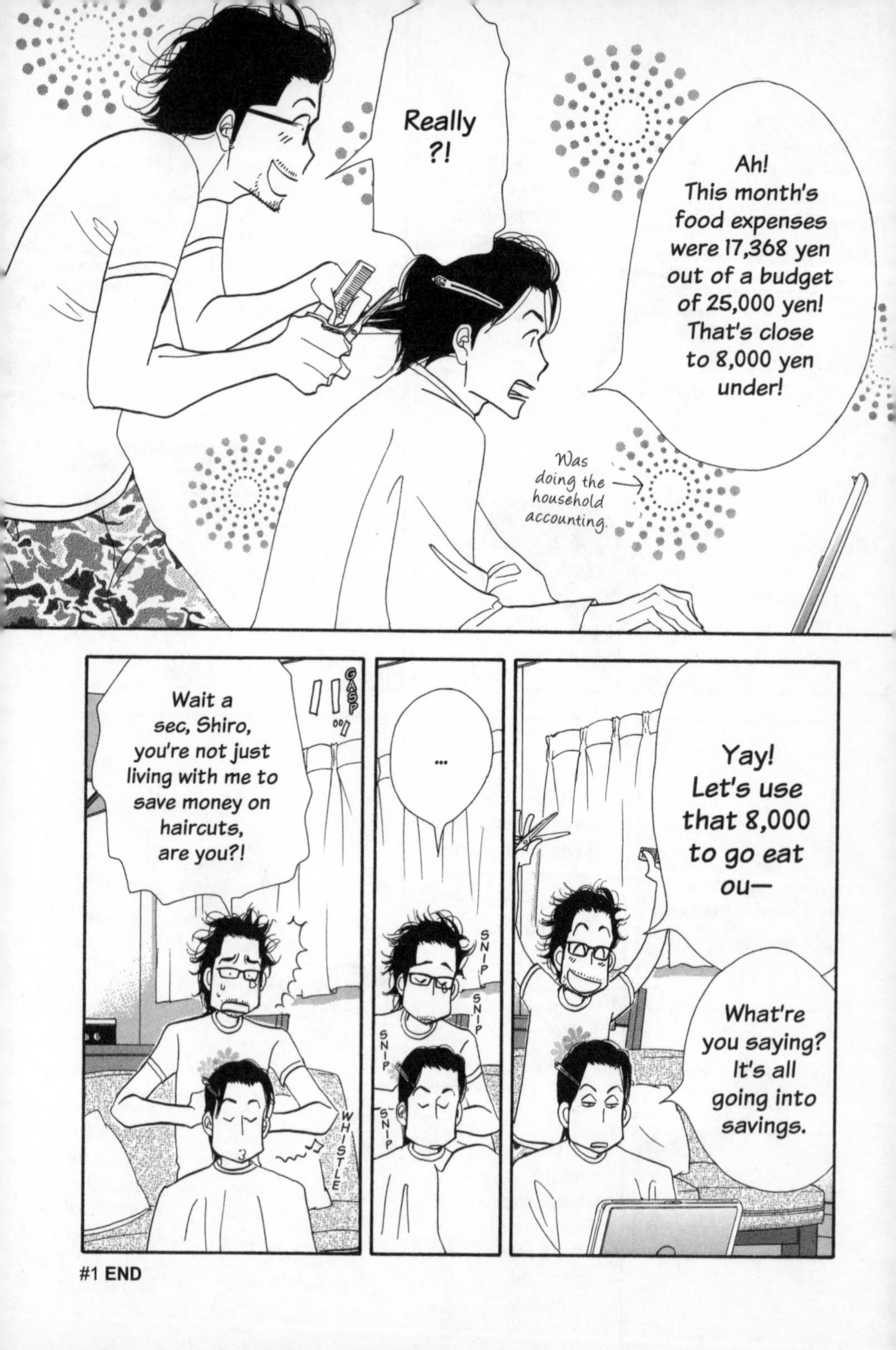
Ah! This month's food expenses were 17,368 yen out of a budget of 25,000 yen! That's close to 8,000 yen under!
Really?!
Was doing the household accounting.
Yay! Let's use that 8,000 to go eat ou—
What're you saying? It's all going into savings.
...
SNIP
SNIP
SNIP
SNIP
GASP
Wait a sec, Shiro, you're not just living with me to save money on haircuts, are you?!
WHISTLE

#1 END

Mitsuba (Japanese parsley) and nori seaweed also go with salmon-and-burdock seasoned mixed rice. Garnish with salmon roe when serving to guests.

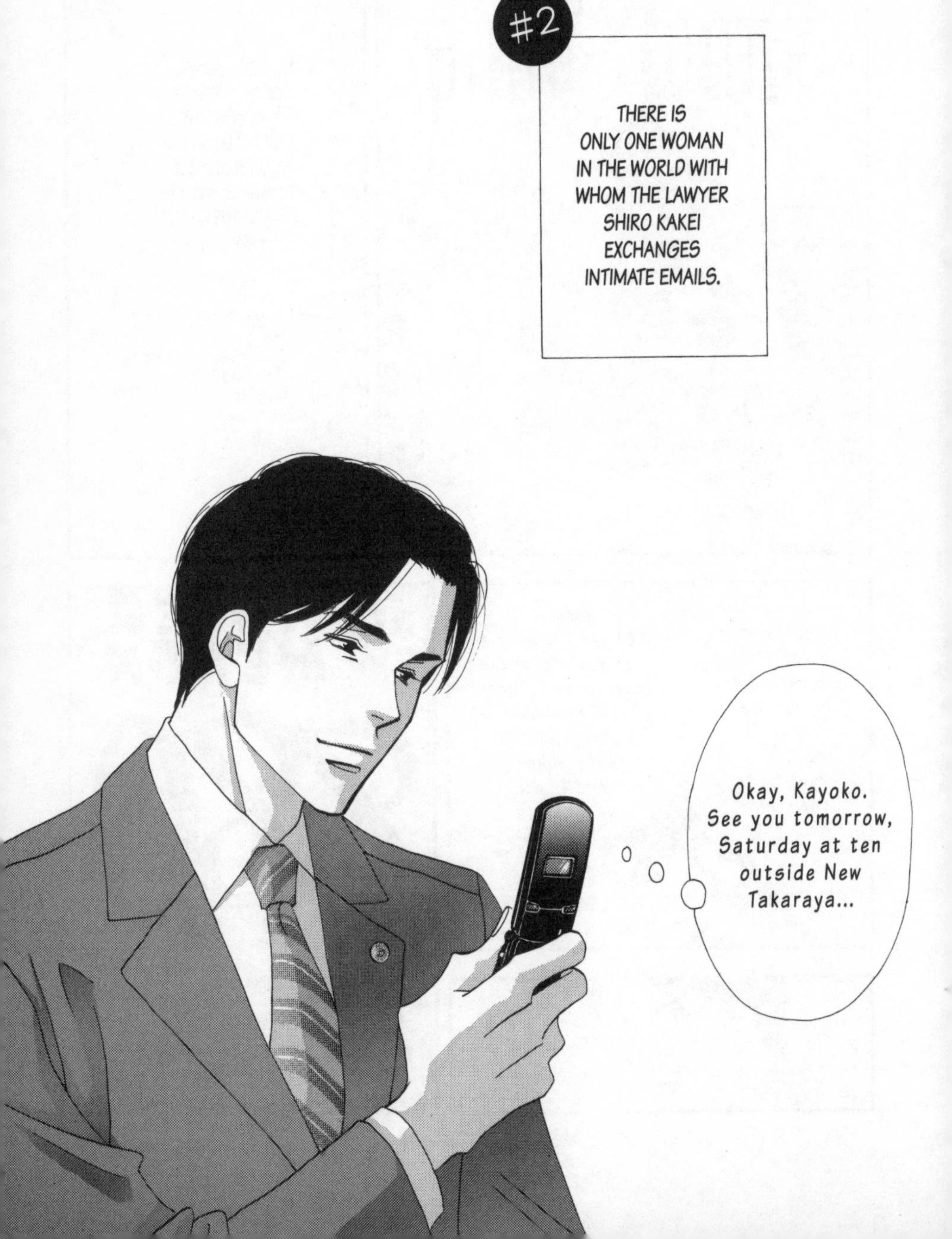
#2
THERE IS ONLY ONE WOMAN IN THE WORLD WITH WHOM THE LAWYER SHIRO KAKEI EXCHANGES INTIMATE EMAILS.
Okay, Kayoko. See you tomorrow, Saturday at ten outside New Takaraya...

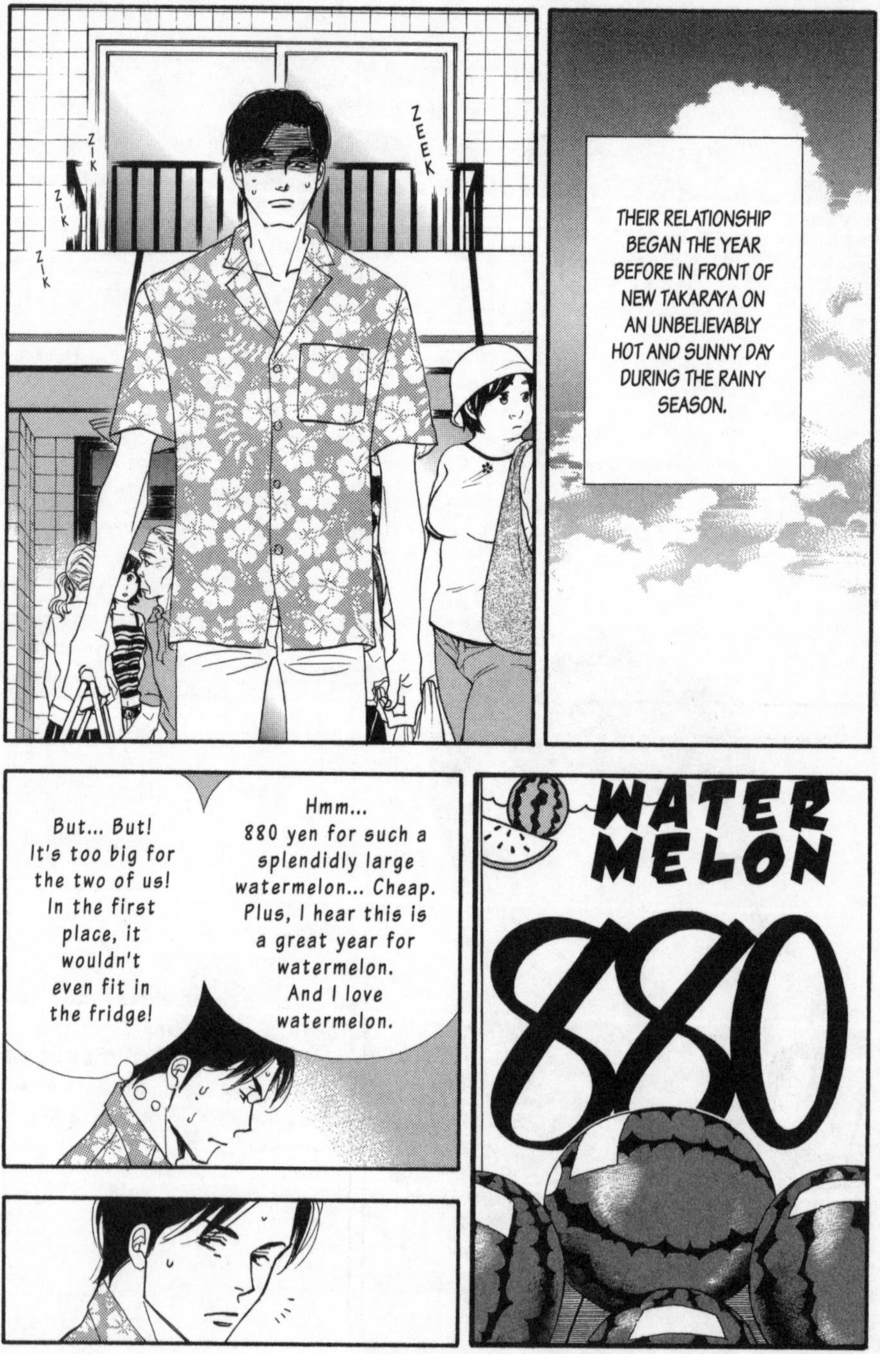
THEIR RELATIONSHIP BEGAN THE YEAR BEFORE IN FRONT OF NEW TAKARAYA ON AN UNBELIEVABLY HOT AND SUNNY DAY DURING THE RAINY SEASON.
ZEEK
ZIK
ZIK
ZIK
WATER MELON
880
Hmm... 880 yen for such a splendidly large watermelon... Cheap. Plus, I hear this is a great year for watermelon. And I love watermelon.
But... But! It's too big for the two of us! In the first place, it wouldn't even fit in the fridge!

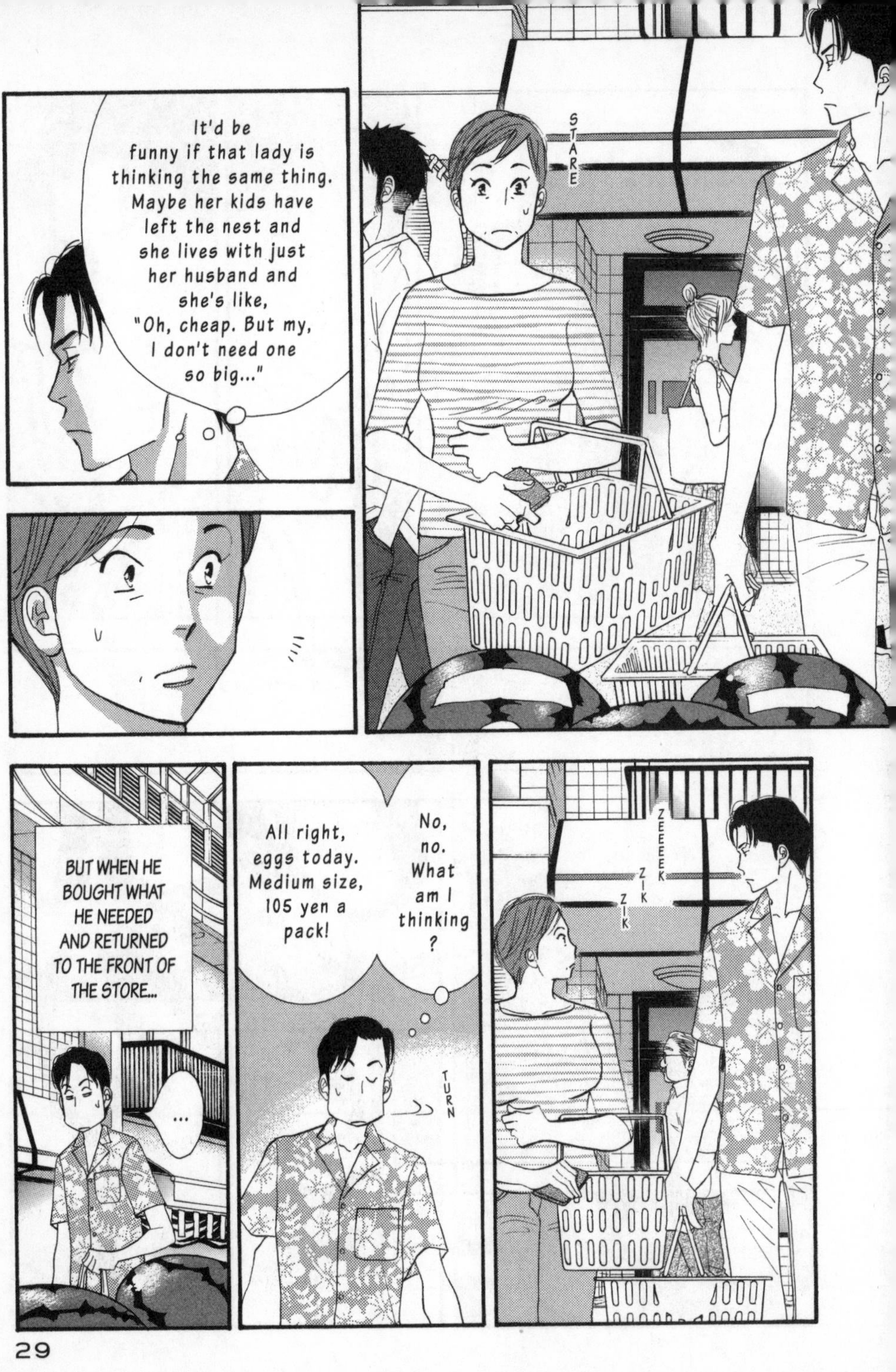
STARE
It'd be funny if that lady is thinking the same thing. Maybe her kids have left the nest and she lives with just her husband and she's like, "Oh, cheap. But my, I don't need one so big..."
ZEEEEK
ZIK
ZIK
No, no. What am I thinking?
All right, eggs today. Medium size, 105 yen a pack!
TURN
BUT WHEN HE BOUGHT WHAT HE NEEDED AND RETURNED TO THE FRONT OF THE STORE...
...

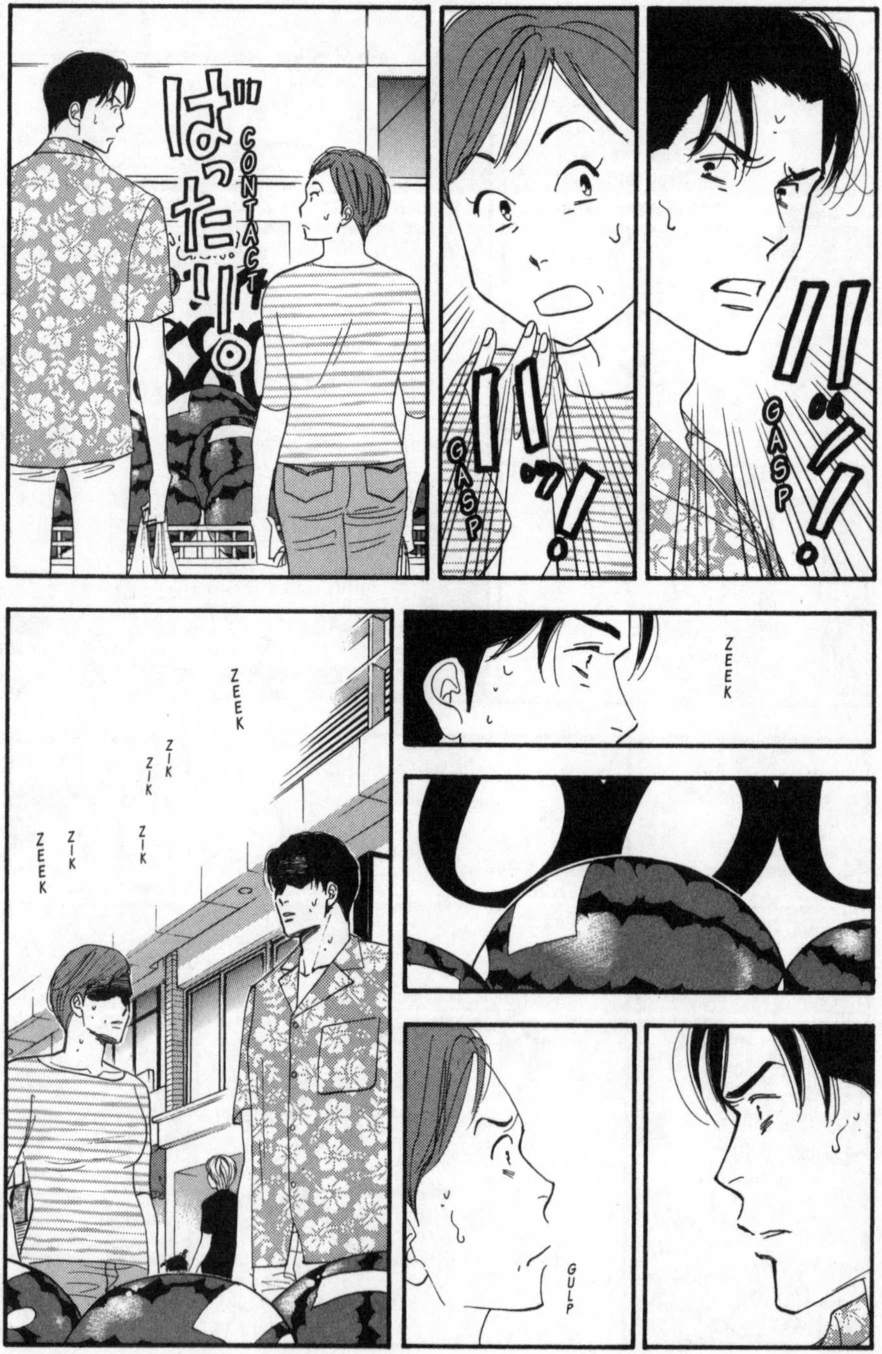
GASP
GASP
ばったり!!
CONTACT
ZEEK
GULP
ZEEK
ZIK
ZIK
ZIK
ZIK
ZEEK

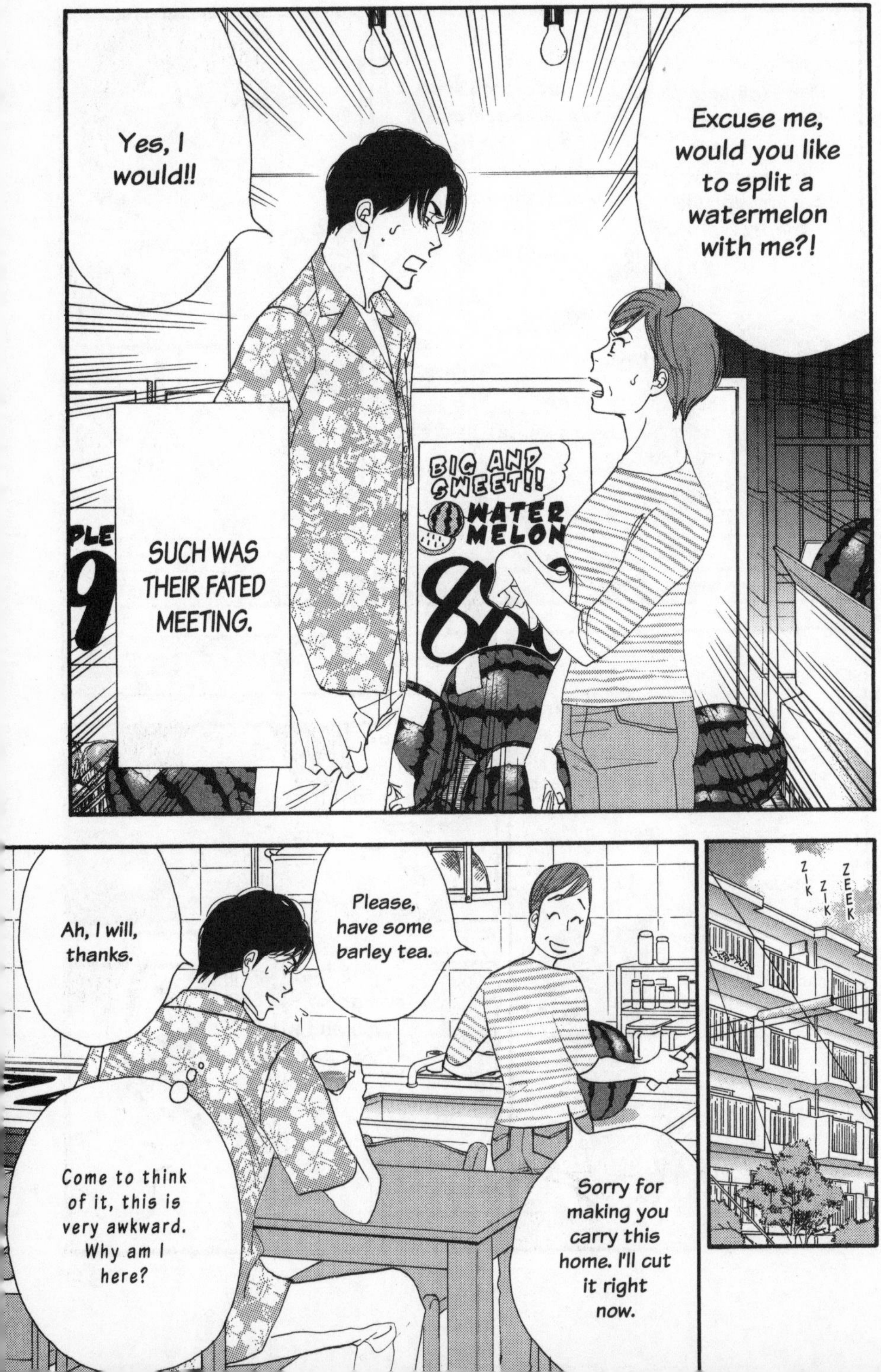
Excuse me, would you like to split a watermelon with me?!
Yes, I would!!
BIG AND SWEET!!
WATERMELON
SUCH WAS THEIR FATED MEETING.
ZEEK
ZIK ZIK
Sorry for making you carry this home. I'll cut it right now.
Please, have some barley tea.
Ah, I will, thanks.
Come to think of it, this is very awkward. Why am I here?

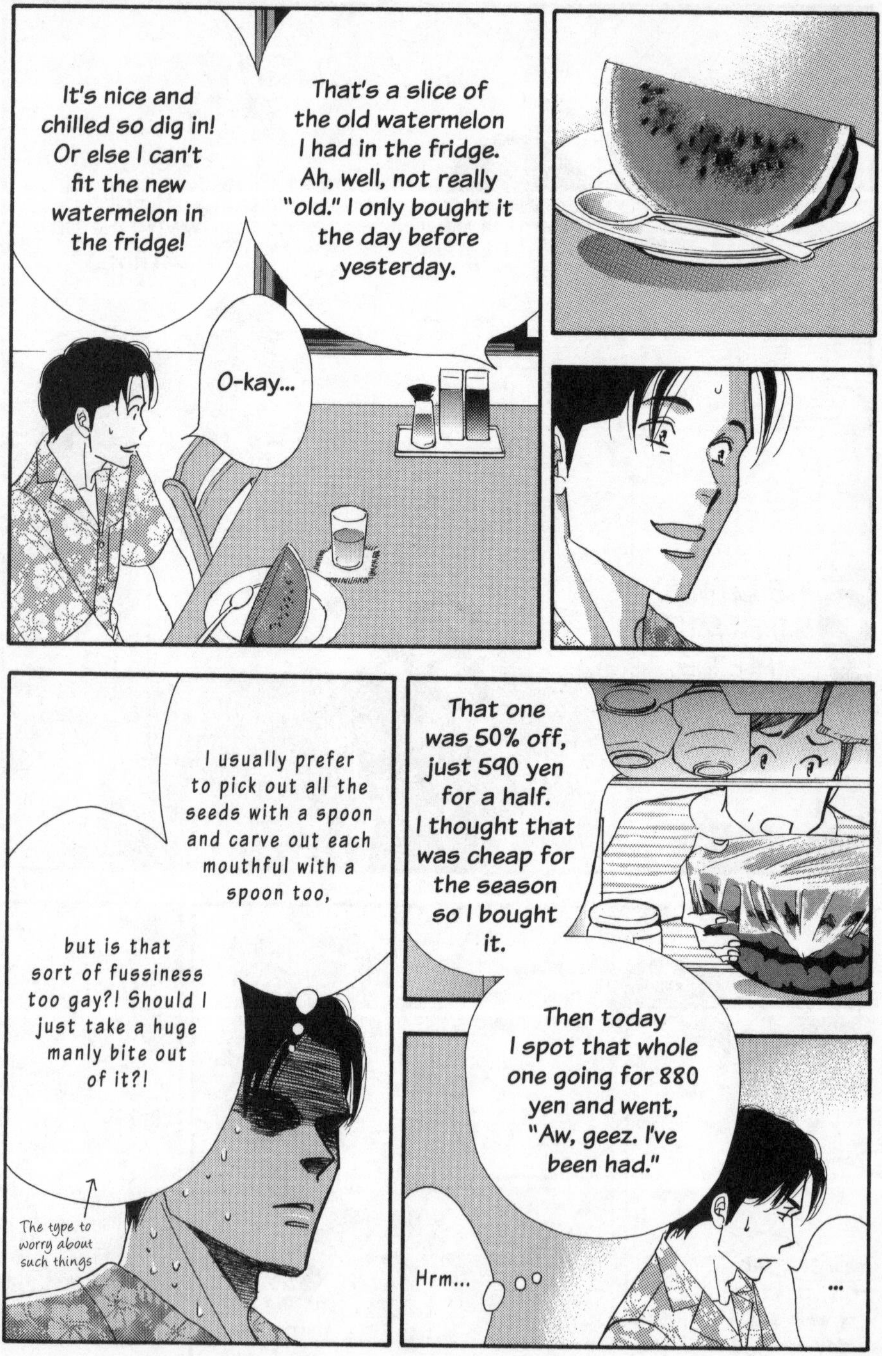
That's a slice of the old watermelon I had in the fridge. Ah, well, not really "old." I only bought it the day before yesterday.
It's nice and chilled so dig in! Or else I can't fit the new watermelon in the fridge!
O-kay...
That one was 50% off, just 590 yen for a half. I thought that was cheap for the season so I bought it.
Then today I spot that whole one going for 880 yen and went, "Aw, geez. I've been had."
...
Hrm...
I usually prefer to pick out all the seeds with a spoon and carve out each mouthful with a spoon too,
but is that sort of fussiness too gay?! Should I just take a huge manly bite out of it?!
The type to worry about such things

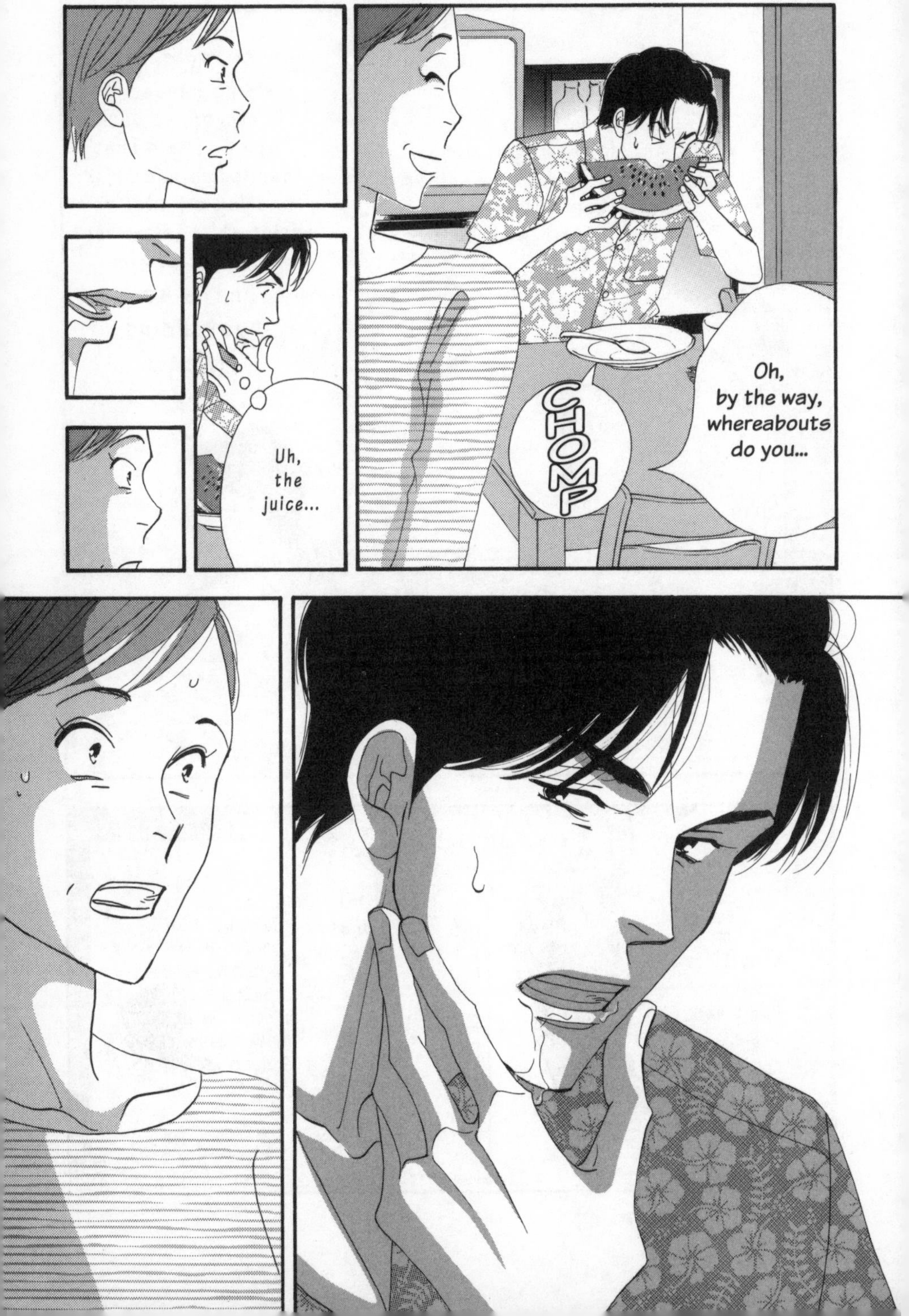
Oh, by the way, whereabouts do you...
CHOMP
Uh, the juice...

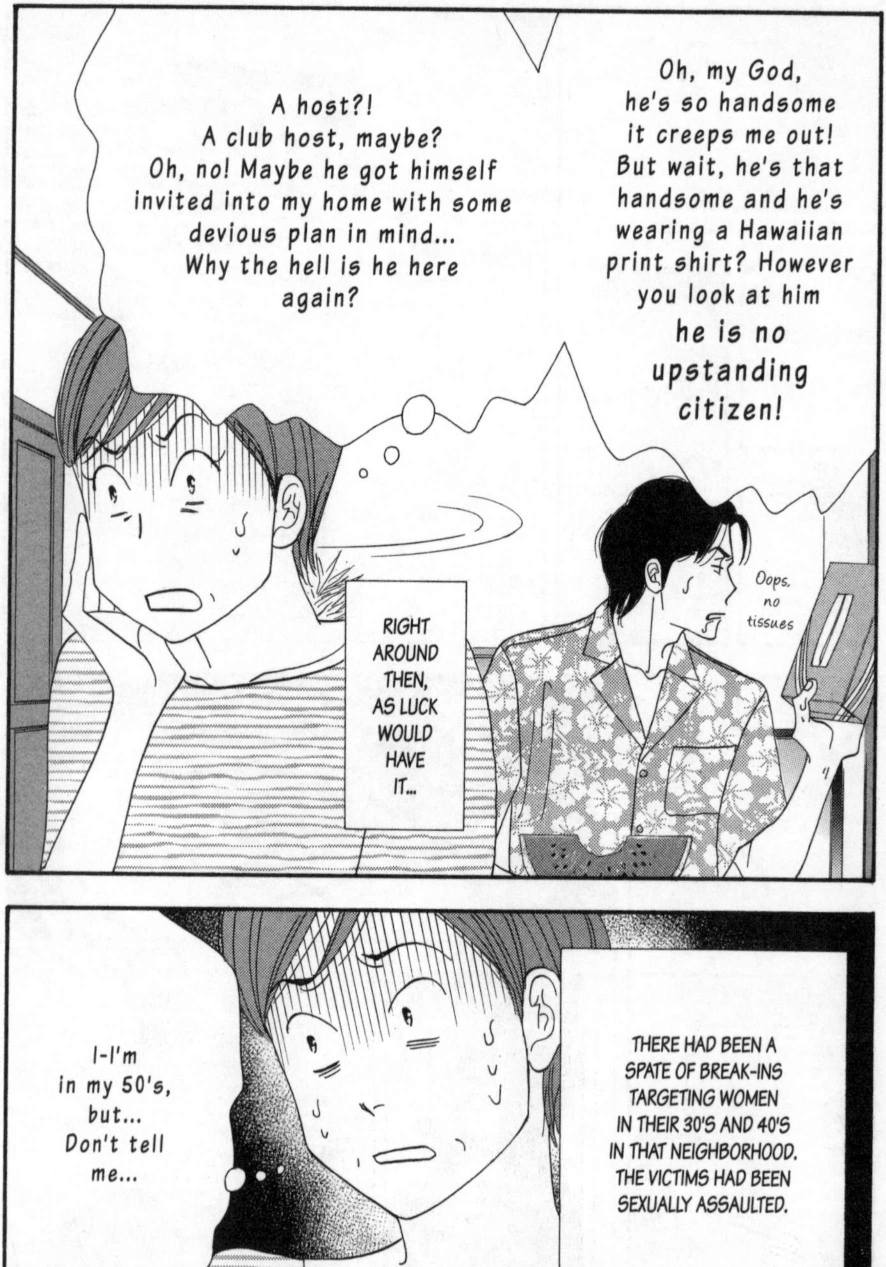
Oh, my God, he's so handsome it creeps me out! But wait, he's that handsome and he's wearing a Hawaiian print shirt? However you look at him he is no upstanding citizen!
A host?! A club host, maybe? Oh, no! Maybe he got himself invited into my home with some devious plan in mind... Why the hell is he here again?
Oops, no tissues
RIGHT AROUND THEN, AS LUCK WOULD HAVE IT...
THERE HAD BEEN A SPATE OF BREAK-INS TARGETING WOMEN IN THEIR 30'S AND 40'S IN THAT NEIGHBORHOOD. THE VICTIMS HAD BEEN SEXUALLY ASSAULTED.
I-I'm in my 50's, but... Don't tell me...

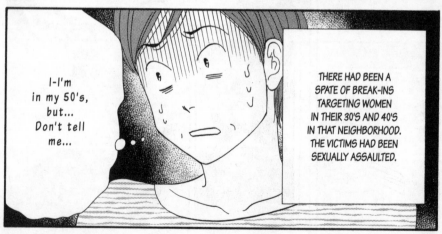

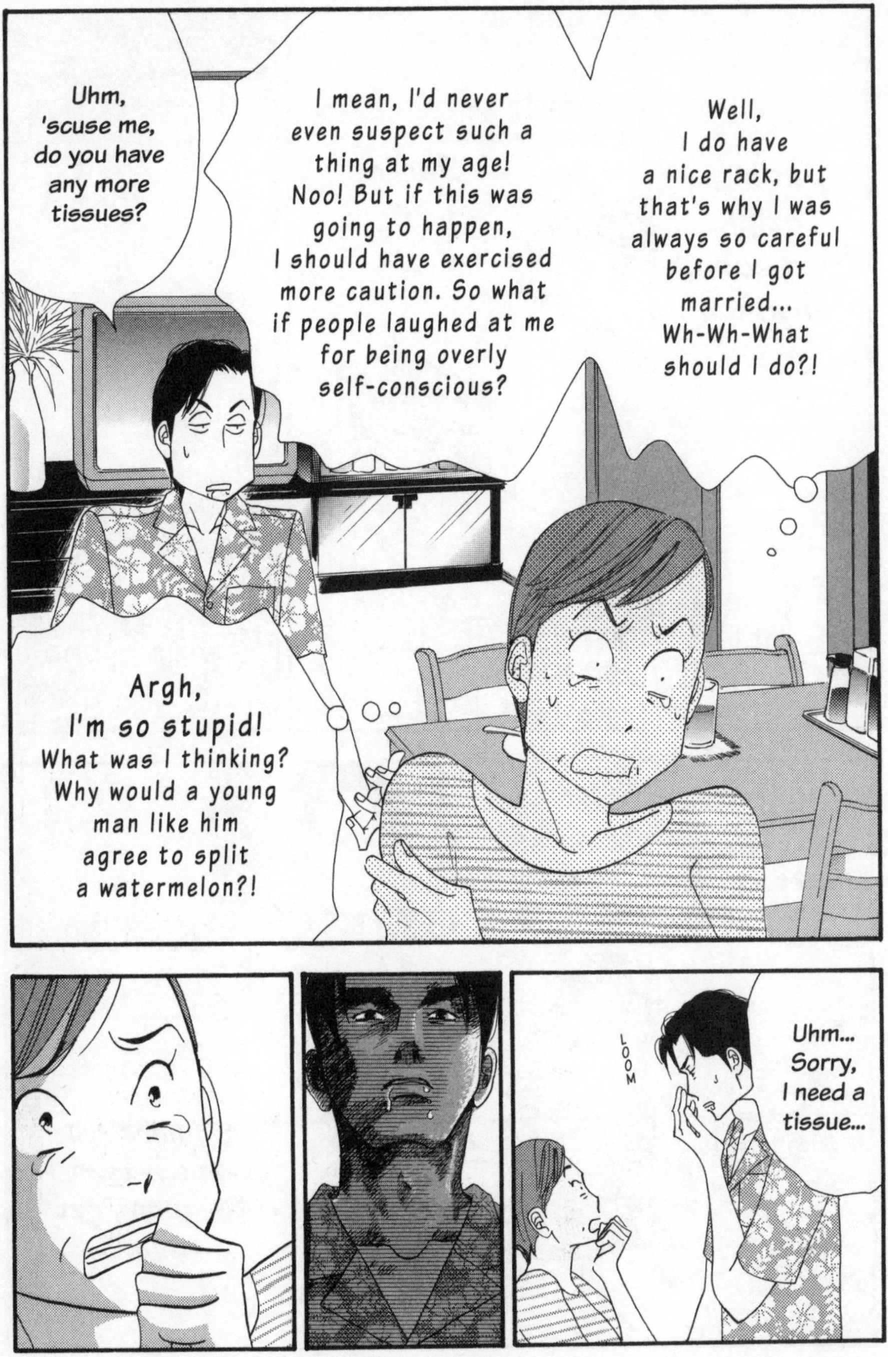
Well, I do have a nice rack, but that's why I was always so careful before I got married... Wh-Wh-What should I do?!
I mean, I'd never even suspect such a thing at my age! Noo! But if this was going to happen, I should have exercised more caution. So what if people laughed at me for being overly self-conscious?
Uhm, 'scuse me, do you have any more tissues?
Argh, I'm so stupid! What was I thinking? Why would a young man like him agree to split a watermelon?!
Uhm... Sorry, I need a tissue...
LOOM

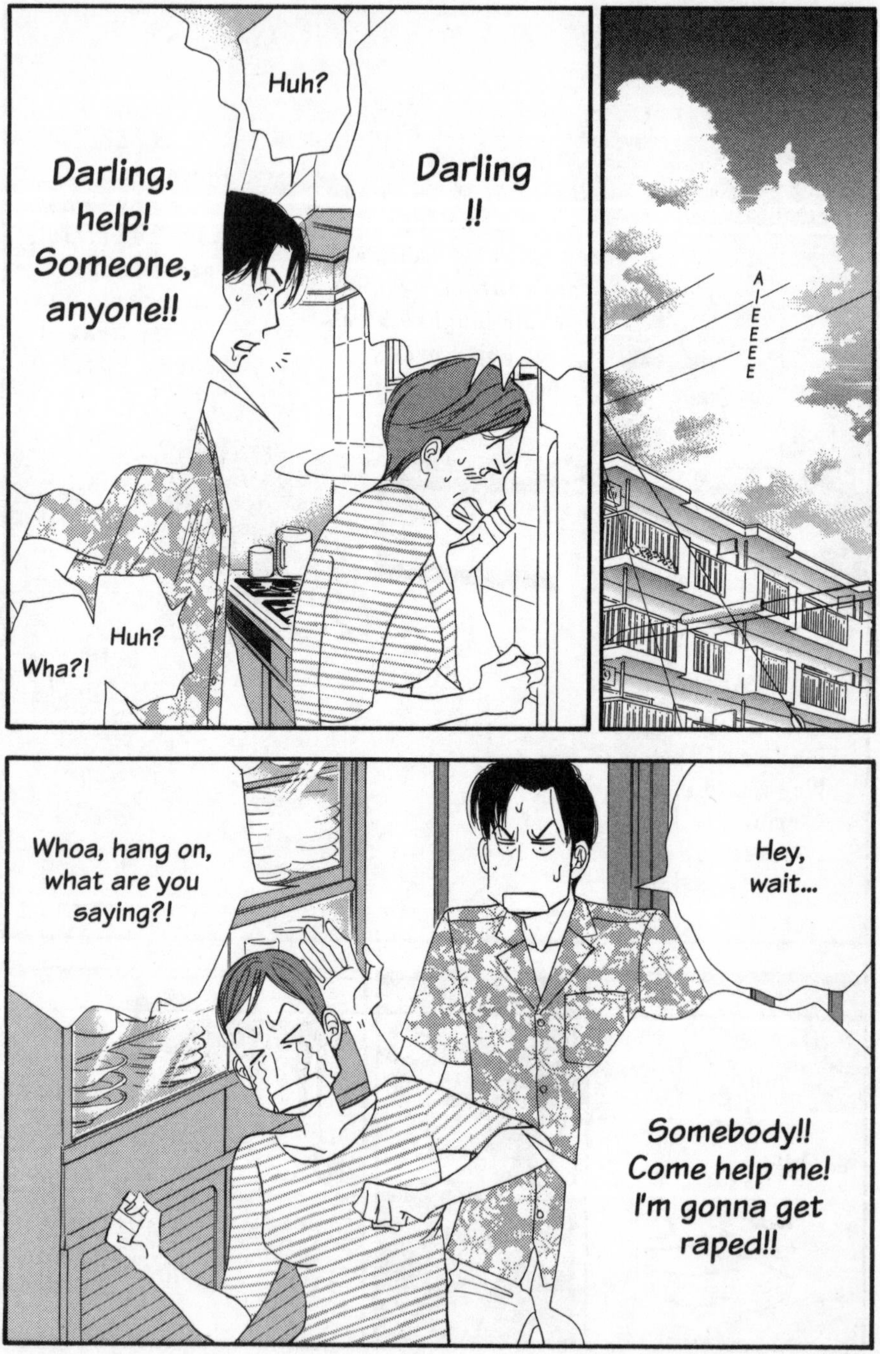
AIEEEE
Darling !!
Huh?
Darling, help! Someone, anyone!!
Huh?
Wha?!
Hey, wait...
Whoa, hang on, what are you saying?!
Somebody!! Come help me! I'm gonna get raped!!

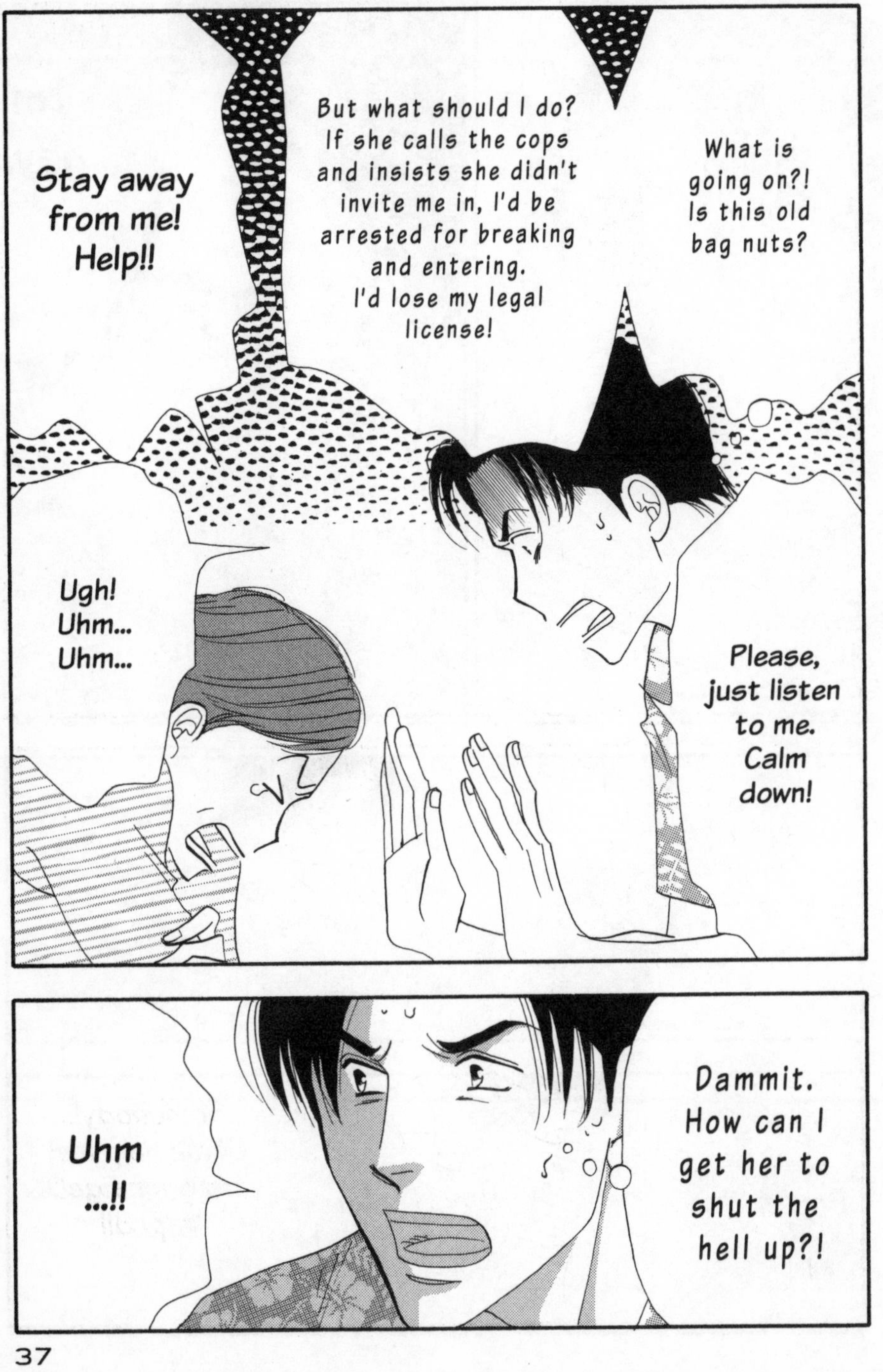
What is going on?! Is this old bag nuts?
But what should I do? If she calls the cops and insists she didn't invite me in, I'd be arrested for breaking and entering. I'd lose my legal license!
Stay away from me! Help!!
Please, just listen to me. Calm down!
Ugh! Uhm... Uhm...
Dammit. How can I get her to shut the hell up?!
Uhm ...!!

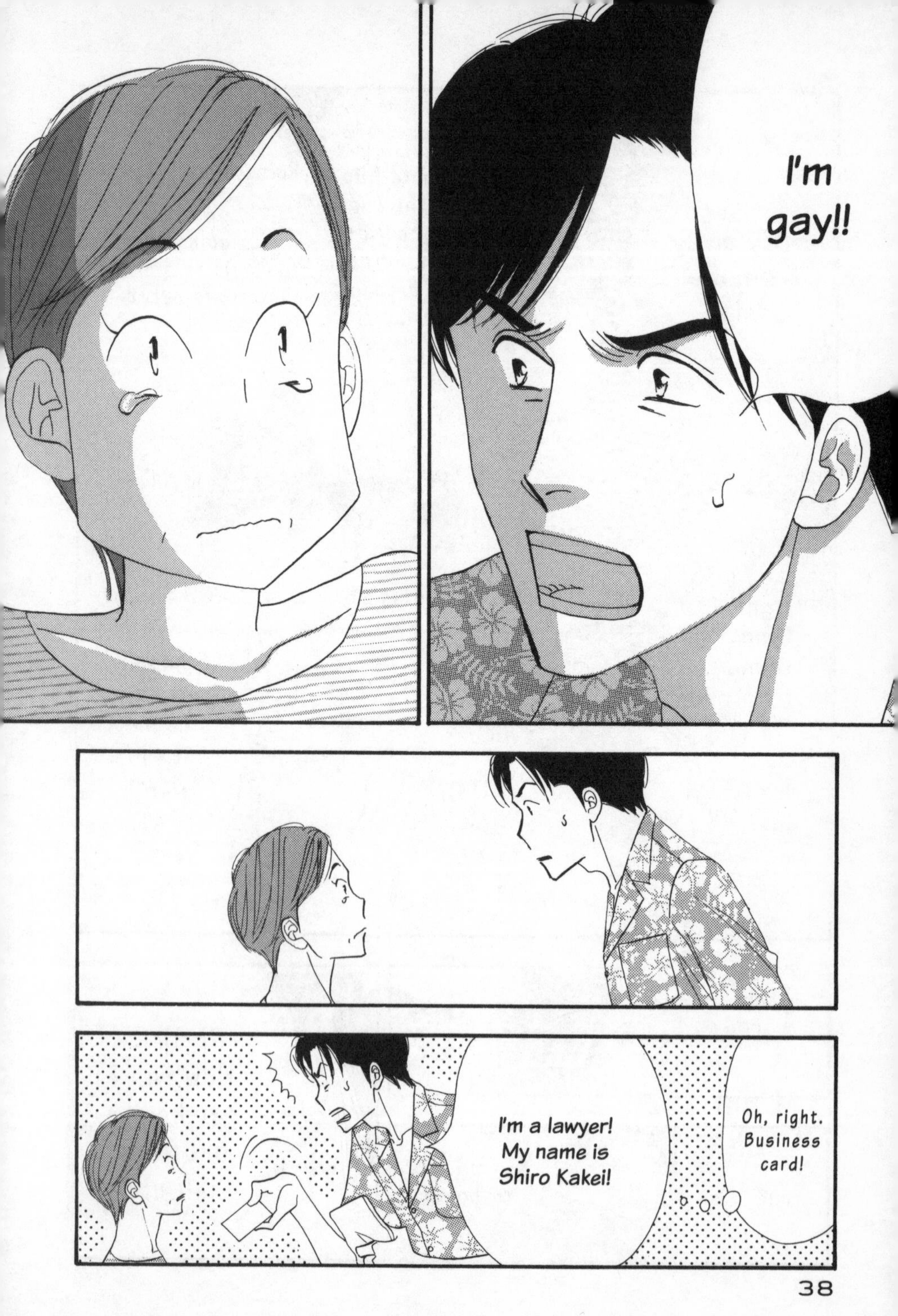
I'm gay!!
Oh, right. Business card!
I'm a lawyer! My name is Shiro Kakei!

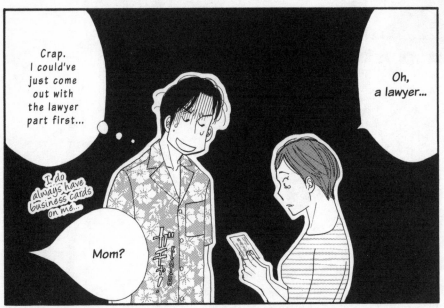

Oh,
a lawyer...
Crap.
I could've
just come
out with
the lawyer
part first...
I do always have business cards on me...
ガチャ! KLATCH
Mom?
New Takaraya's selling watermelons whole for 880 yen each, so I thought we could split one... Hm?
?
Uhm...
Oh! I am...
Suspiciously handsome...
Don't worry, Michiru. He says he's gay!
I'm home!
Hm?

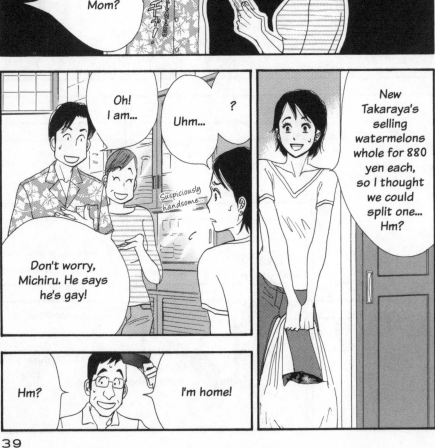

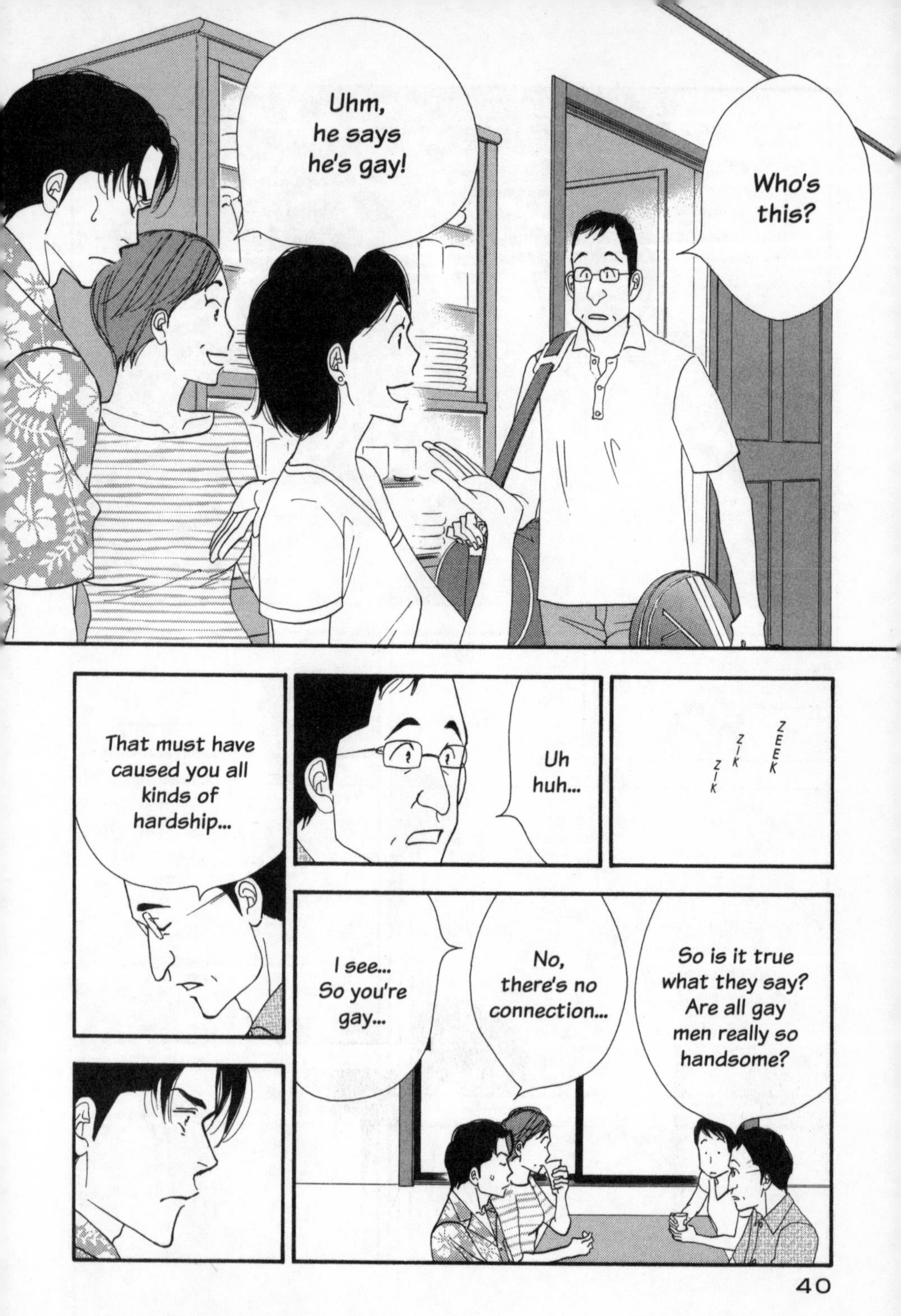

Who's this?
Uhm, he says he's gay!
ZIK ZIK ZEEK
Uh huh...
That must have caused you all kinds of hardship...
So is it true what they say? Are all gay men really so handsome?
No, there's no connection...
I see... So you're gay...

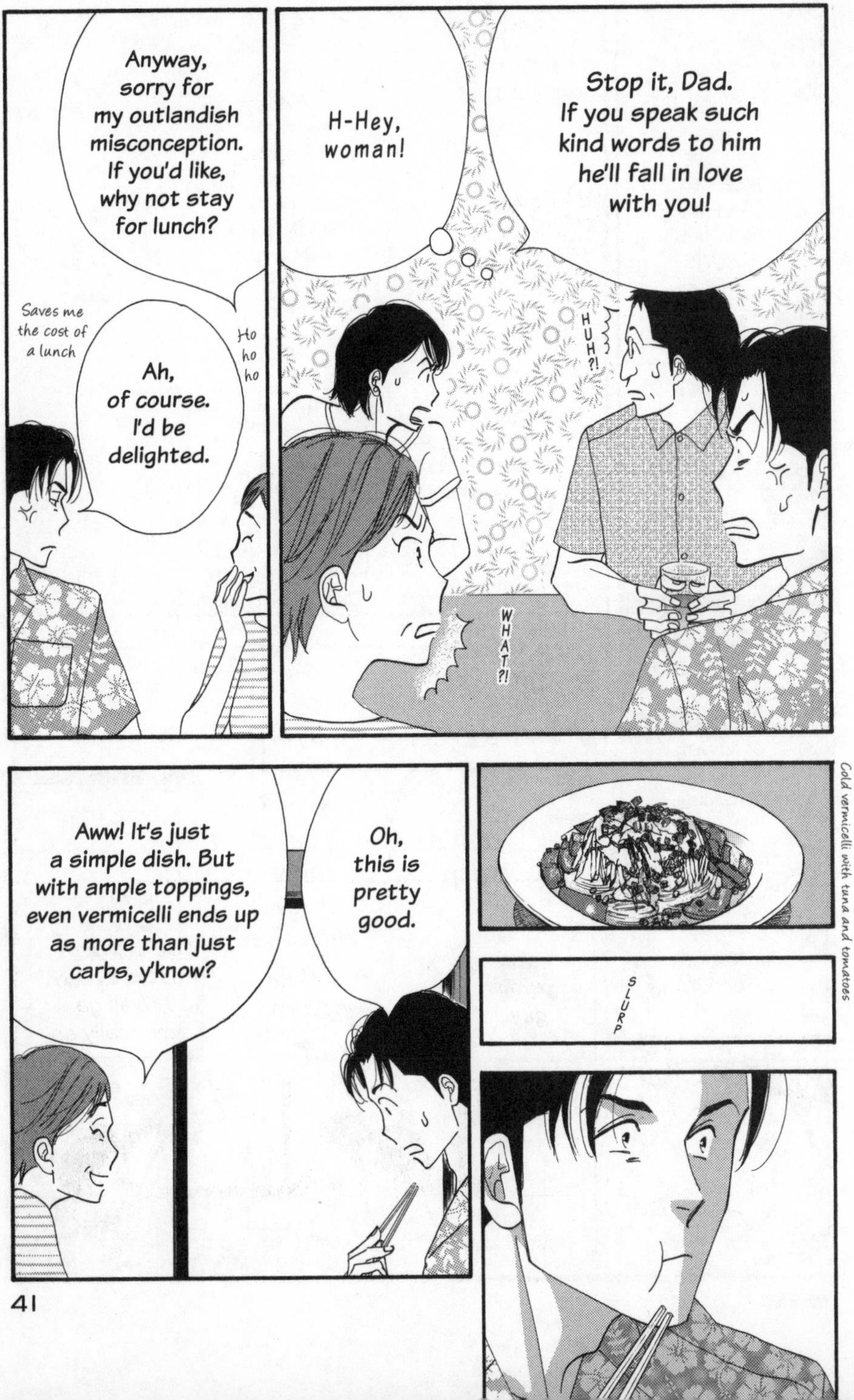

Stop it, Dad. If you speak such kind words to him he'll fall in love with you!
H-Hey, woman!
HUH?!
WHAT?!
Anyway, sorry for my outlandish misconception. If you'd like, why not stay for lunch?
Ho ho ho
Ah, of course. I'd be delighted.
Saves me the cost of a lunch
Cold vermicelli with tuna and tomatoes
SLURP
Oh, this is pretty good.
Aww! It's just a simple dish. But with ample toppings, even vermicelli ends up as more than just carbs, y'know?

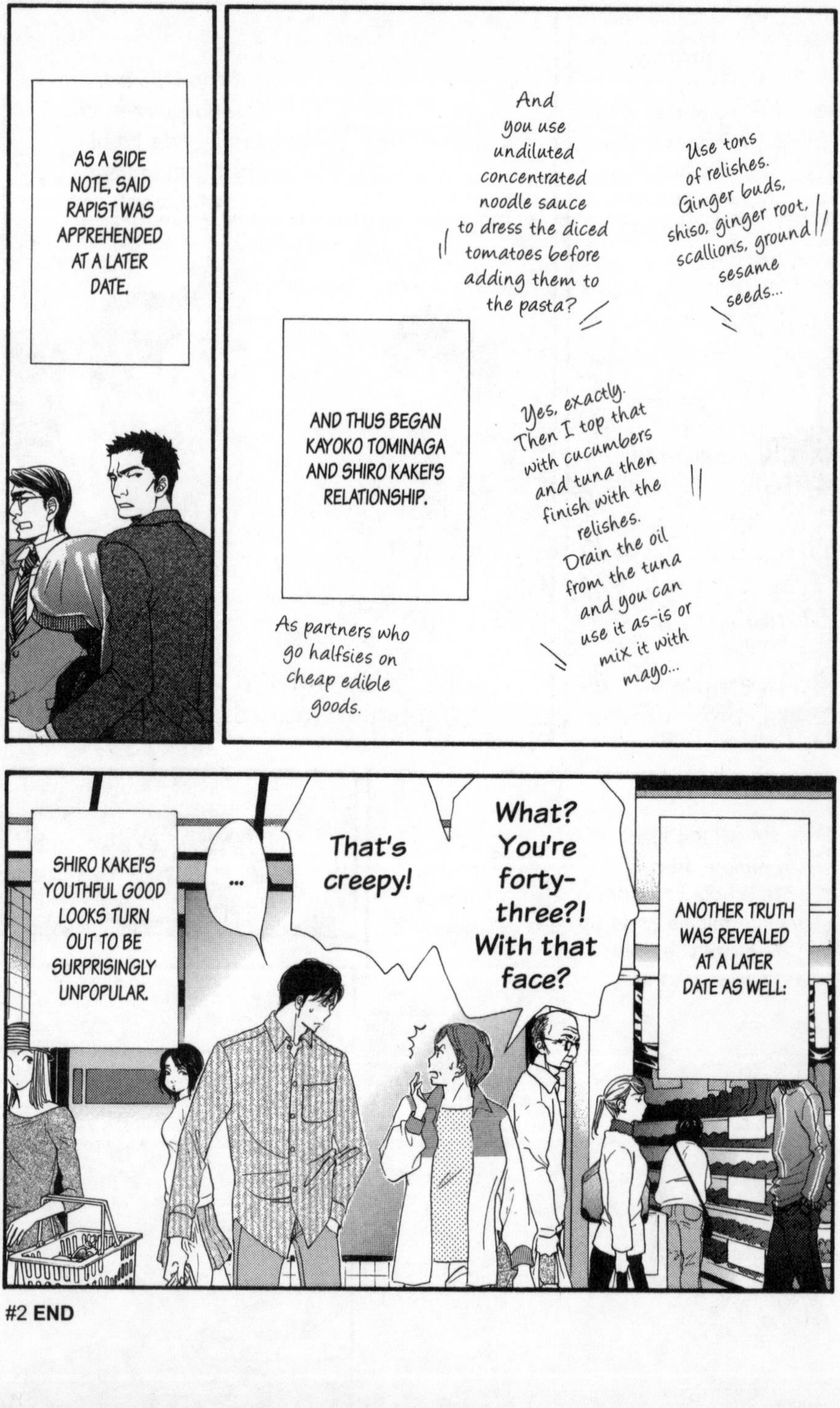
Use tons of relishes. Ginger buds, shiso, ginger root, scallions, ground sesame seeds...
And you use undiluted concentrated noodle sauce to dress the diced tomatoes before adding them to the pasta?
Yes, exactly. Then I top that with cucumbers and tuna then finish with the relishes. Drain the oil from the tuna and you can use it as-is or mix it with mayo...
AND THUS BEGAN KAYOKO TOMINAGA AND SHIRO KAKEI'S RELATIONSHIP.
As partners who go halfsies on cheap edible goods.
AS A SIDE NOTE, SAID RAPIST WAS APPREHENDED AT A LATER DATE.
ANOTHER TRUTH WAS REVEALED AT A LATER DATE AS WELL:
What? You're forty-three?! With that face?
That's creepy!
...
SHIRO KAKEI'S YOUTHFUL GOOD LOOKS TURN OUT TO BE SURPRISINGLY UNPOPULAR.

#2 END

Cold Vermicelli with Tuna and Tomatoes (serves 2)

5 1/4 oz (150 g (3 bunches)) vermicelli (*soumen*)
Half can oil-packed tuna, drained
   and mixed with mayonnaise
1 large tomato, diced
1/2 cucumber, julienned
5-6 leaves *shiso* leaves
4 scallions, finely chopped
1 ginger bud, cut lengthwise then sliced on the bias
Ground white sesame seeds, to taste
Grated ginger, to taste
Mentsuyu (noodle sauce), to taste

Boil vermicelli, rinse then soak in ice water to set. Drain.
Plate, then simply top with remaining ingredients.

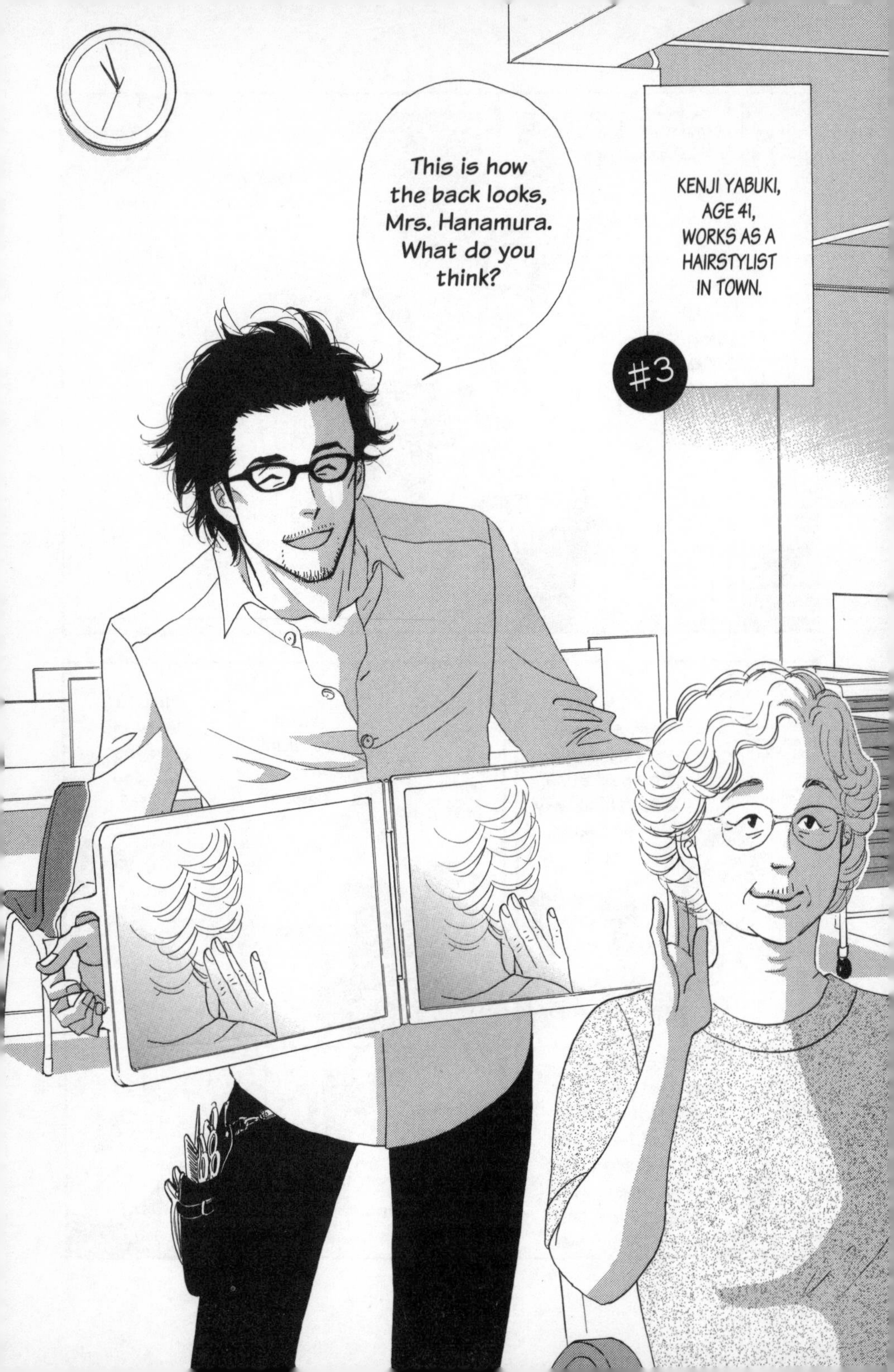
KENJI YABUKI, AGE 41, WORKS AS A HAIRSTYLIST IN TOWN.
#3
This is how the back looks, Mrs. Hanamura. What do you think?

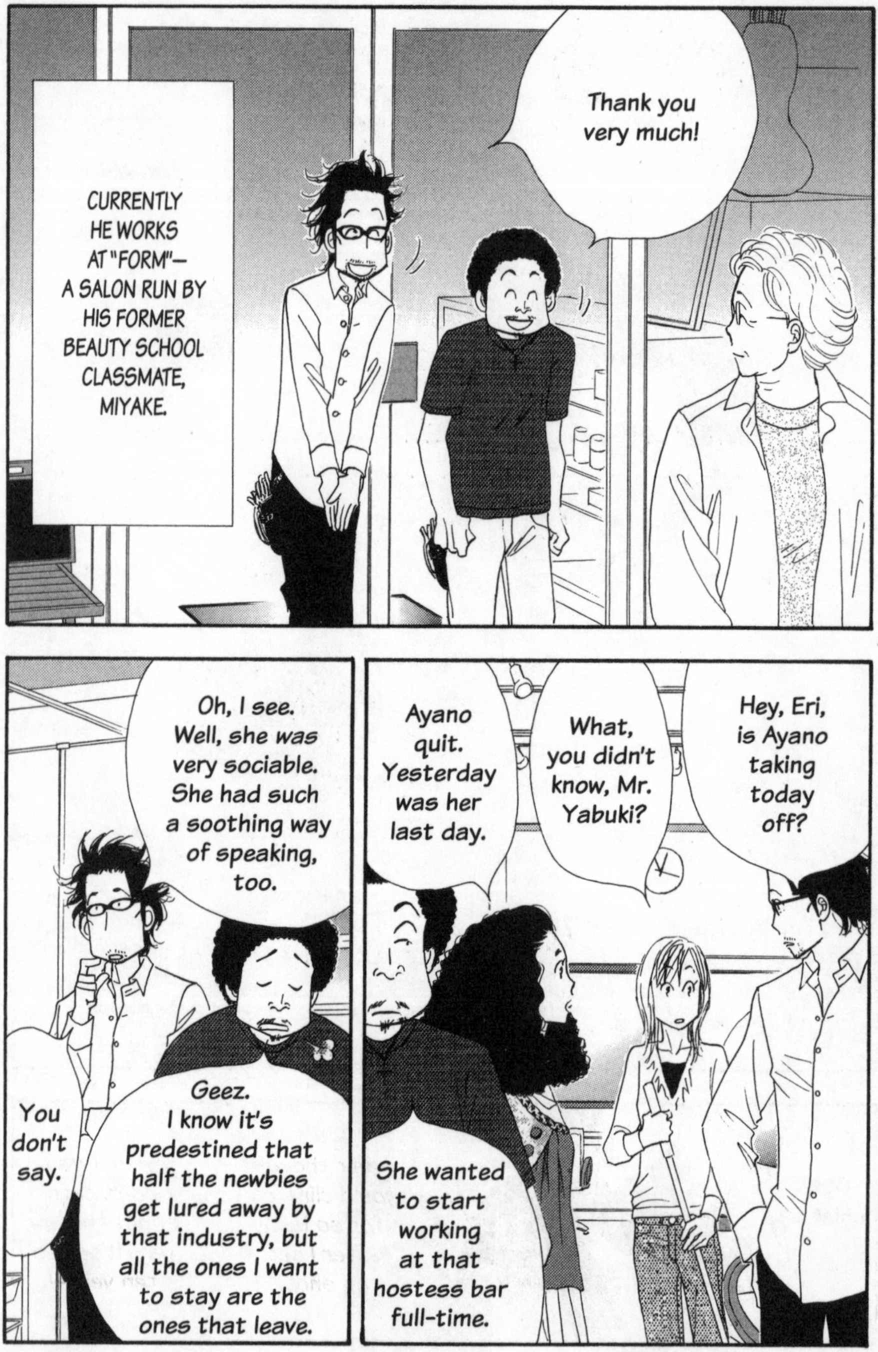
Thank you very much!
CURRENTLY HE WORKS AT "FORM"— A SALON RUN BY HIS FORMER BEAUTY SCHOOL CLASSMATE, MIYAKE.
Hey, Eri, is Ayano taking today off?
What, you didn't know, Mr. Yabuki?
Ayano quit. Yesterday was her last day.
She wanted to start working at that hostess bar full-time.
Oh, I see. Well, she was very sociable. She had such a soothing way of speaking, too.
Geez. I know it's predestined that half the newbies get lured away by that industry, but all the ones I want to stay are the ones that leave.
You don't say.

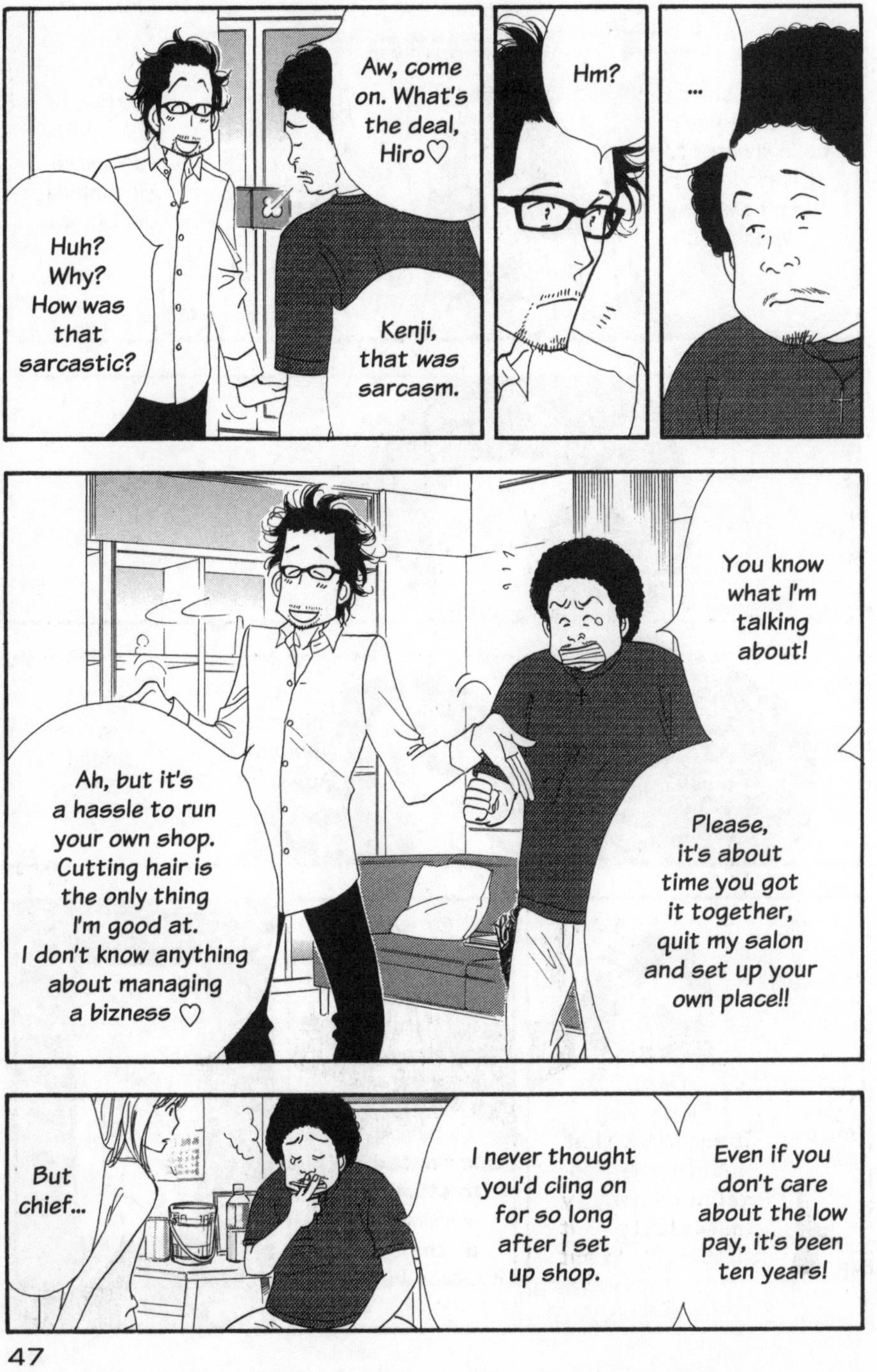
...
Hm?
Aw, come on. What's the deal, Hiro♡
Kenji, that was sarcasm.
Huh? Why? How was that sarcastic?
You know what I'm talking about!
Please, it's about time you got it together, quit my salon and set up your own place!!
Ah, but it's a hassle to run your own shop. Cutting hair is the only thing I'm good at. I don't know anything about managing a bizness ♡
Even if you don't care about the low pay, it's been ten years!
I never thought you'd cling on for so long after I set up shop.
But chief...

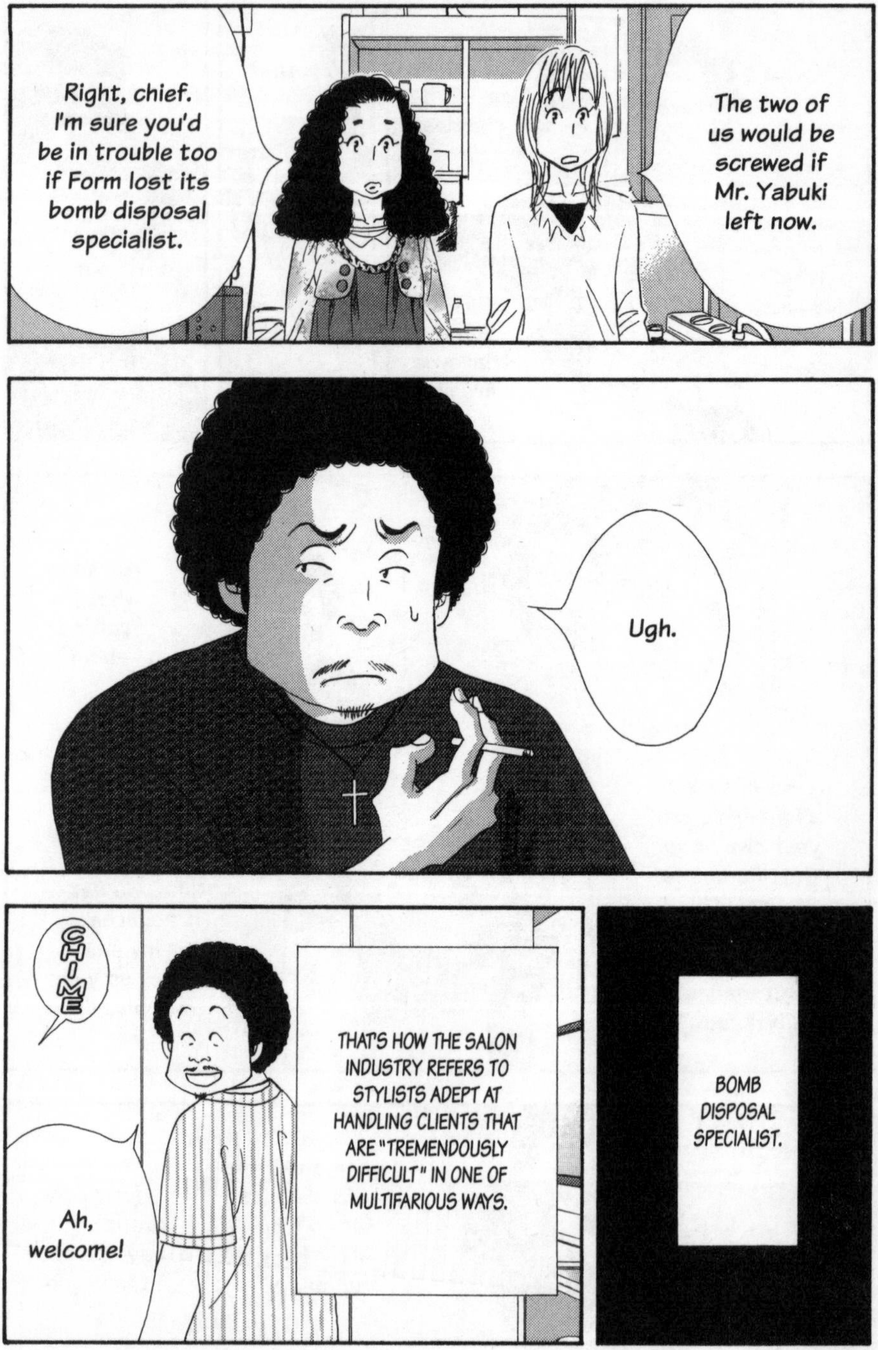
The two of us would be screwed if Mr. Yabuki left now.
Right, chief. I'm sure you'd be in trouble too if Form lost its bomb disposal specialist.
Ugh.
BOMB DISPOSAL SPECIALIST.
THAT'S HOW THE SALON INDUSTRY REFERS TO STYLISTS ADEPT AT HANDLING CLIENTS THAT ARE "TREMENDOUSLY DIFFICULT" IN ONE OF MULTIFARIOUS WAYS.
CHIME
Ah, welcome!

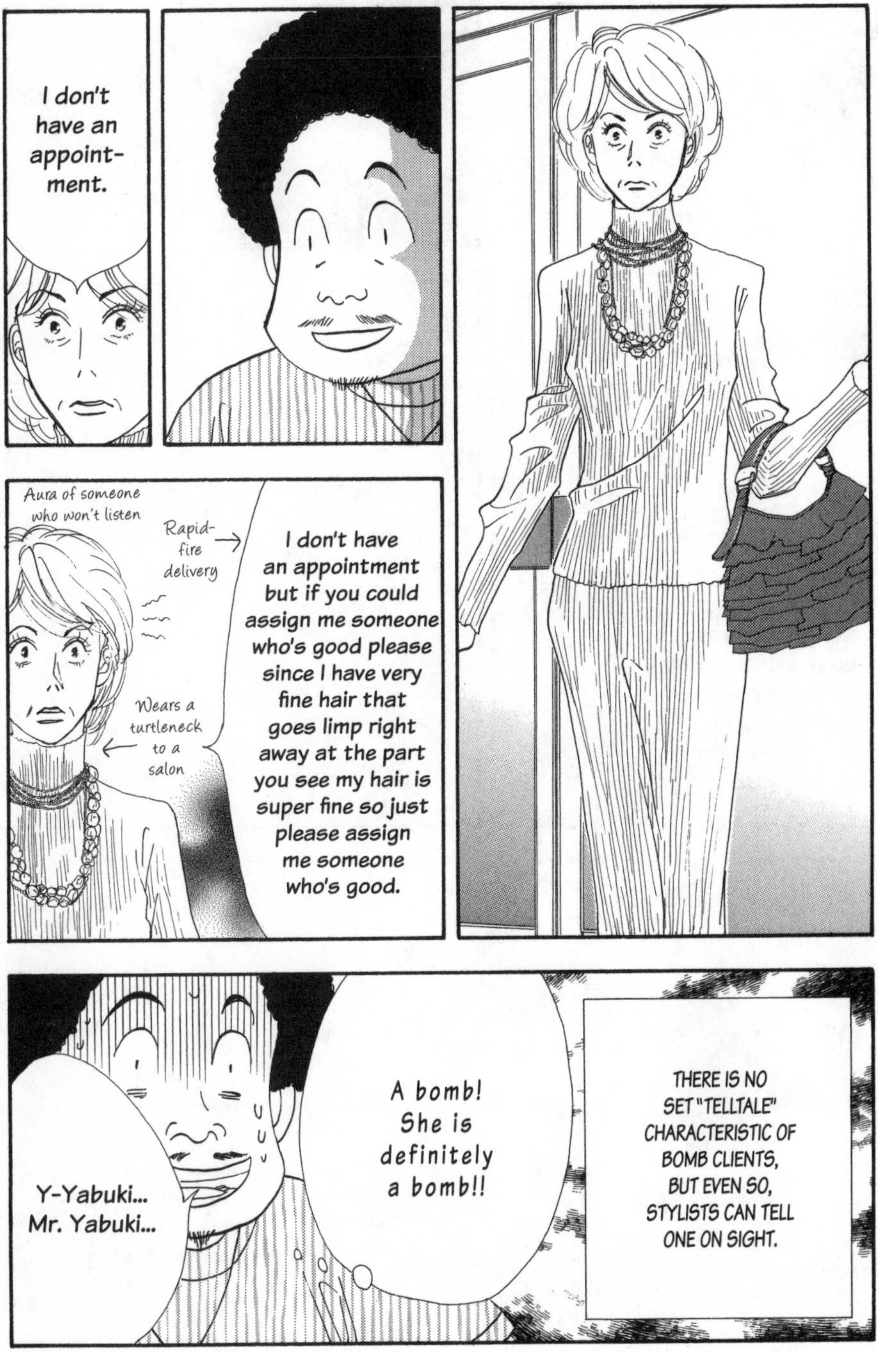
I don't have an appoint-ment.
I don't have an appointment but if you could assign me someone who's good please since I have very fine hair that goes limp right away at the part you see my hair is super fine so just please assign me someone who's good.
Rapid-fire delivery
Aura of someone who won't listen
Wears a turtleneck to a salon
THERE IS NO SET "TELLTALE" CHARACTERISTIC OF BOMB CLIENTS, BUT EVEN SO, STYLISTS CAN TELL ONE ON SIGHT.
A bomb! She is definitely a bomb!!
Y-Yabuki... Mr. Yabuki...

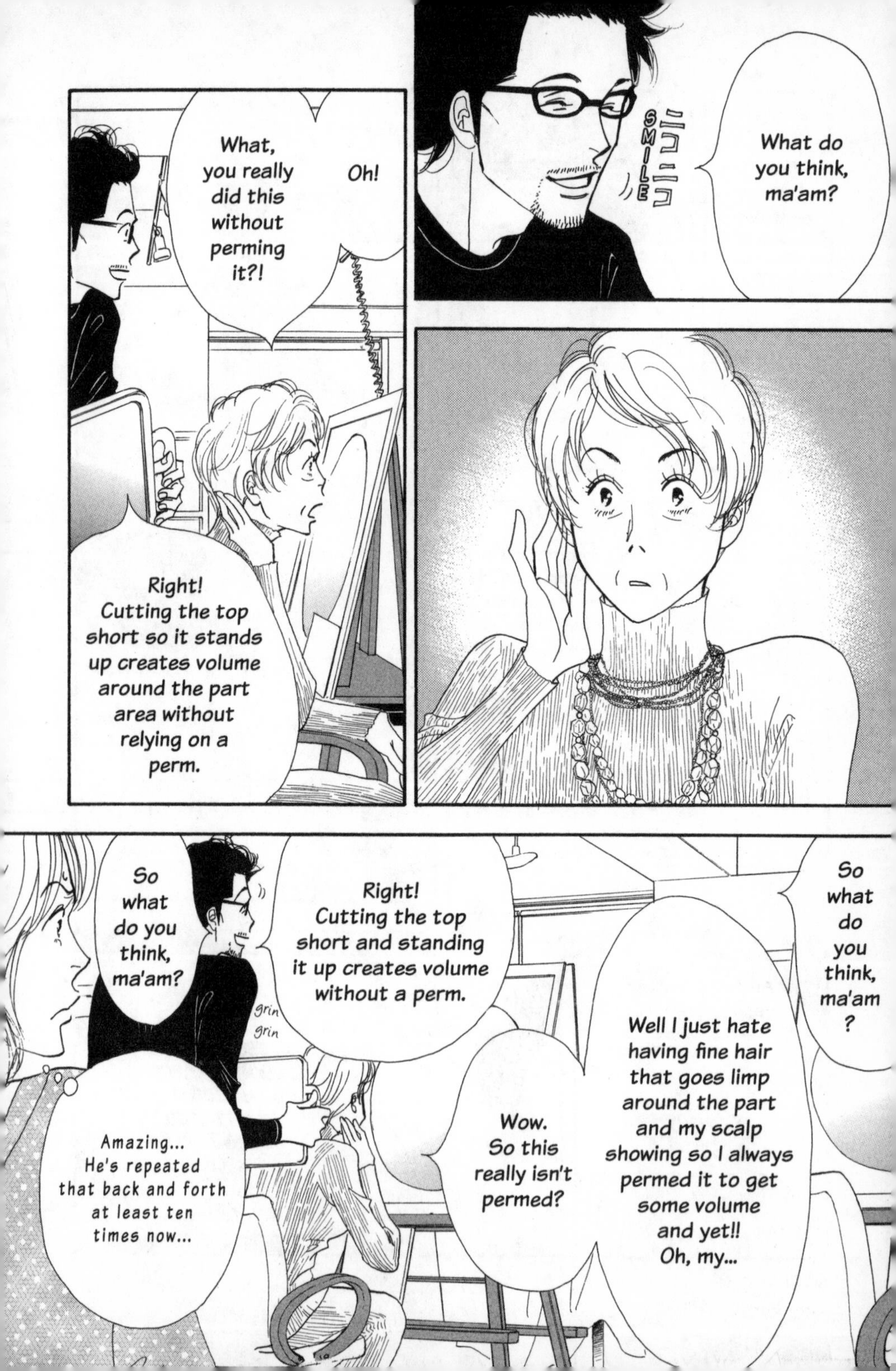

What do you think, ma'am?
ニコニコ SMILE
Oh!
What, you really did this without perming it?!
Right! Cutting the top short so it stands up creates volume around the part area without relying on a perm.
So what do you think, ma'am?
Well I just hate having fine hair that goes limp around the part and my scalp showing so I always permed it to get some volume and yet!! Oh, my...
Wow. So this really isn't permed?
Right! Cutting the top short and standing it up creates volume without a perm.
grin grin
So what do you think, ma'am?
Amazing... He's repeated that back and forth at least ten times now...

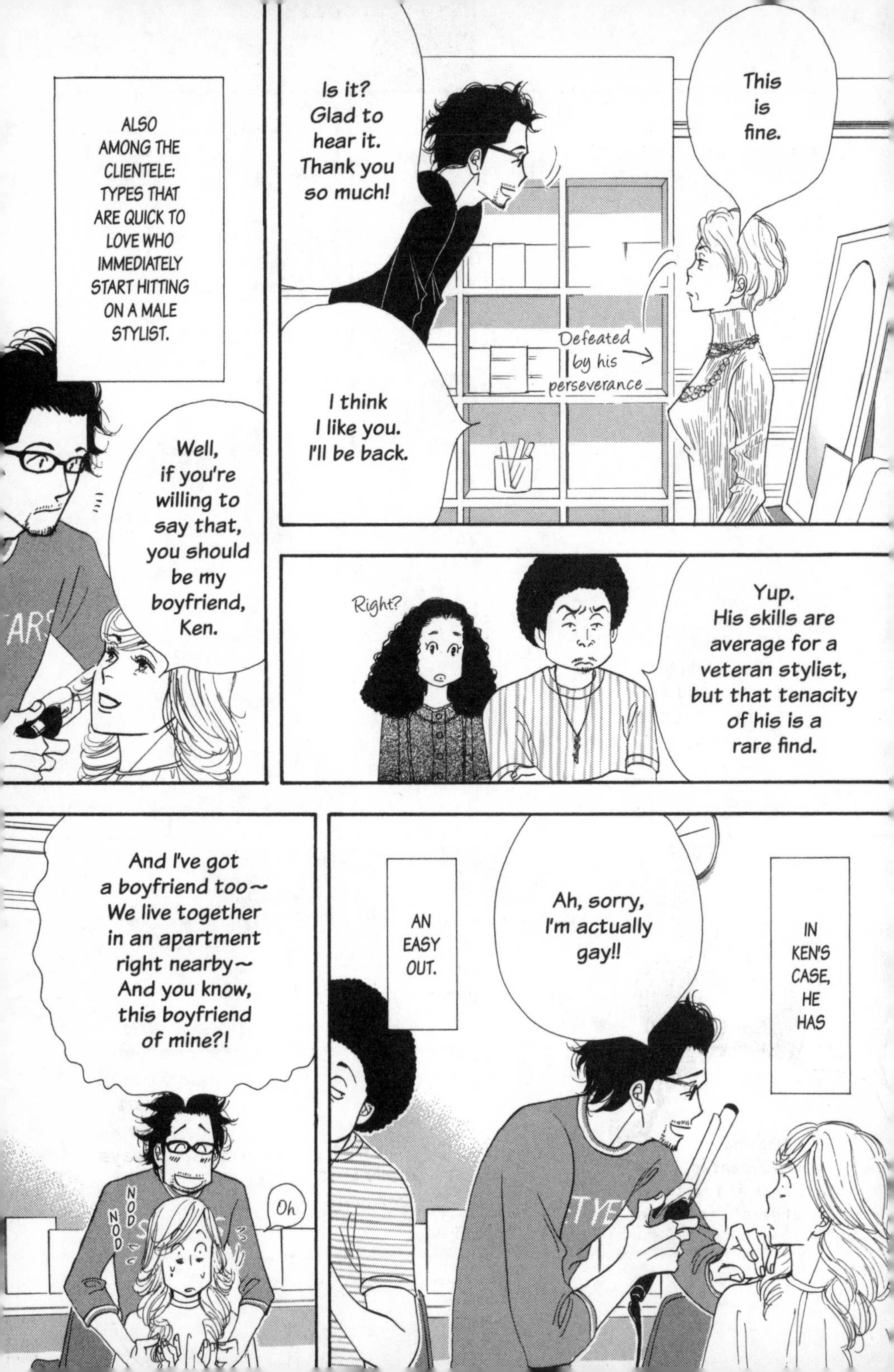

This is fine.
Is it? Glad to hear it. Thank you so much!
Defeated by his perseverance
I think I like you. I'll be back.
Yup. His skills are average for a veteran stylist, but that tenacity of his is a rare find.
Right?
ALSO AMONG THE CLIENTELE: TYPES THAT ARE QUICK TO LOVE WHO IMMEDIATELY START HITTING ON A MALE STYLIST.
Well, if you're willing to say that, you should be my boyfriend, Ken.
IN KEN'S CASE, HE HAS
Ah, sorry, I'm actually gay!!
AN EASY OUT.
And I've got a boyfriend too~ We live together in an apartment right nearby~ And you know, this boyfriend of mine?!
NOD NOD
Oh

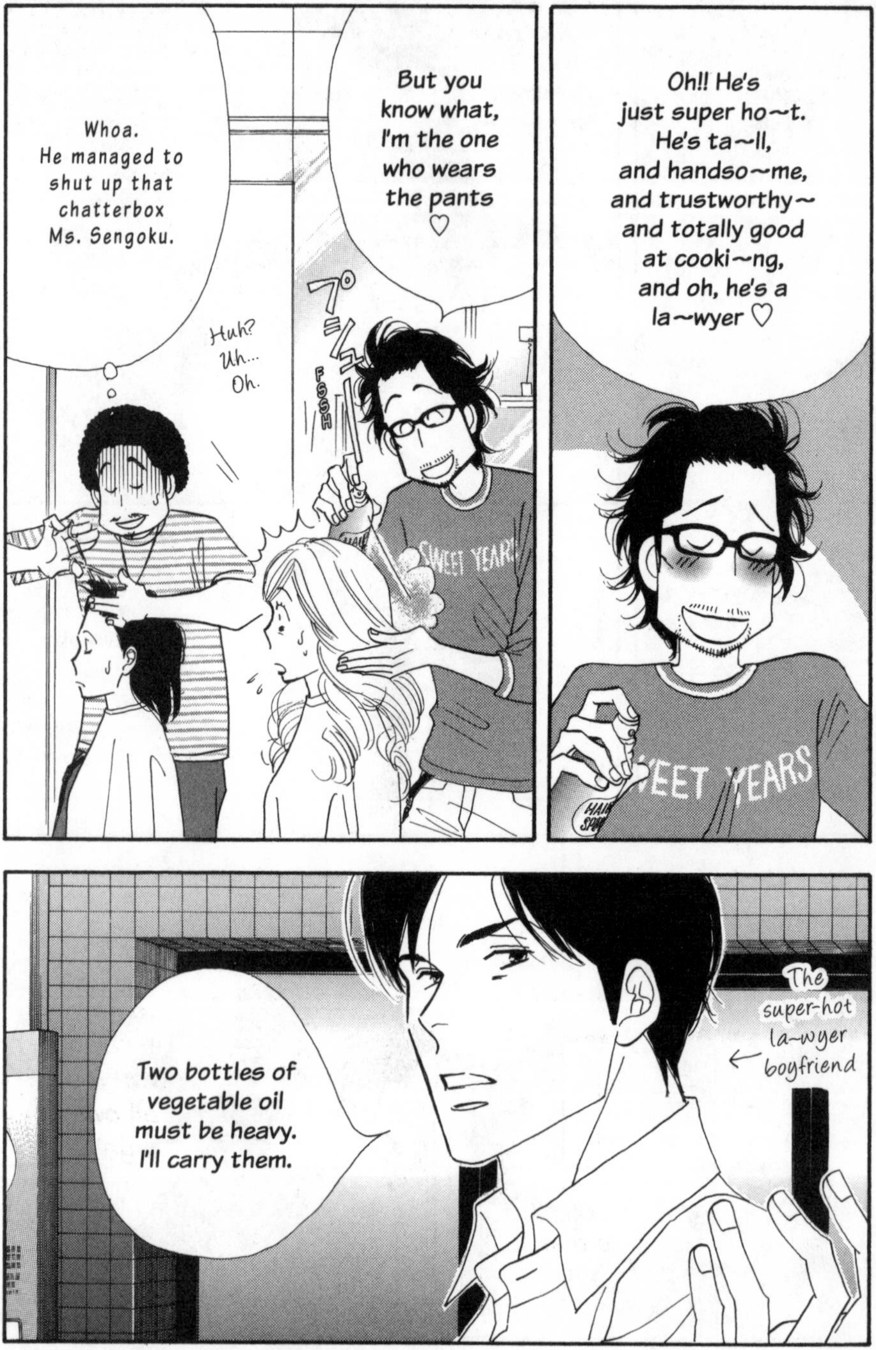
Oh!! He's just super ho~t. He's ta~ll, and handso~me, and trustworthy~ and totally good at cooki~ng, and oh, he's a la~wyer ♡
But you know what, I'm the one who wears the pants ♡
Whoa. He managed to shut up that chatterbox Ms. Sengoku.
FSSH
Huh? Uh... Oh.
SWEET YEARS
The super-hot la~wyer boyfriend
Two bottles of vegetable oil must be heavy. I'll carry them.

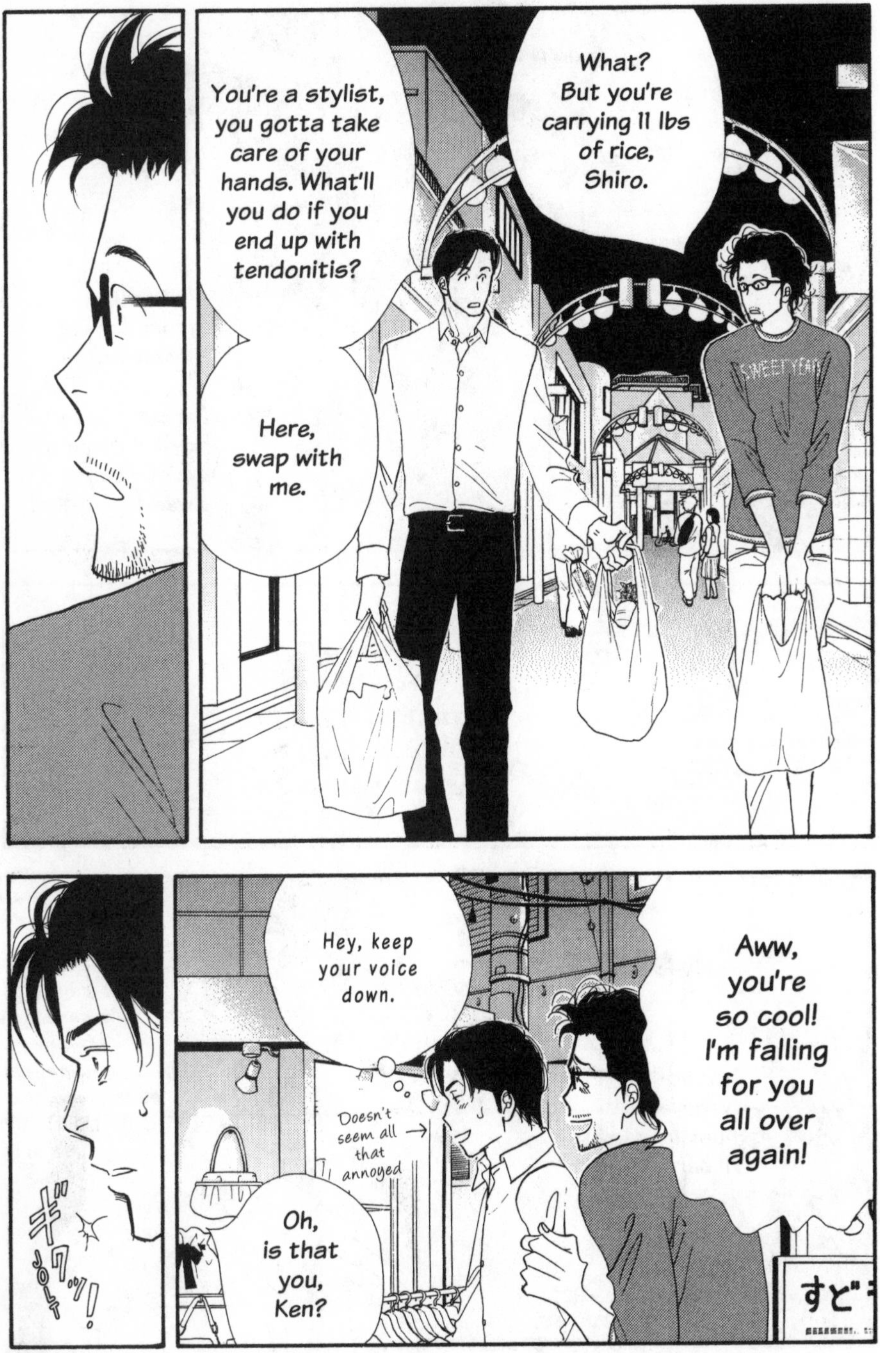
What? But you're carrying 11 lbs of rice, Shiro.
You're a stylist, you gotta take care of your hands. What'll you do if you end up with tendonitis?
Here, swap with me.
Aww, you're so cool! I'm falling for you all over again!
Hey, keep your voice down.
Doesn't seem all that annoyed
Oh, is that you, Ken?
ギクッ!
JOLT

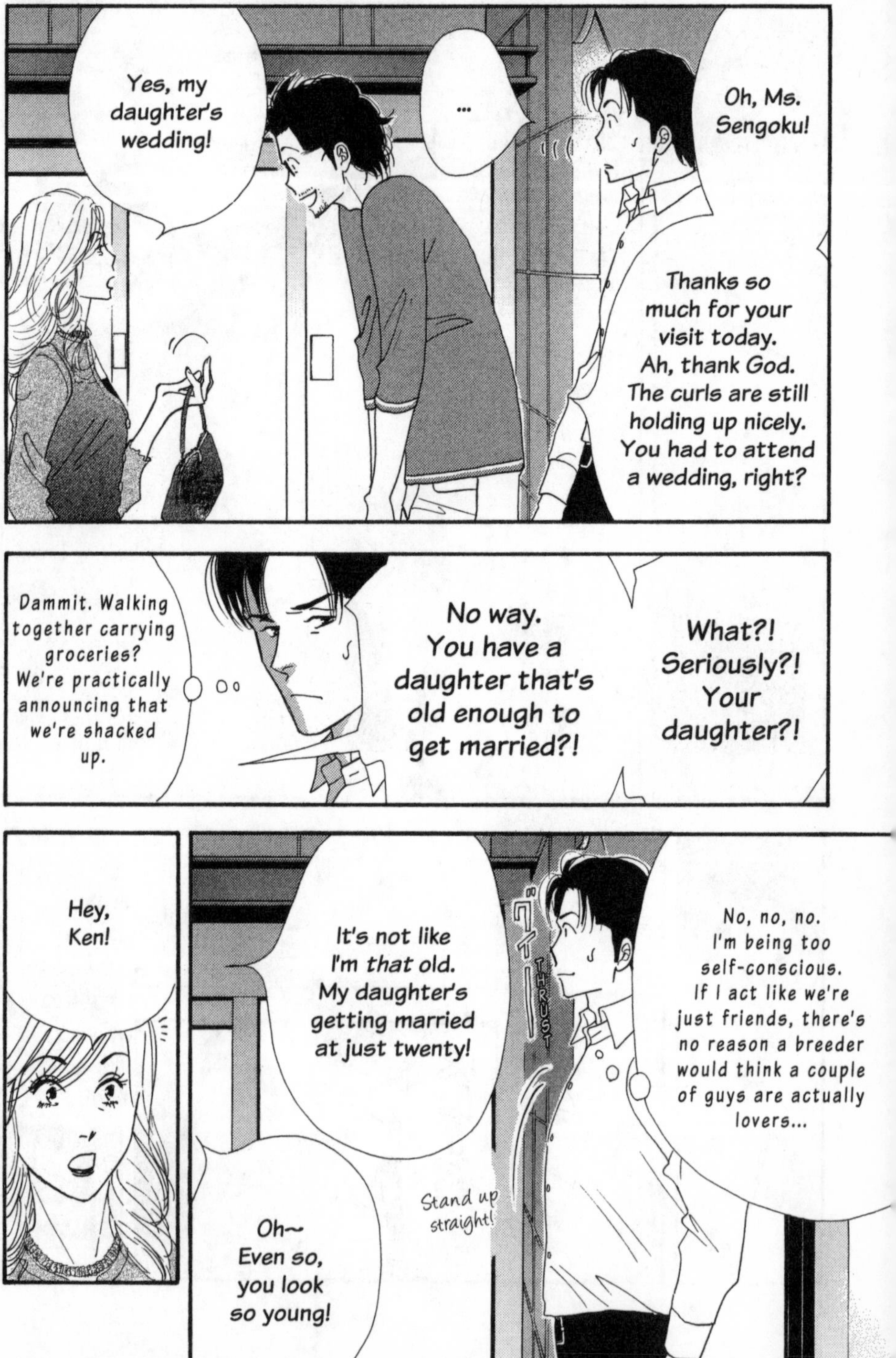
Oh, Ms. Sengoku!
Thanks so much for your visit today. Ah, thank God. The curls are still holding up nicely. You had to attend a wedding, right?
...
Yes, my daughter's wedding!
What?! Seriously?! Your daughter?!
No way. You have a daughter that's old enough to get married?!
Dammit. Walking together carrying groceries? We're practically announcing that we're shacked up.
No, no, no. I'm being too self-conscious. If I act like we're just friends, there's no reason a breeder would think a couple of guys are actually lovers...
THRUST
It's not like I'm *that* old. My daughter's getting married at just twenty!
Stand up straight!
Oh~ Even so, you look so young!
Hey, Ken!

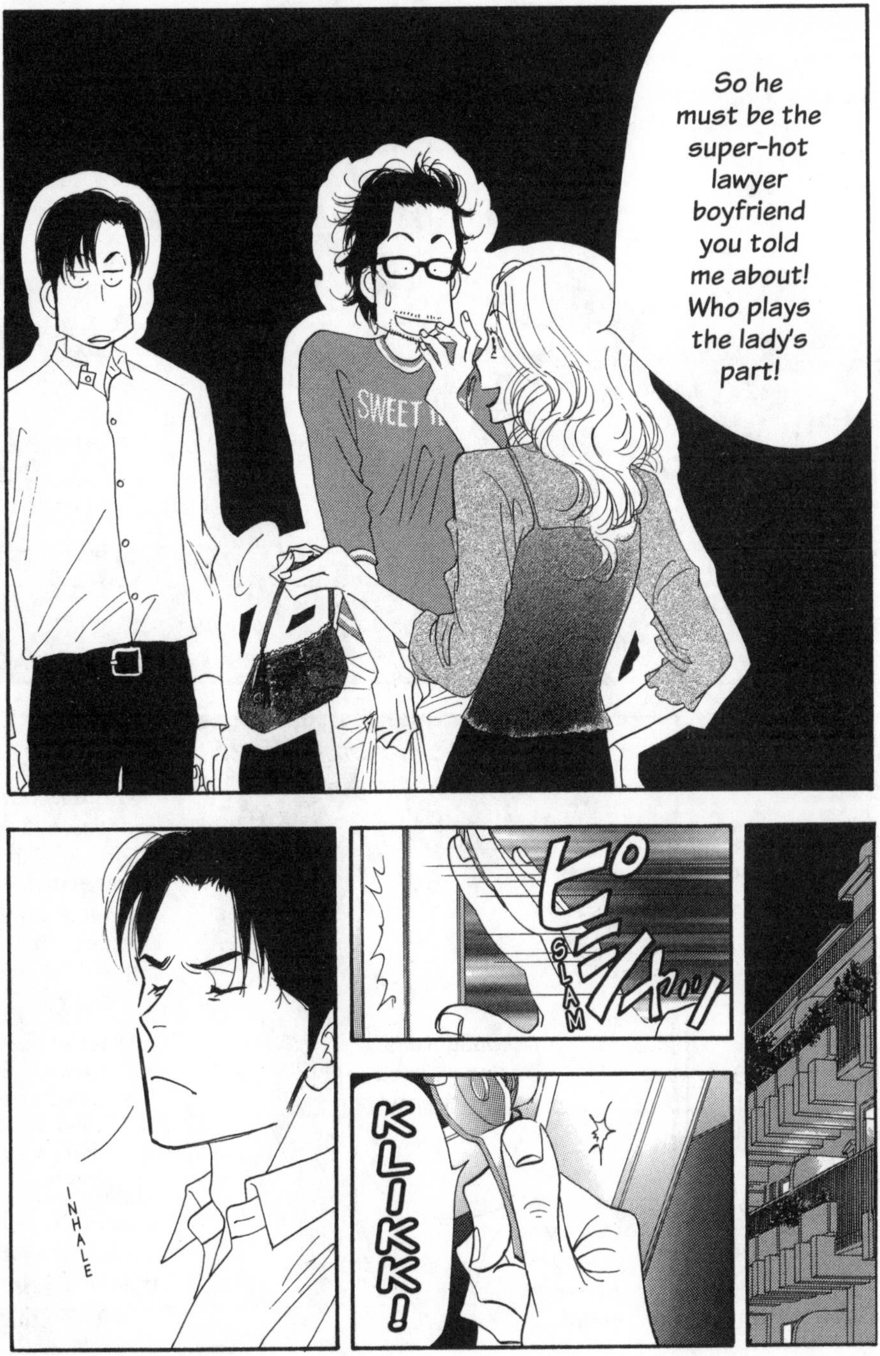
So he must be the super-hot lawyer boyfriend you told me about! Who plays the lady's part!
ピシャッ
SLAM
KLIKK!
INHALE

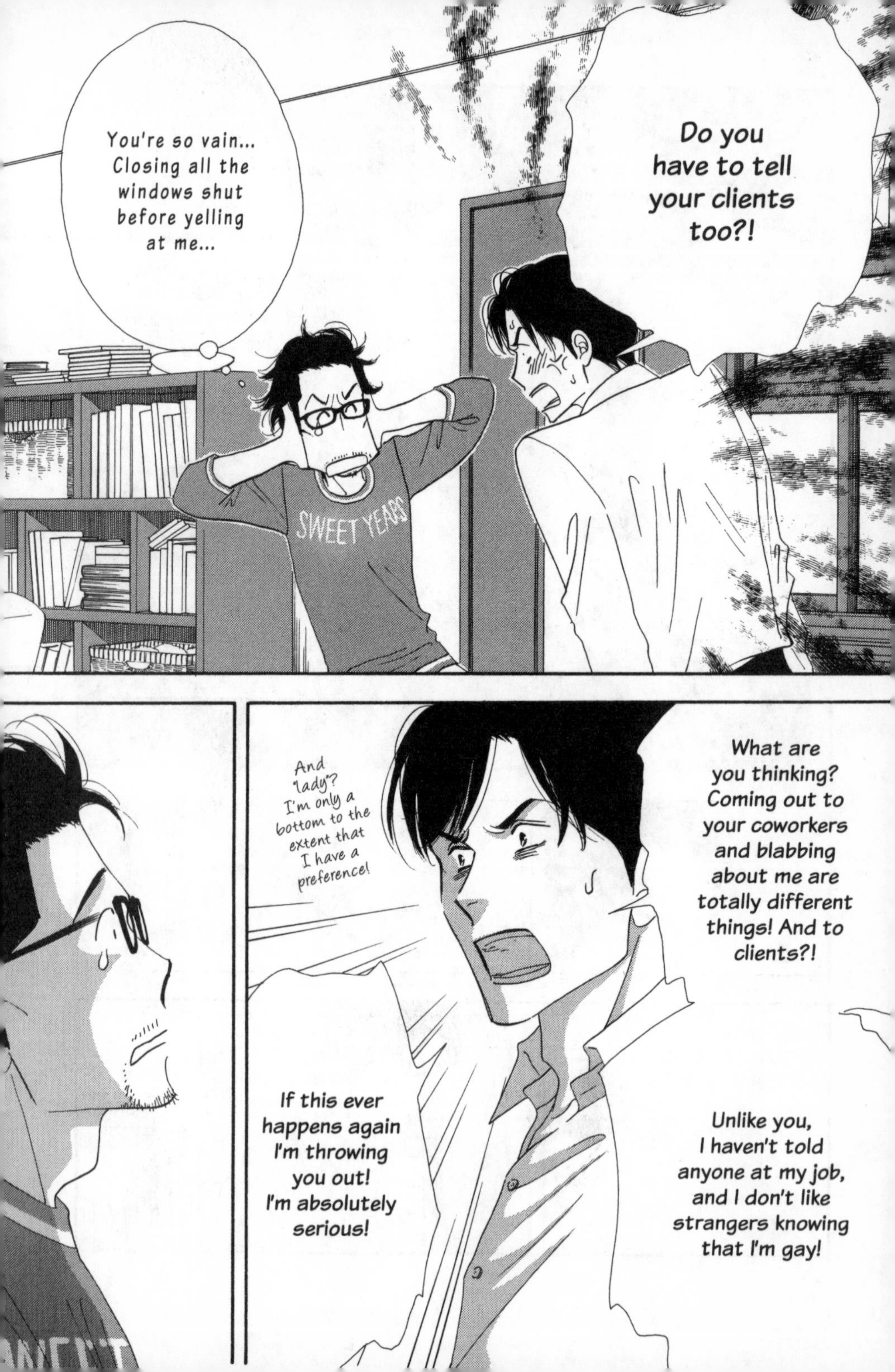
Do you have to tell your clients too?!
You're so vain... Closing all the windows shut before yelling at me...
SWEET YEARS
What are you thinking? Coming out to your coworkers and blabbing about me are totally different things! And to clients?!
And "lady"? I'm only a bottom to the extent that I have a preference!
Unlike you, I haven't told anyone at my job, and I don't like strangers knowing that I'm gay!
If this ever happens again I'm throwing you out! I'm absolutely serious!

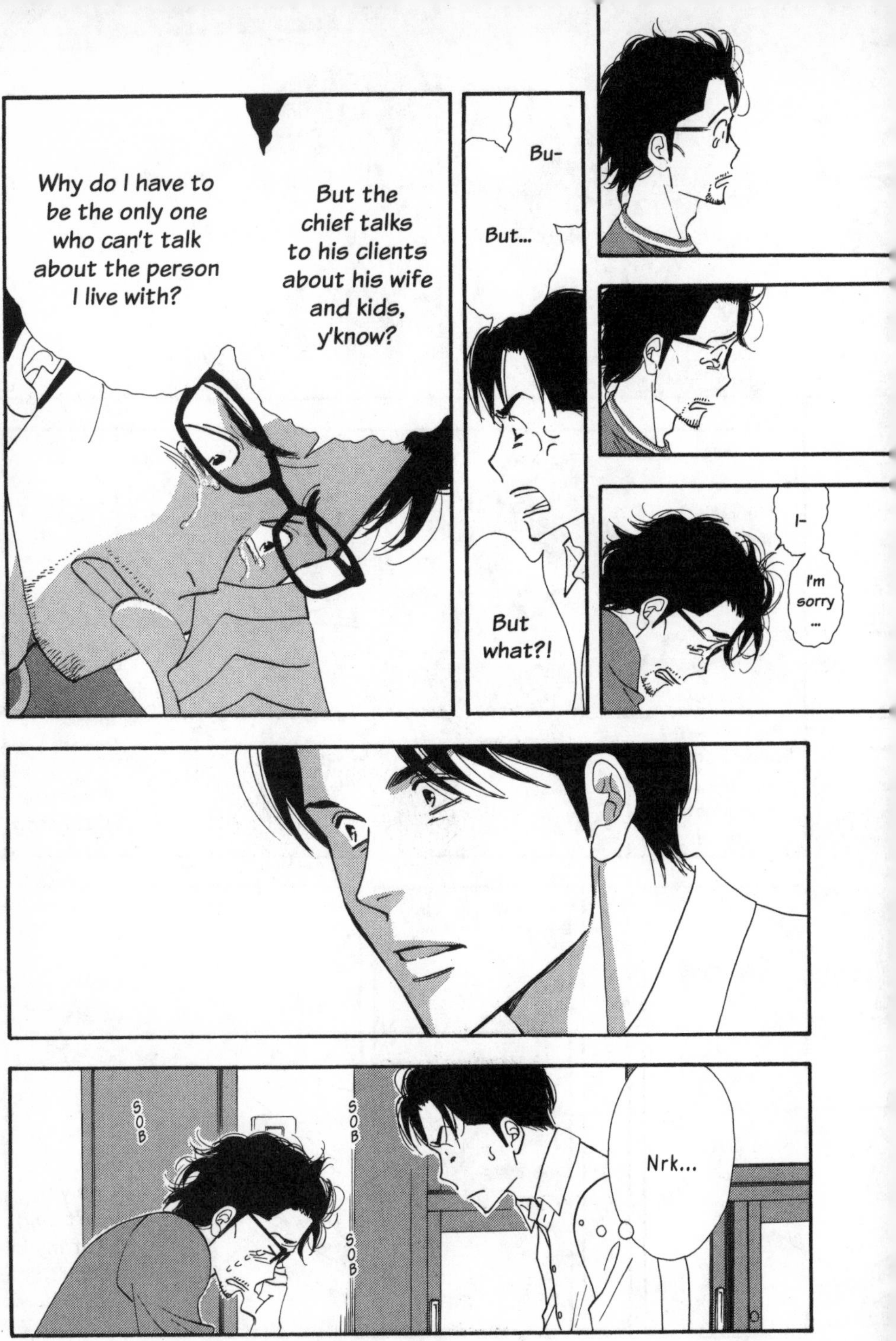
I-
I'm sorry...
Bu-
But...
But what?!
Why do I have to be the only one who can't talk about the person I live with?
But the chief talks to his clients about his wife and kids, y'know?
Nrk...
SOB
SOB
SOB

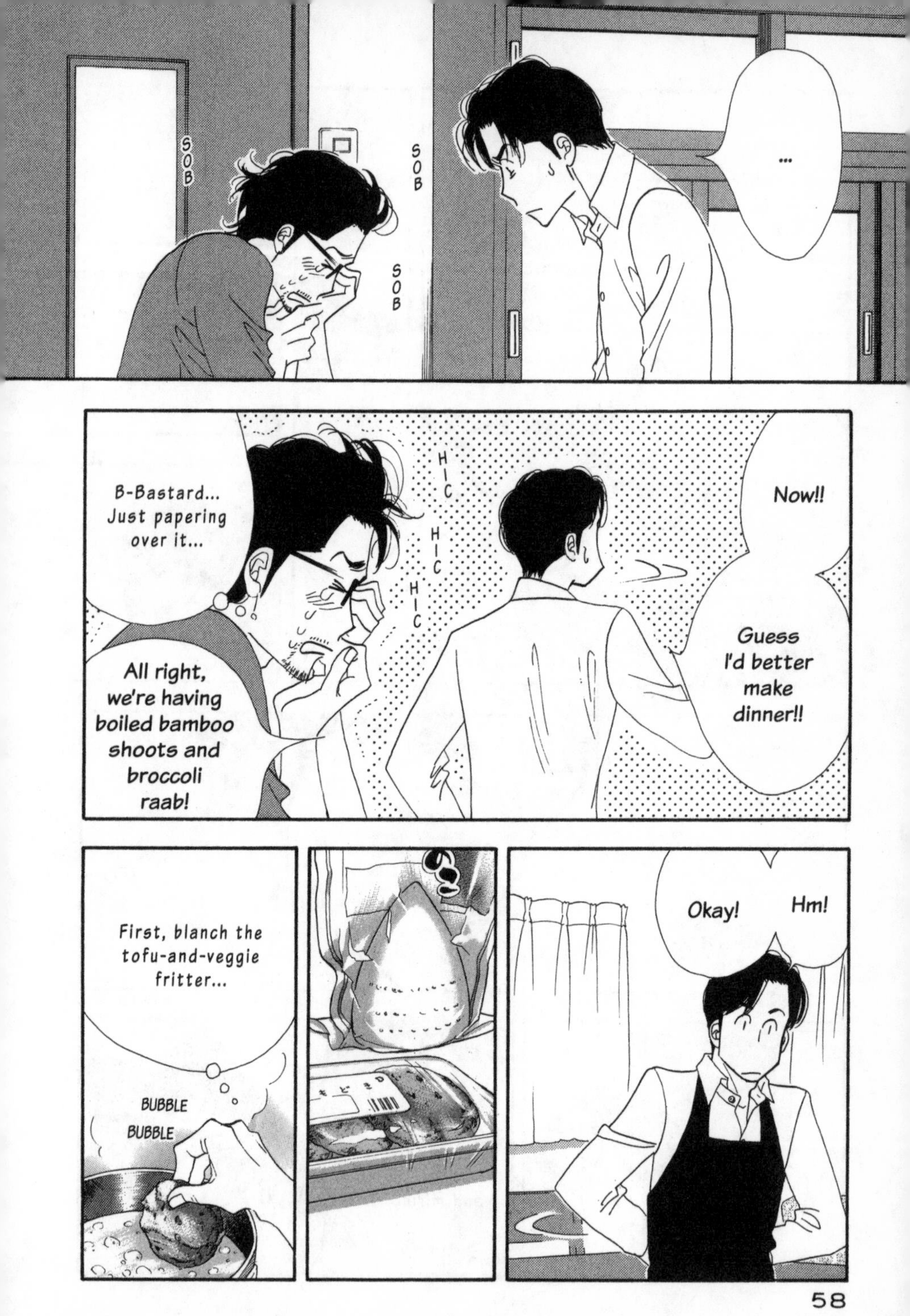
...
SOB
SOB
SOB
Now!!
Guess I'd better make dinner!!
HIC
HIC
HIC
B-Bastard... Just papering over it...
All right, we're having boiled bamboo shoots and broccoli raab!
Okay! Hm!
First, blanch the tofu-and-veggie fritter...
BUBBLE
BUBBLE

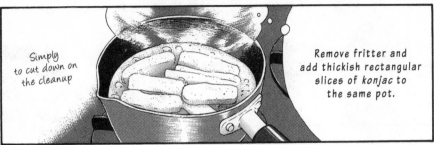

Remove fritter and add thickish rectangular slices of *konjac* to the same pot.
Simply to cut down on the cleanup
Slice open the middle of the *konjac* block half an inch from each end.
Tuck one end through opening and pull through to get...
TWIST
It's called braided konjac
This way the flavors seep into the *konjac* more easily.
Add roughly chopped bamboo shoots and the fritter to the pot and pour in water to cover.
Season with noodle broth base and mirin.
KLATTER
KLATTER

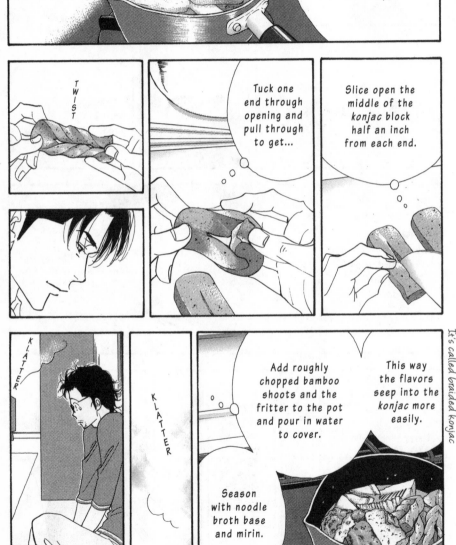

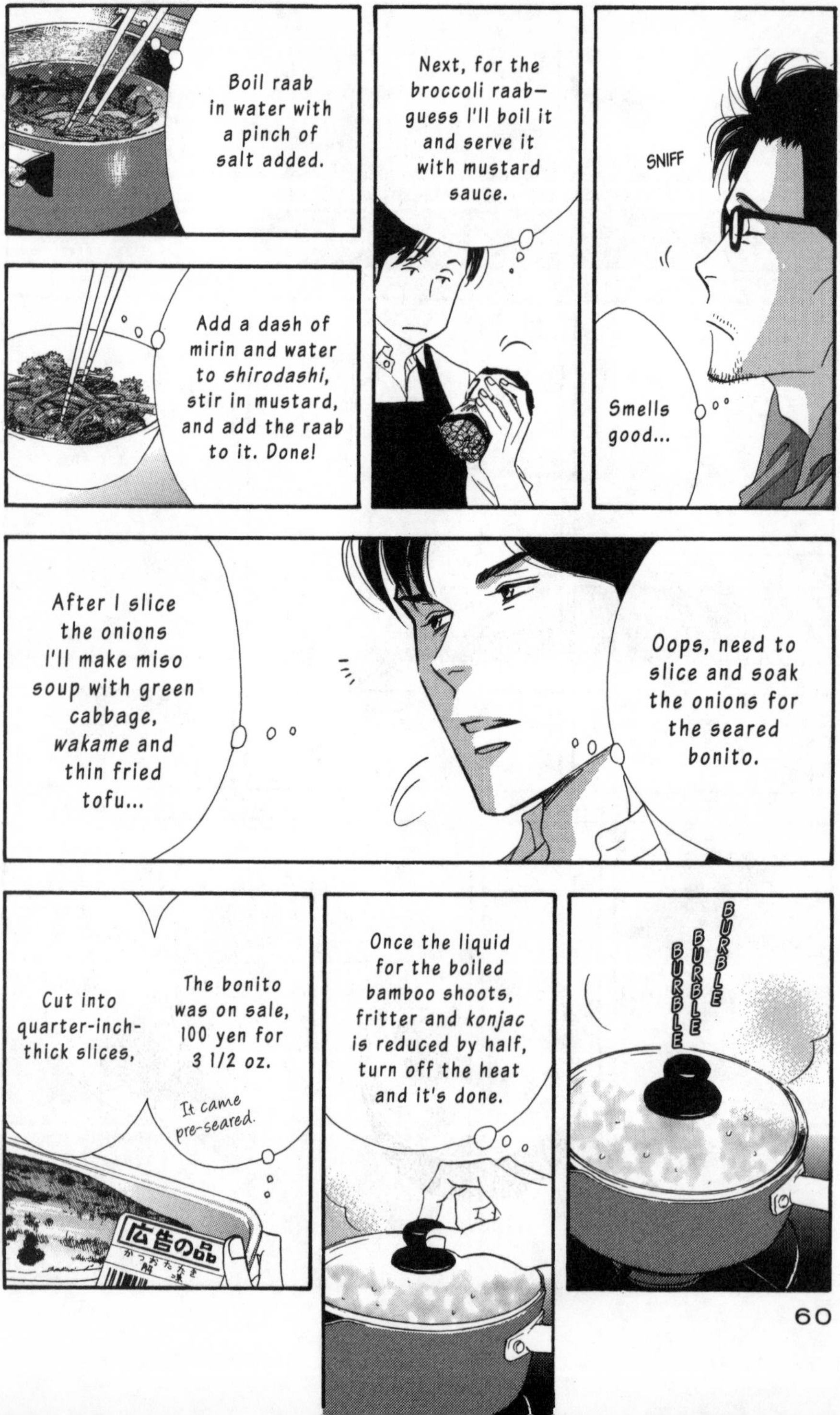

SNIFF
Smells good...
Next, for the broccoli raab—guess I'll boil it and serve it with mustard sauce.
Boil raab in water with a pinch of salt added.
Add a dash of mirin and water to *shirodashi*, stir in mustard, and add the raab to it. Done!
Oops, need to slice and soak the onions for the seared bonito.
After I slice the onions I'll make miso soup with green cabbage, *wakame* and thin fried tofu...
BURBLE
BURBLE
BURBLE
Once the liquid for the boiled bamboo shoots, fritter and *konjac* is reduced by half, turn off the heat and it's done.
The bonito was on sale, 100 yen for 3 1/2 oz.
It came pre-seared.
Cut into quarter-inch-thick slices,
広告の品

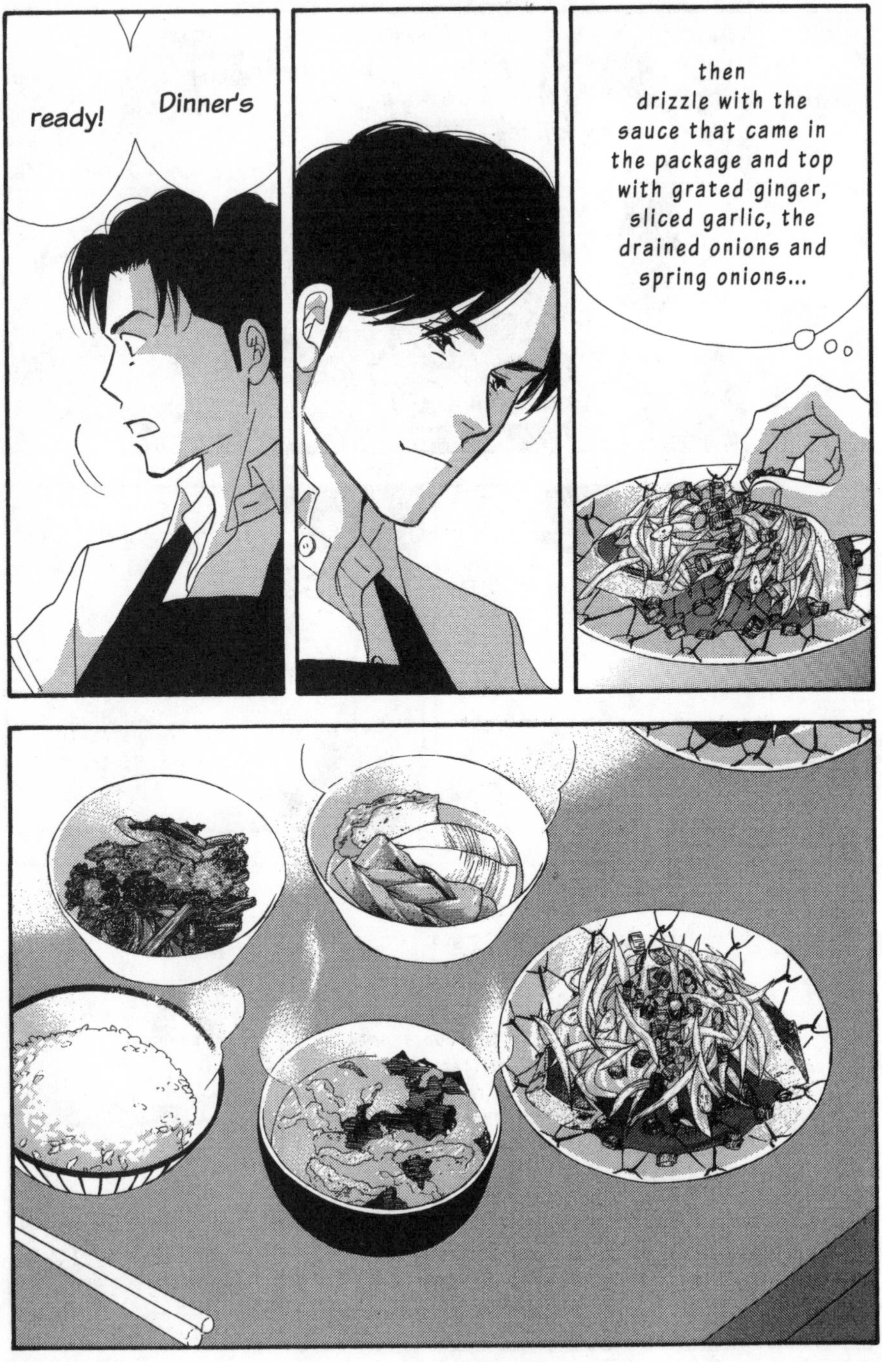
then drizzle with the sauce that came in the package and top with grated ginger, sliced garlic, the drained onions and spring onions...
Dinner's ready!

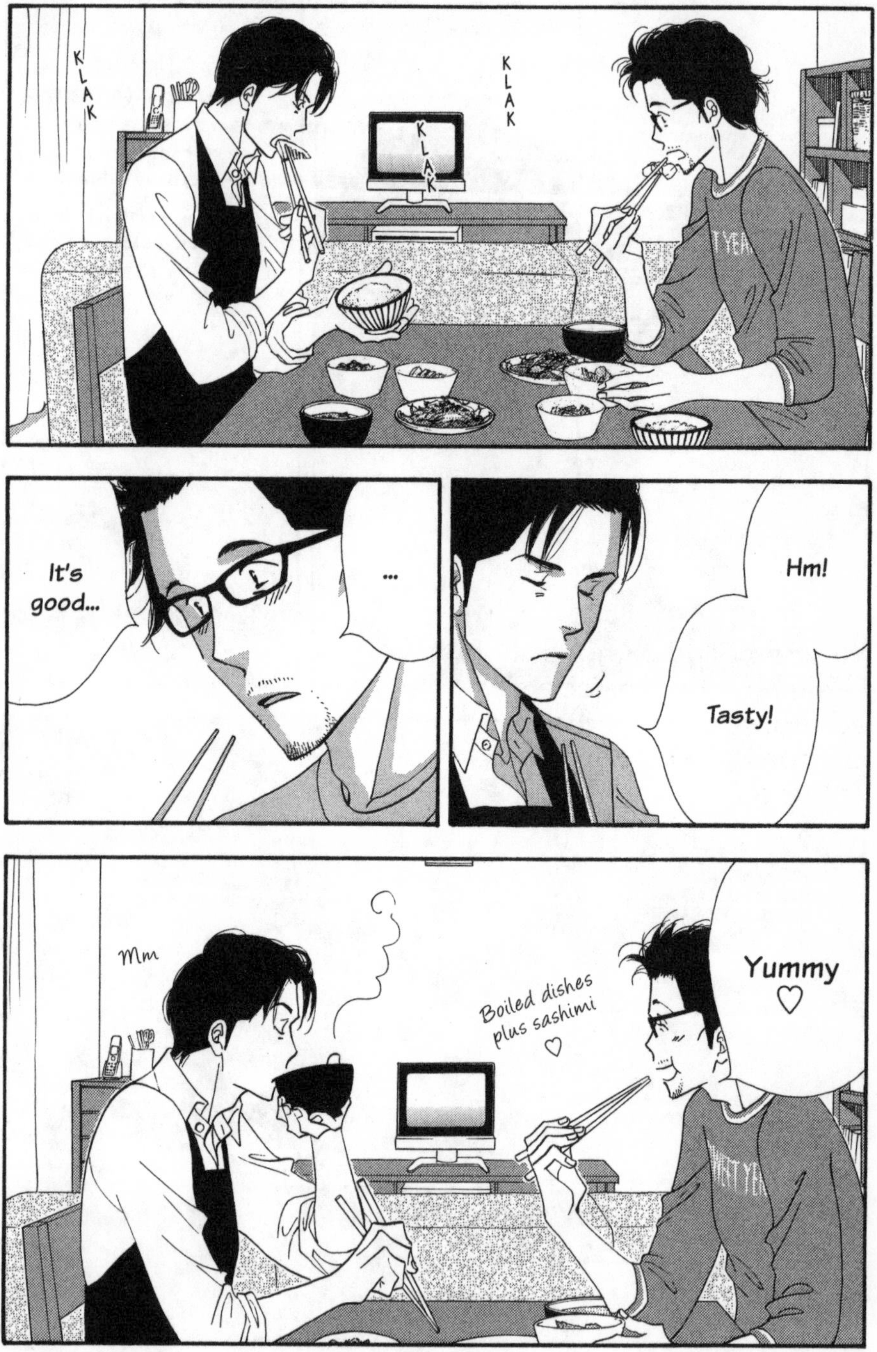
KLAK
KLAK
KLAK
Hm!
Tasty!
...
It's good...
Yummy ♡
Boiled dishes plus sashimi ♡
Mm

#3 END

For the boiled bamboo shoots, if you omit the *konjac* and add soaked, drained and chopped *wakame* seaweed at the very end of the cooking process, you'll have *wakatake-ni* ("boiled young bamboo").

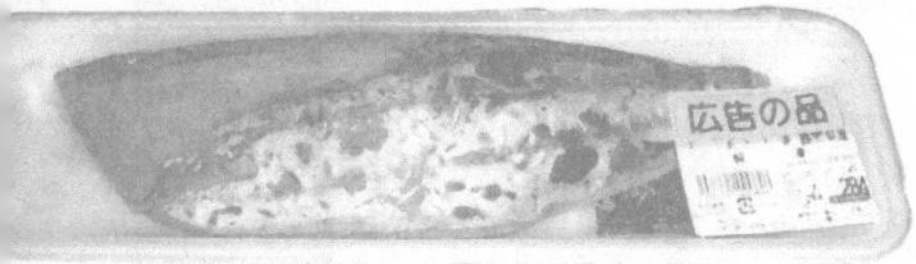
広告の品

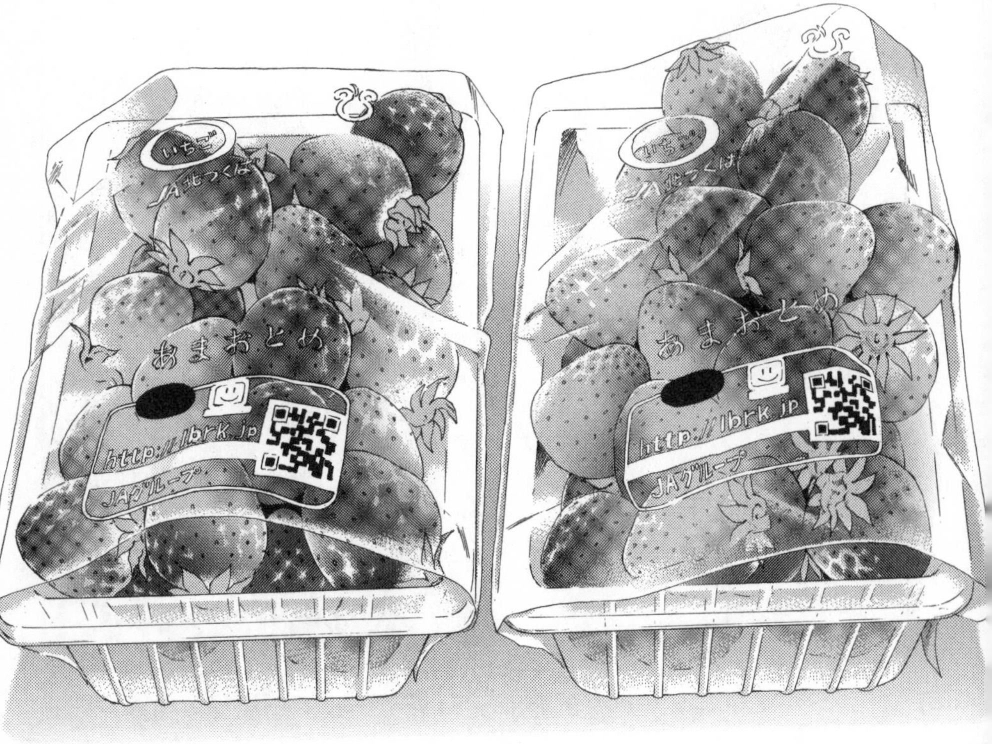
いちご
JA北つくば
あまおとめ
http://lbrk.jp
JAグループ
いちご
JA北つくば
あまおとめ
http://lbrk.jp
JAグループ

#4

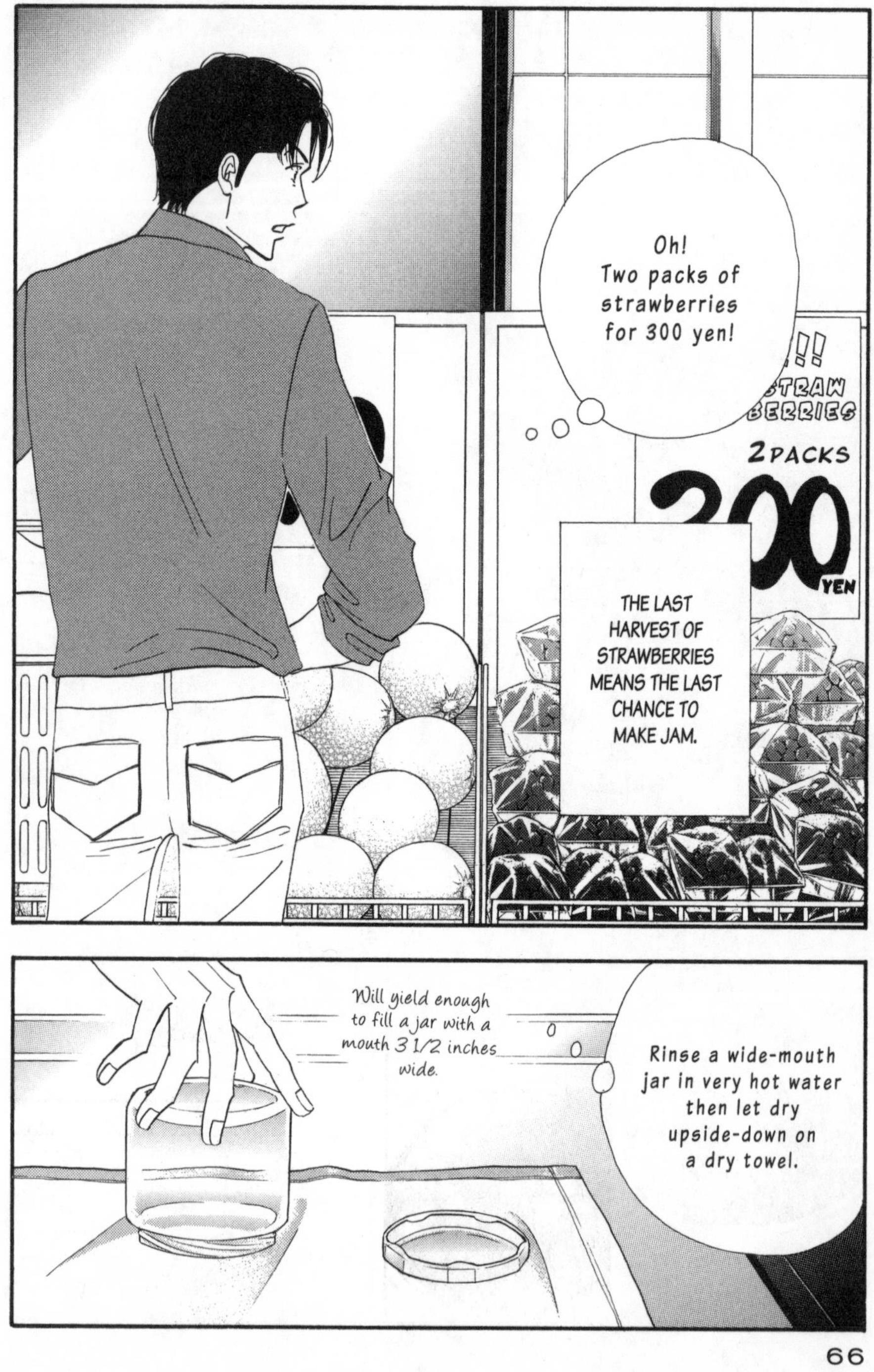

Oh! Two packs of strawberries for 300 yen!
STRAW BERRIES
2 PACKS
YEN
THE LAST HARVEST OF STRAWBERRIES MEANS THE LAST CHANCE TO MAKE JAM.
Rinse a wide-mouth jar in very hot water then let dry upside-down on a dry towel.
Will yield enough to fill a jar with a mouth 3 1/2 inches wide.

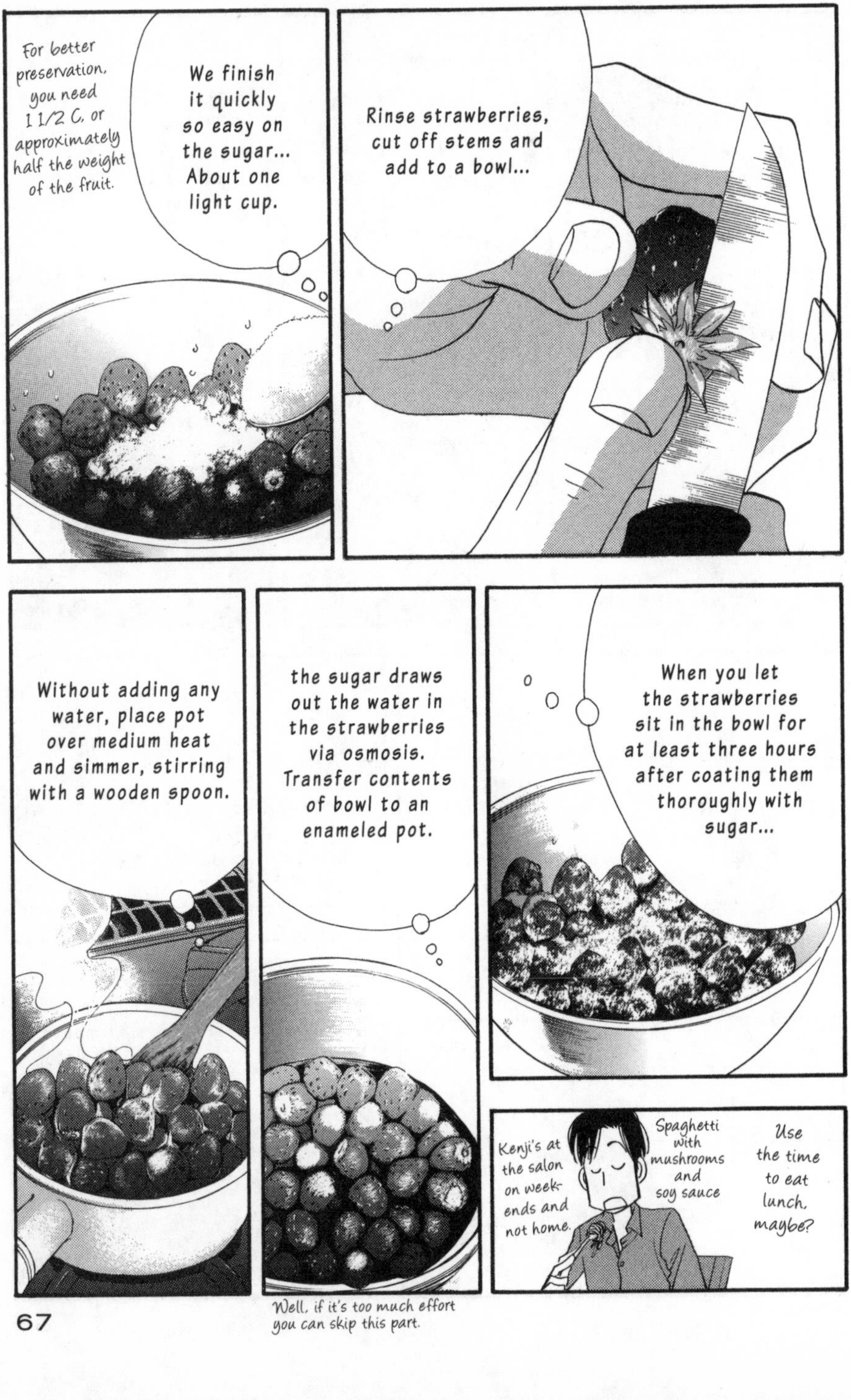
Rinse strawberries, cut off stems and add to a bowl...
We finish it quickly so easy on the sugar... About one light cup.
For better preservation, you need 1 1/2 C, or approximately half the weight of the fruit.
When you let the strawberries sit in the bowl for at least three hours after coating them thoroughly with sugar...
Use the time to eat lunch, maybe?
Spaghetti with mushrooms and soy sauce
Kenji's at the salon on week-ends and not home.
the sugar draws out the water in the strawberries via osmosis. Transfer contents of bowl to an enameled pot.
Well, if it's too much effort you can skip this part.
Without adding any water, place pot over medium heat and simmer, stirring with a wooden spoon.

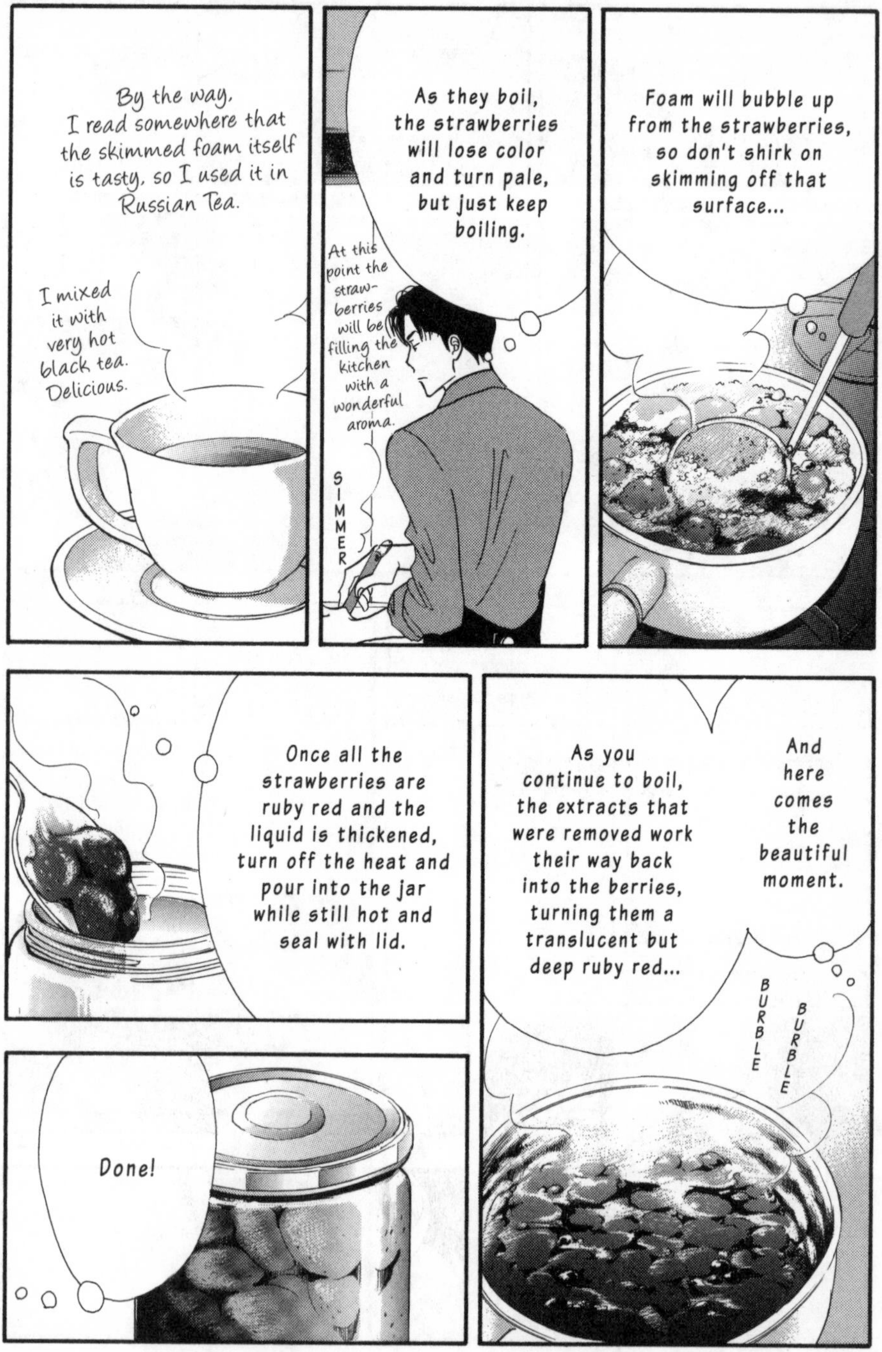

Foam will bubble up from the strawberries, so don't shirk on skimming off that surface...
As they boil, the strawberries will lose color and turn pale, but just keep boiling.
At this point the straw-berries will be filling the kitchen with a wonderful aroma.
SIMMER
By the way, I read somewhere that the skimmed foam itself is tasty, so I used it in Russian Tea.
I mixed it with very hot black tea. Delicious.
And here comes the beautiful moment.
As you continue to boil, the extracts that were removed work their way back into the berries, turning them a translucent but deep ruby red...
BURBLE
BURBLE
Once all the strawberries are ruby red and the liquid is thickened, turn off the heat and pour into the jar while still hot and seal with lid.
Done!

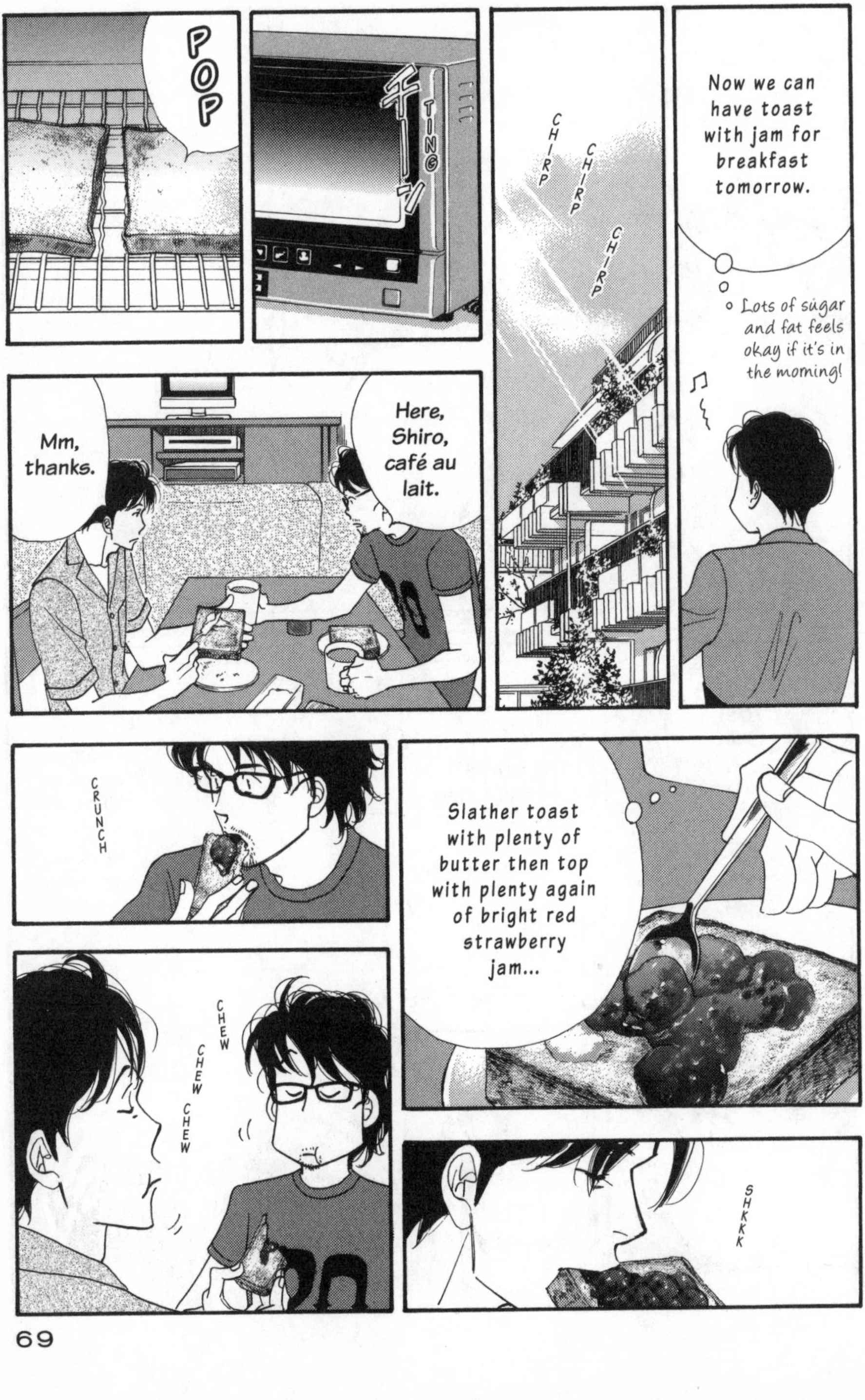

Now we can have toast with jam for breakfast tomorrow.
Lots of sugar and fat feels okay if it's in the morning!
CHIRP
CHIRP
CHIRP
チーン
TING
POP
Here, Shiro, café au lait.
Mm, thanks.
Slather toast with plenty of butter then top with plenty again of bright red strawberry jam...
SHKKK
CRUNCH
CHEW
CHEW
CHEW

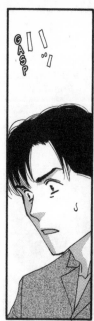

Ahh, the sweet and tart jam and slightly salty butter makes it so delicious!
I. AM. SO. LUCKY~ ♡
GASP
W-Wait, I only made jam because strawberries are in season, it's not my hobby or anything! I can't make marmalade or anything complicated like that!
Marmalade? No ordinary guy bothers to make any kind of jam.
SURE SURE
But Shiro,
...
when it comes to bread, you go to a real bakery.

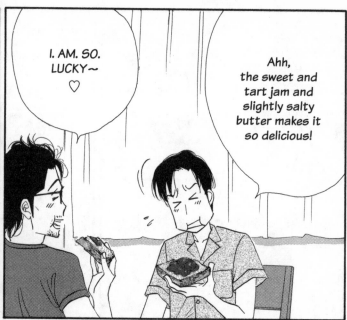

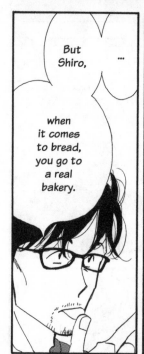

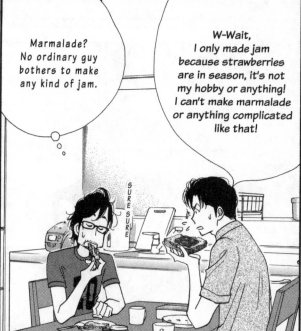

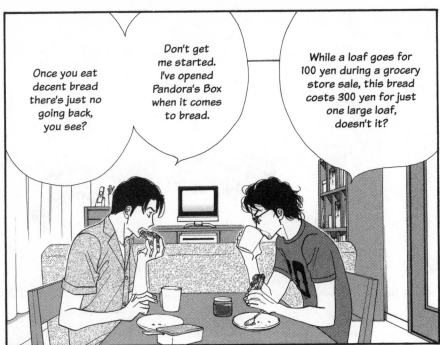

While a loaf goes for 100 yen during a grocery store sale, this bread costs 300 yen for just one large loaf, doesn't it?
Don't get me started. I've opened Pandora's Box when it comes to bread.
Once you eat decent bread there's just no going back, you see?
Still, for real bread from a bakery, this place is on the cheap side, y'know? And it's tasty.
I mean why not? I buy sprouted brown rice too, but we're keeping within the monthly food budget of 25,000 yen for the two of us.
...

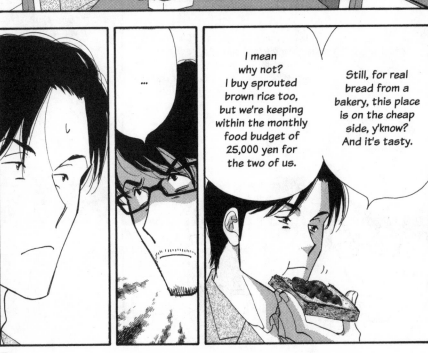

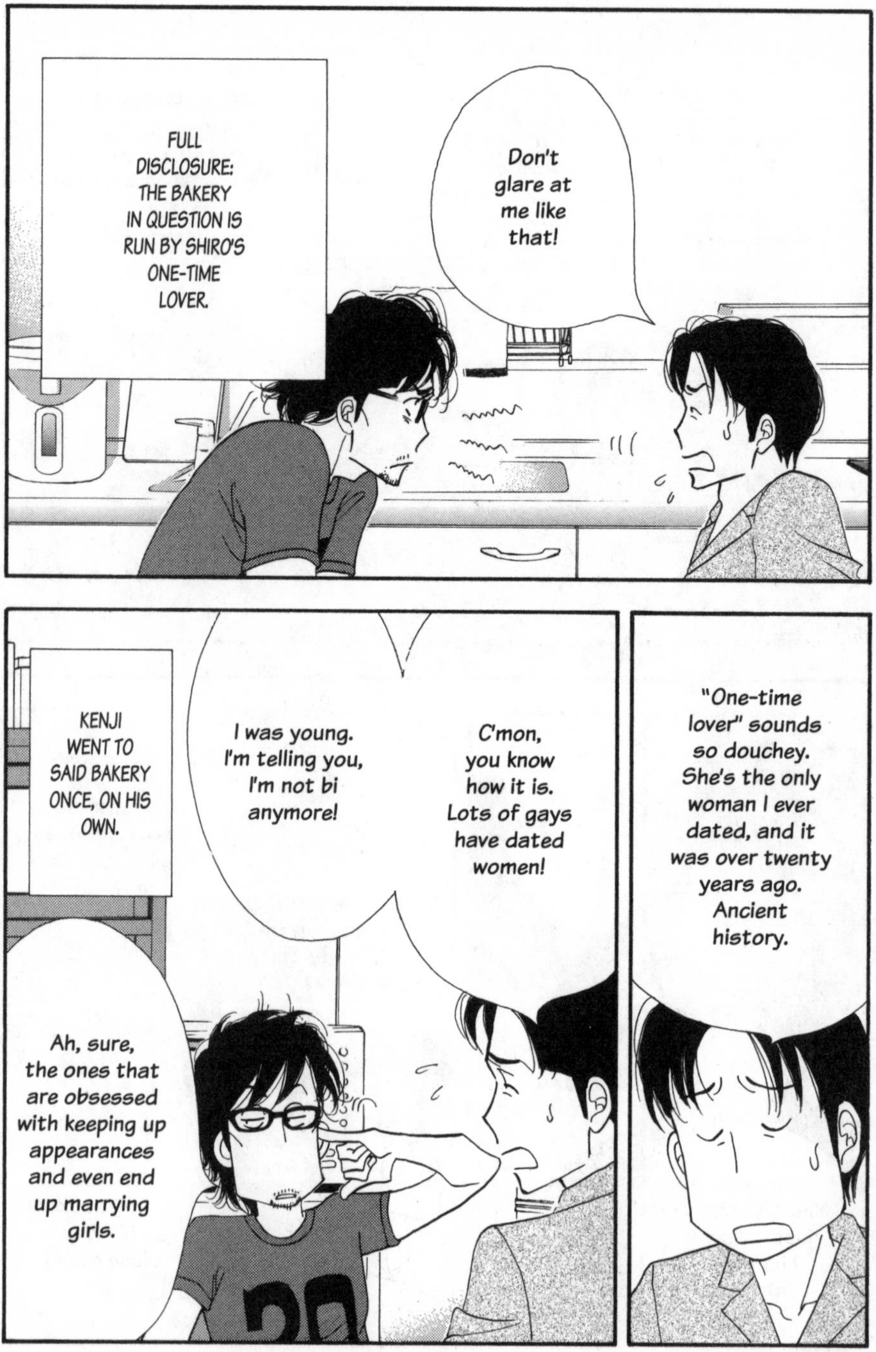
Don't glare at me like that!
FULL DISCLOSURE: THE BAKERY IN QUESTION IS RUN BY SHIRO'S ONE-TIME LOVER.
"One-time lover" sounds so douchey. She's the only woman I ever dated, and it was over twenty years ago. Ancient history.
C'mon, you know how it is. Lots of gays have dated women!
I was young. I'm telling you, I'm not bi anymore!
KENJI WENT TO SAID BAKERY ONCE, ON HIS OWN.
Ah, sure, the ones that are obsessed with keeping up appearances and even end up marrying girls.

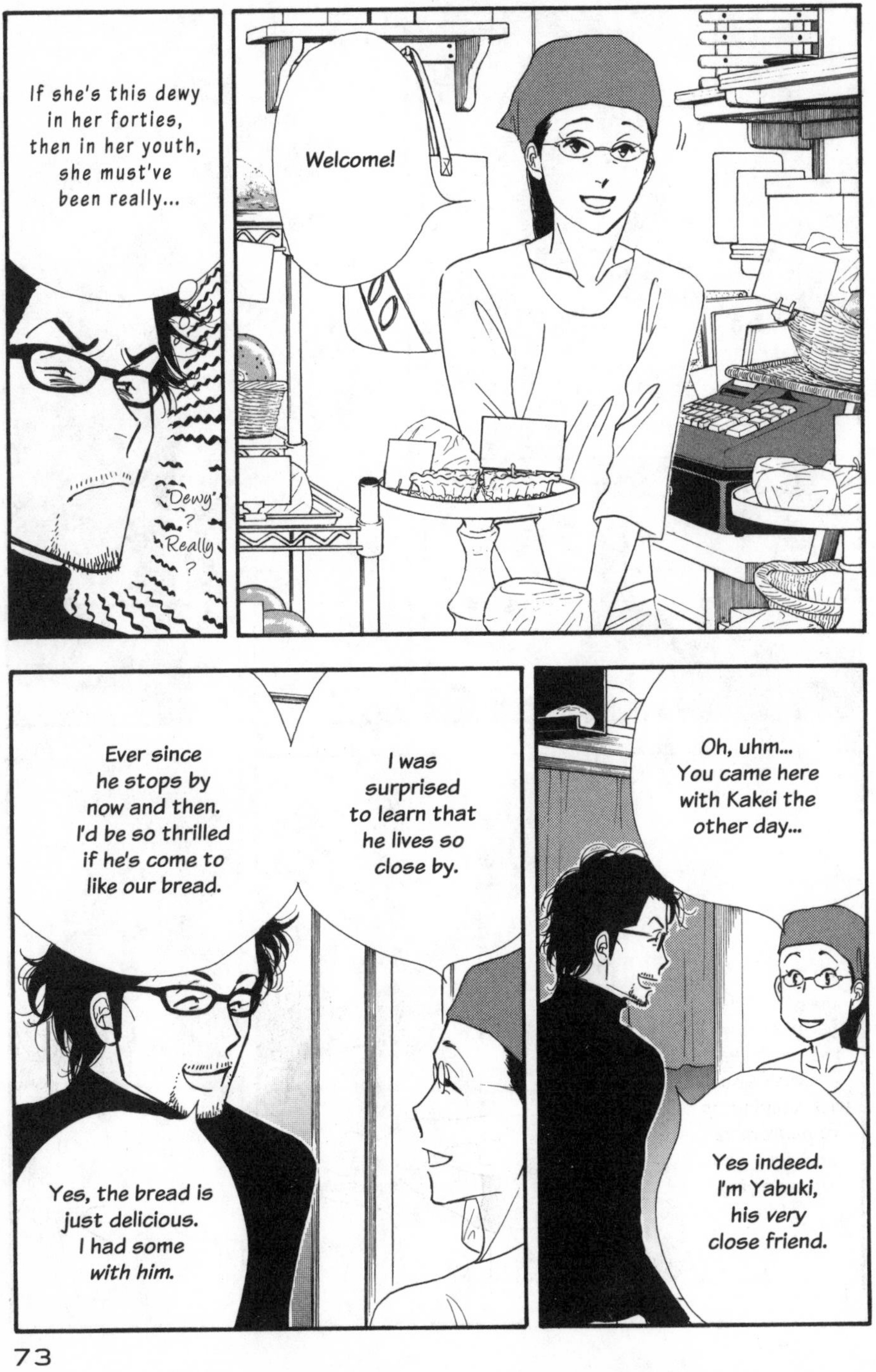
Welcome!
If she's this dewy in her forties, then in her youth, she must've been really...
'Dewy'? Really?
Oh, uhm... You came here with Kakei the other day...
Yes indeed. I'm Yabuki, his *very* close friend.
I was surprised to learn that he lives so close by.
Ever since he stops by now and then. I'd be so thrilled if he's come to like our bread.
Yes, the bread is just delicious. I had some *with him.*

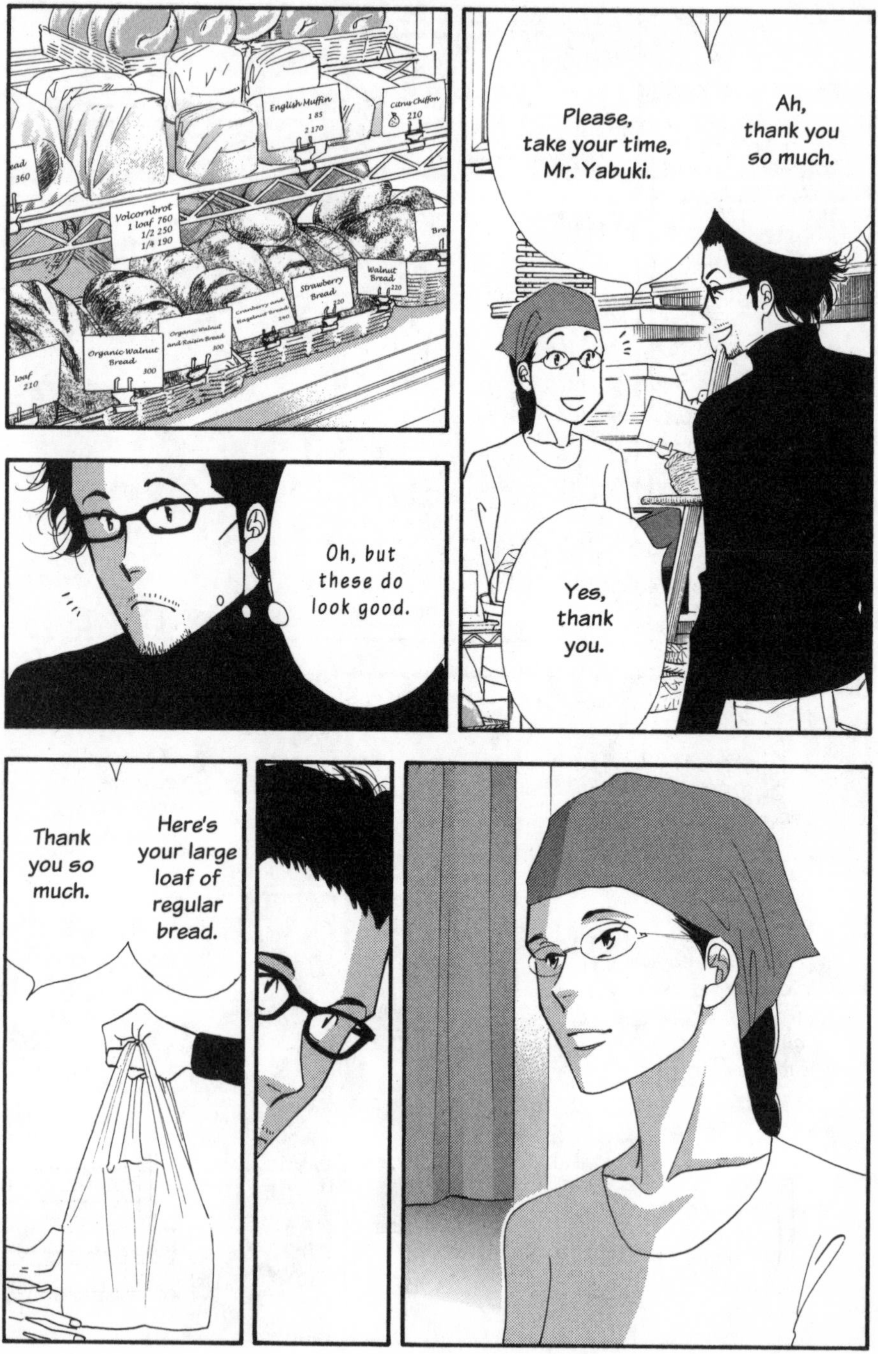
Ah, thank you so much.
Please, take your time, Mr. Yabuki.
Yes, thank you.
English Muffin 1 85 2 170
Citrus Chiffon 210
Volcornbrot 1 loaf 760 1/2 250 1/4 190
Walnut Bread 220
Strawberry Bread 220
Cranberry and Hazelnut Bread 240
Organic Walnut and Raisin Bread 300
Organic Walnut Bread 300
Oh, but these do look good.
Here's your large loaf of regular bread.
Thank you so much.

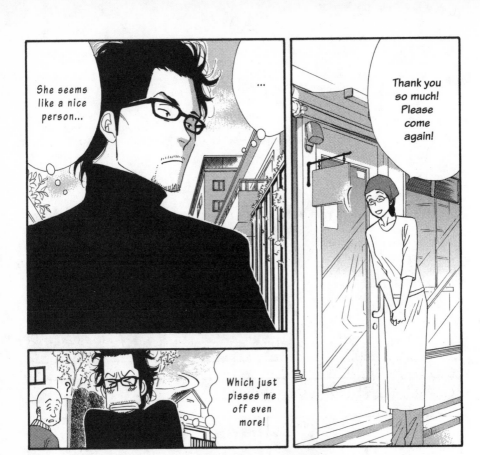

Thank you so much! Please come again!
...
She seems like a nice person...
Which just pisses me off even more!
You'll never understand how wretched I felt that day, Shiro...
tissue
Um, how am I to respond to you feeling like a wife who just scouted out her husband's mistress's little eatery?

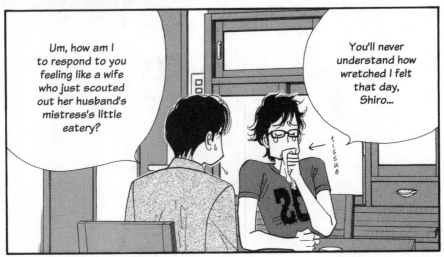

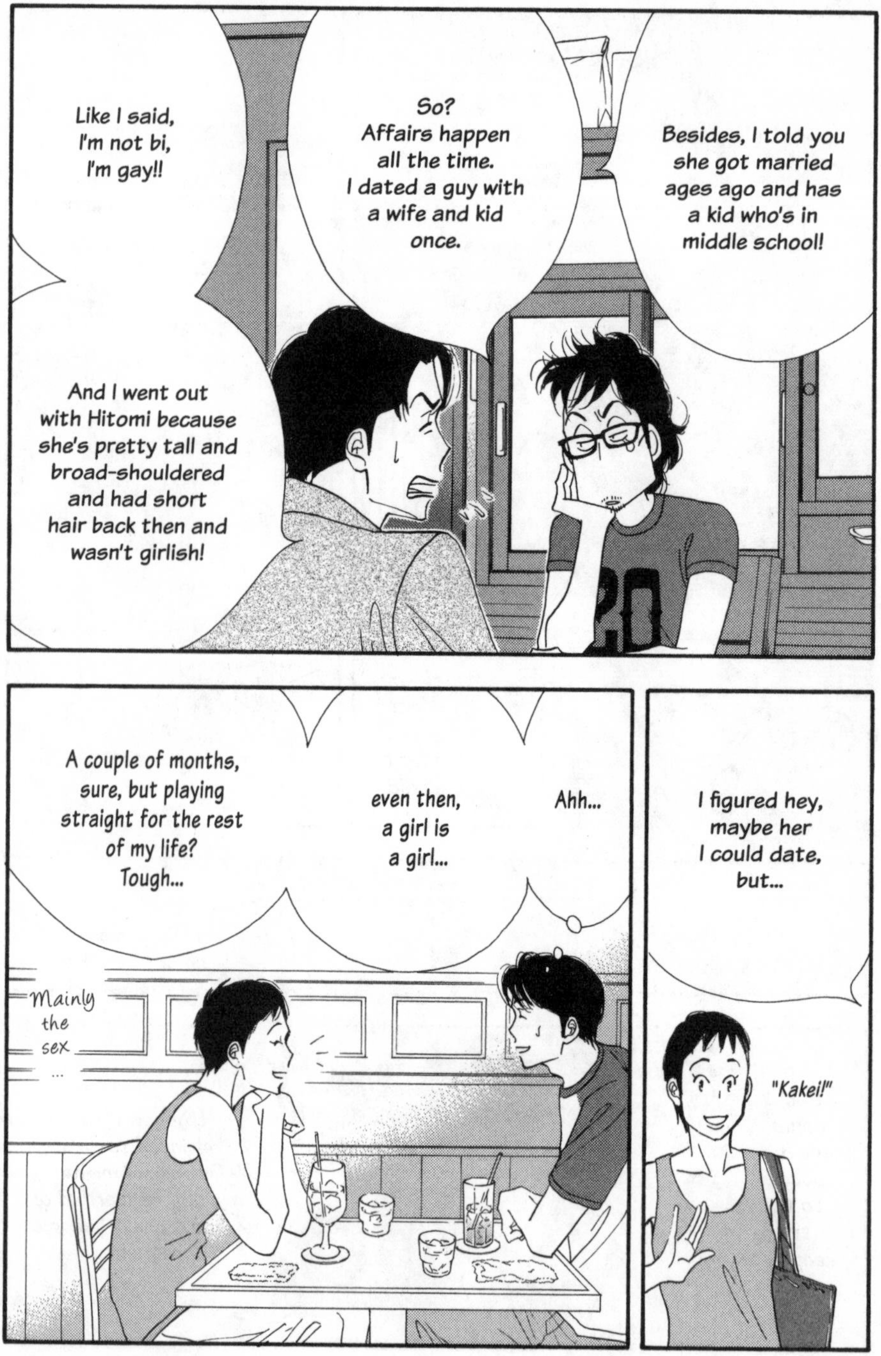

Besides, I told you she got married ages ago and has a kid who's in middle school!
So? Affairs happen all the time. I dated a guy with a wife and kid once.
Like I said, I'm not bi, I'm gay!!
And I went out with Hitomi because she's pretty tall and broad-shouldered and had short hair back then and wasn't girlish!
I figured hey, maybe her I could date, but...
"Kakei!"
Ahh...
even then, a girl is a girl...
A couple of months, sure, but playing straight for the rest of my life? Tough...
Mainly the sex ...

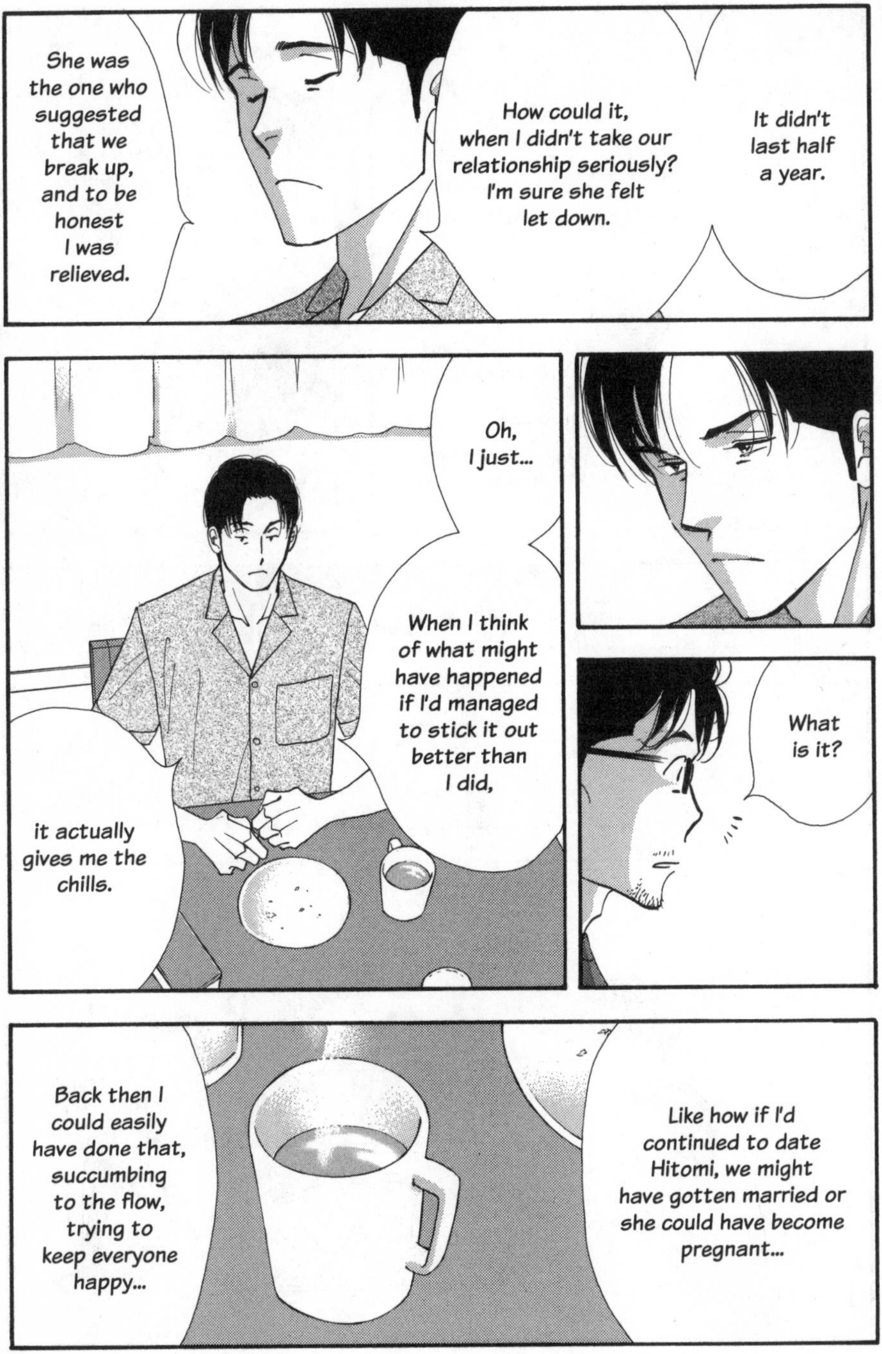

It didn't last half a year.
How could it, when I didn't take our relationship seriously? I'm sure she felt let down.
She was the one who suggested that we break up, and to be honest I was relieved.
What is it?
Oh, I just...
When I think of what might have happened if I'd managed to stick it out better than I did,
it actually gives me the chills.
Like how if I'd continued to date Hitomi, we might have gotten married or she could have become pregnant...
Back then I could easily have done that, succumbing to the flow, trying to keep everyone happy...

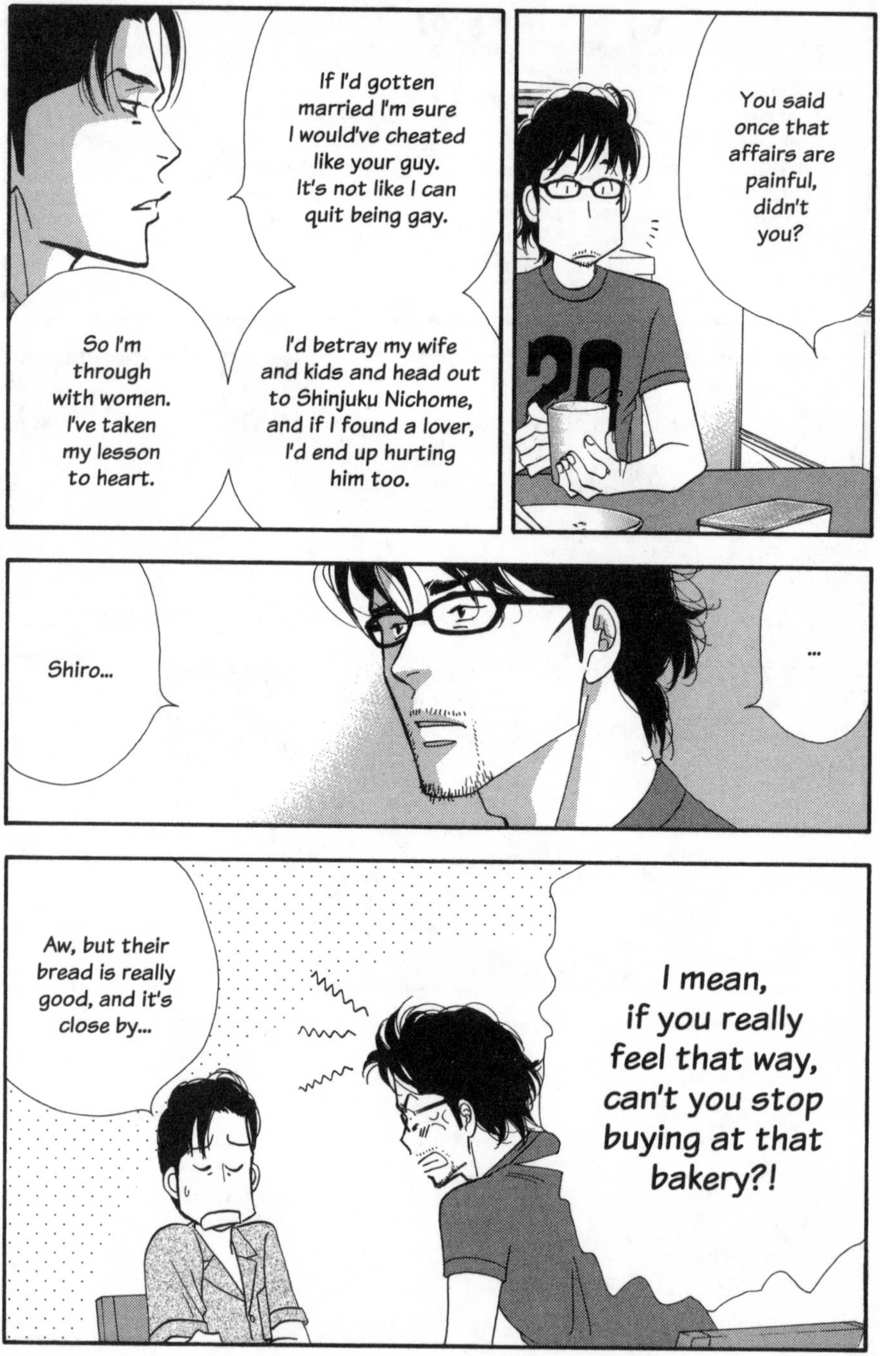
You said once that affairs are painful, didn't you?
If I'd gotten married I'm sure I would've cheated like your guy. It's not like I can quit being gay.
I'd betray my wife and kids and head out to Shinjuku Nichome, and if I found a lover, I'd end up hurting him too.
So I'm through with women. I've taken my lesson to heart.
...
Shiro...
I mean, if you really feel that way, can't you stop buying at that bakery?!
Aw, but their bread is really good, and it's close by...

#4 END

In the summer you can make
simple yet delicious jam from
plums and nectarines as well. Rinse
thoroughly but leave skins on.
Slice all the way around the pit
then twist apart halves.
Leave pits in place and as with
the strawberries boil with sugar
(1/2 weight of fruit).
The pits will naturally pull away
from the fruit so remove at the end
of the cooking process.

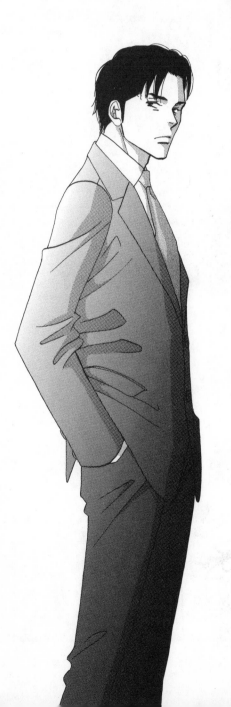

#5

SHIRO KAKEI IS
INDEED VERY
HANDSOME.

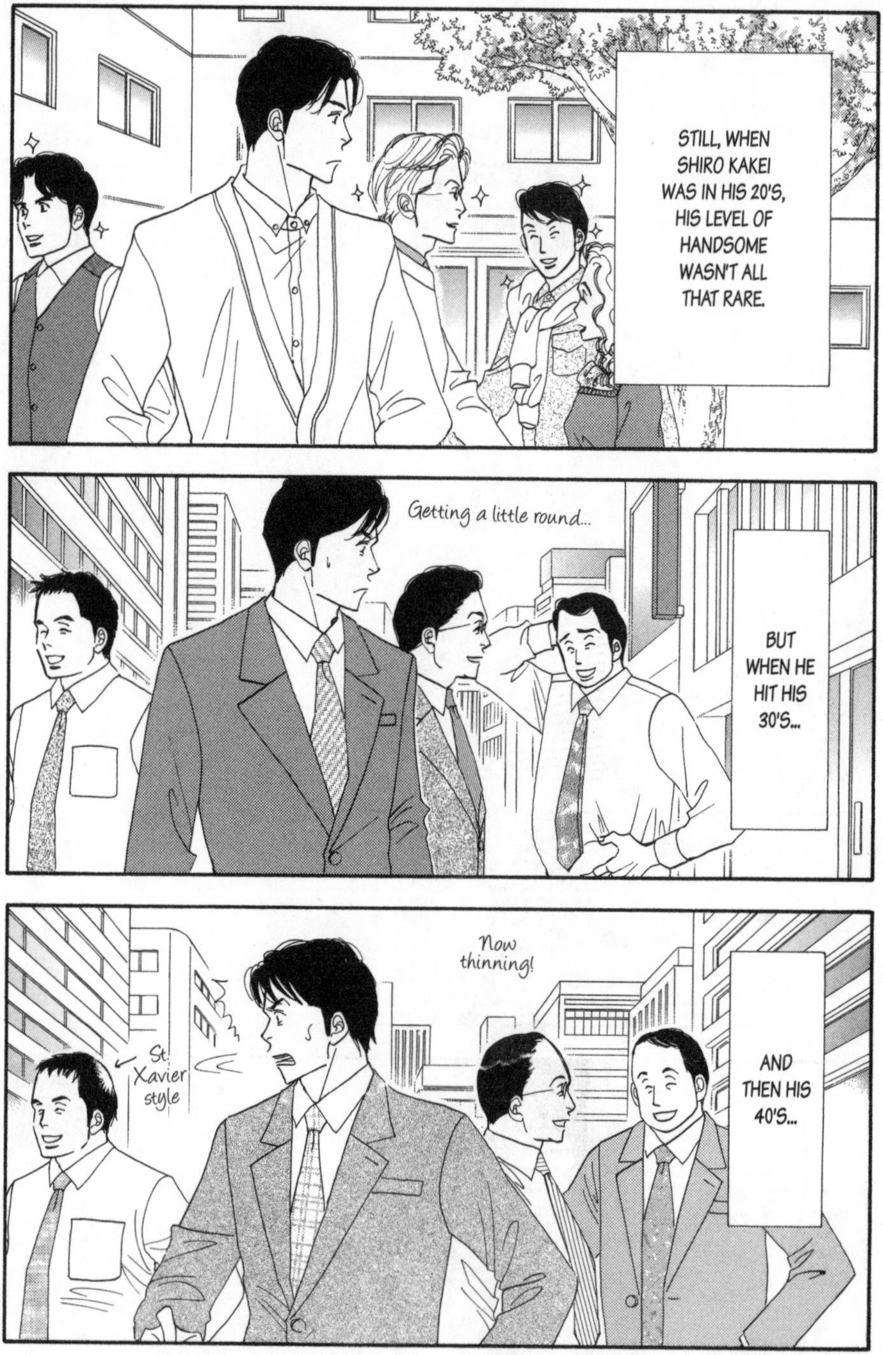
STILL, WHEN SHIRO KAKEI WAS IN HIS 20'S, HIS LEVEL OF HANDSOME WASN'T ALL THAT RARE.
BUT WHEN HE HIT HIS 30'S...
Getting a little round...
AND THEN HIS 40'S...
Now thinning!
St. Xavier style

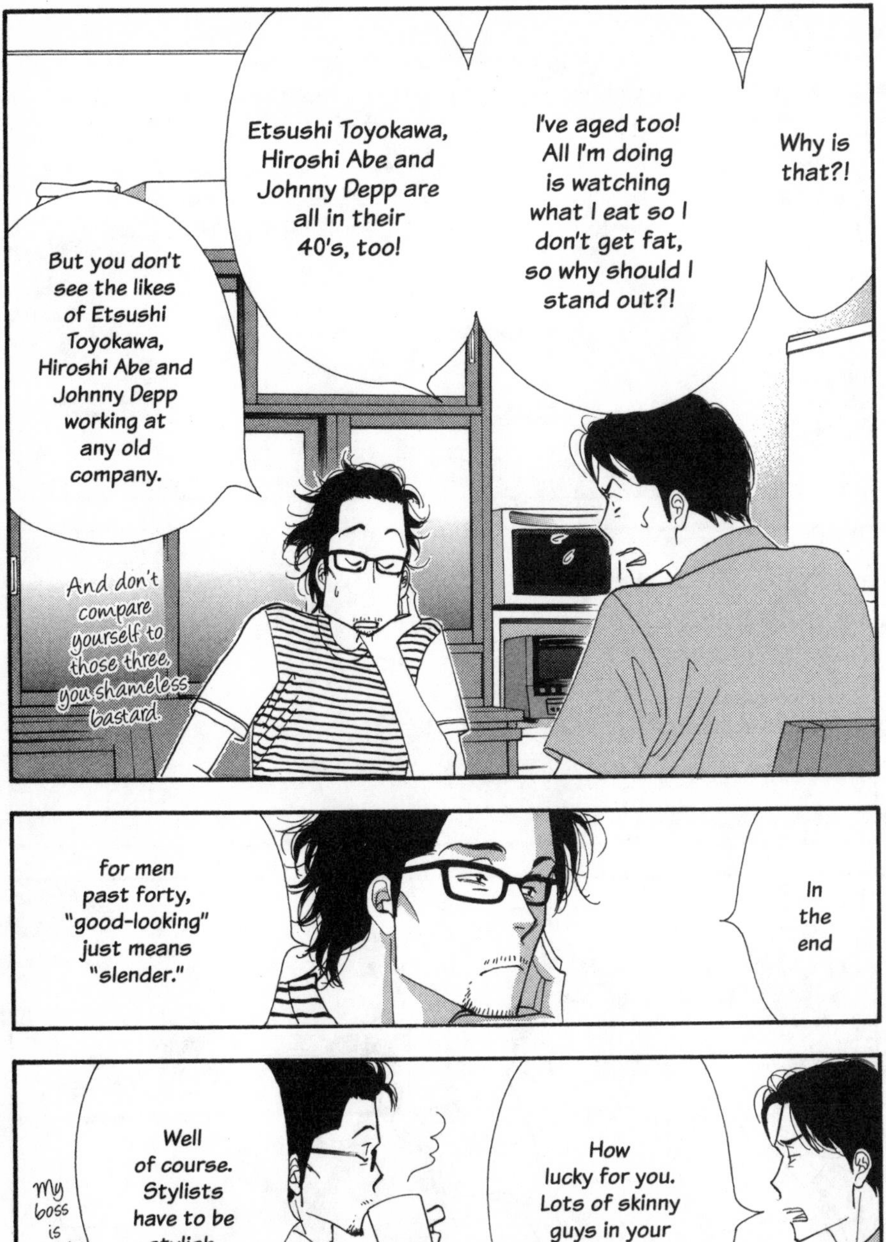
Why is that?!
I've aged too! All I'm doing is watching what I eat so I don't get fat, so why should I stand out?!
Etsushi Toyokawa, Hiroshi Abe and Johnny Depp are all in their 40's, too!
But you don't see the likes of Etsushi Toyokawa, Hiroshi Abe and Johnny Depp working at any old company.
And don't compare yourself to those three, you shameless bastard.
In the end
for men past forty, "good-looking" just means "slender."
How lucky for you. Lots of skinny guys in your industry!
Well of course. Stylists have to be stylish.
My boss is chubby though.

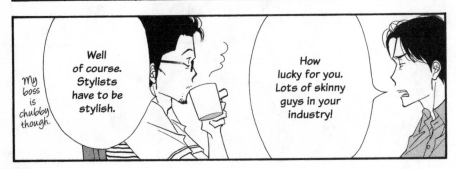

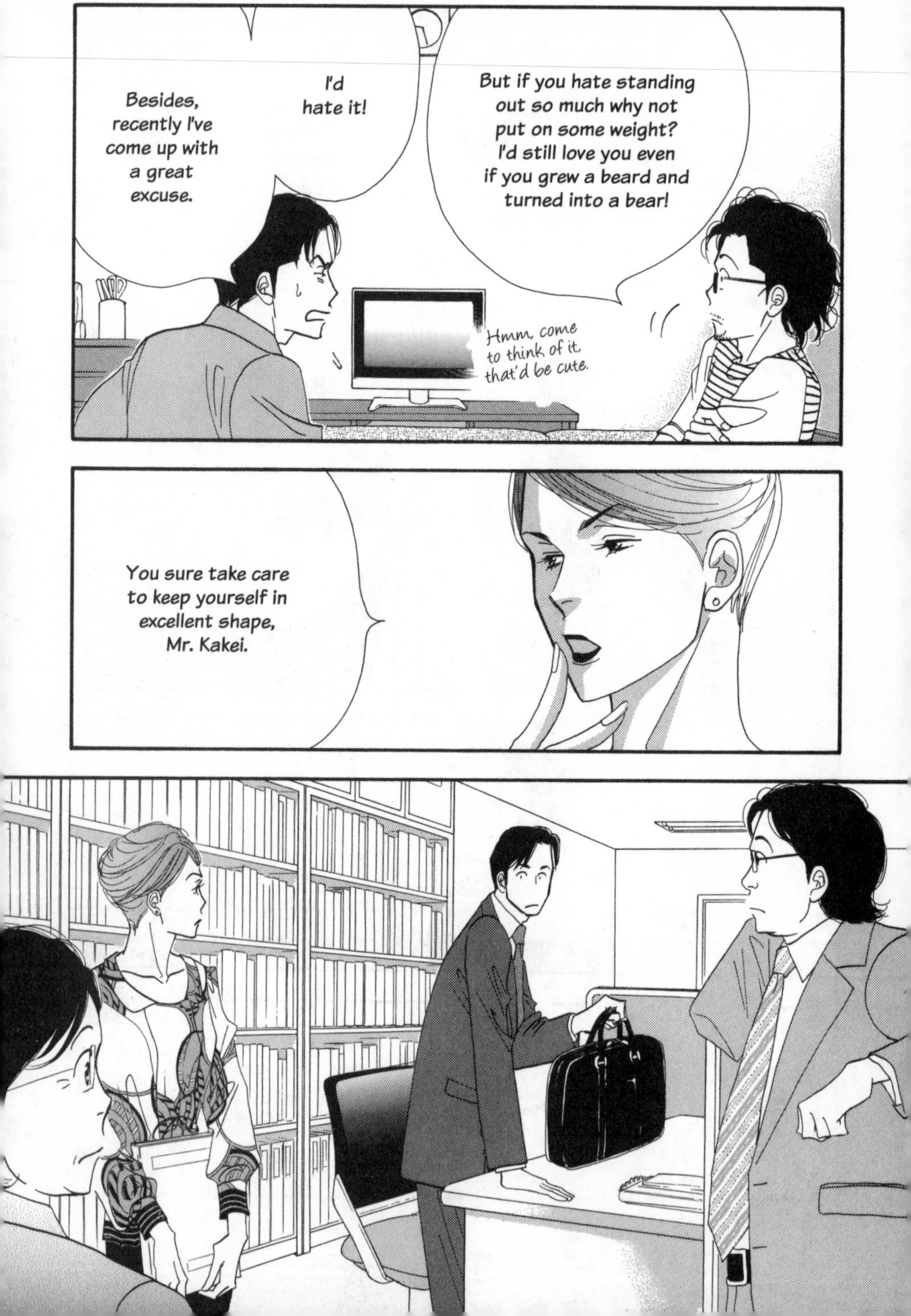

But if you hate standing out so much why not put on some weight? I'd still love you even if you grew a beard and turned into a bear!
Hmm, come to think of it, that'd be cute.
I'd hate it!
Besides, recently I've come up with a great excuse.
You sure take care to keep yourself in excellent shape, Mr. Kakei.

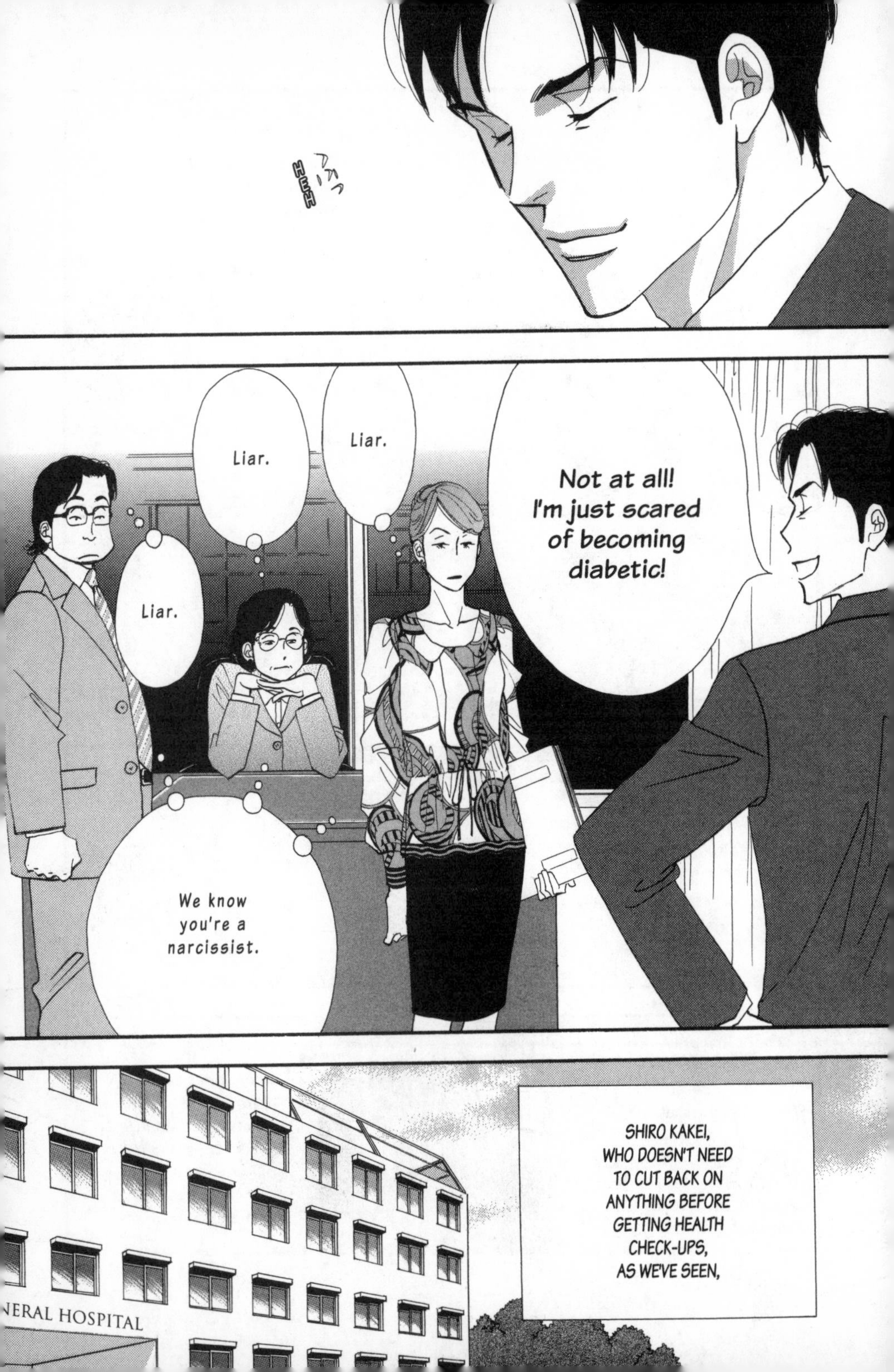
HEH
Not at all! I'm just scared of becoming diabetic!
Liar.
Liar.
Liar.
We know you're a narcissist.
SHIRO KAKEI, WHO DOESN'T NEED TO CUT BACK ON ANYTHING BEFORE GETTING HEALTH CHECK-UPS, AS WE'VE SEEN,
NERAL HOSPITAL

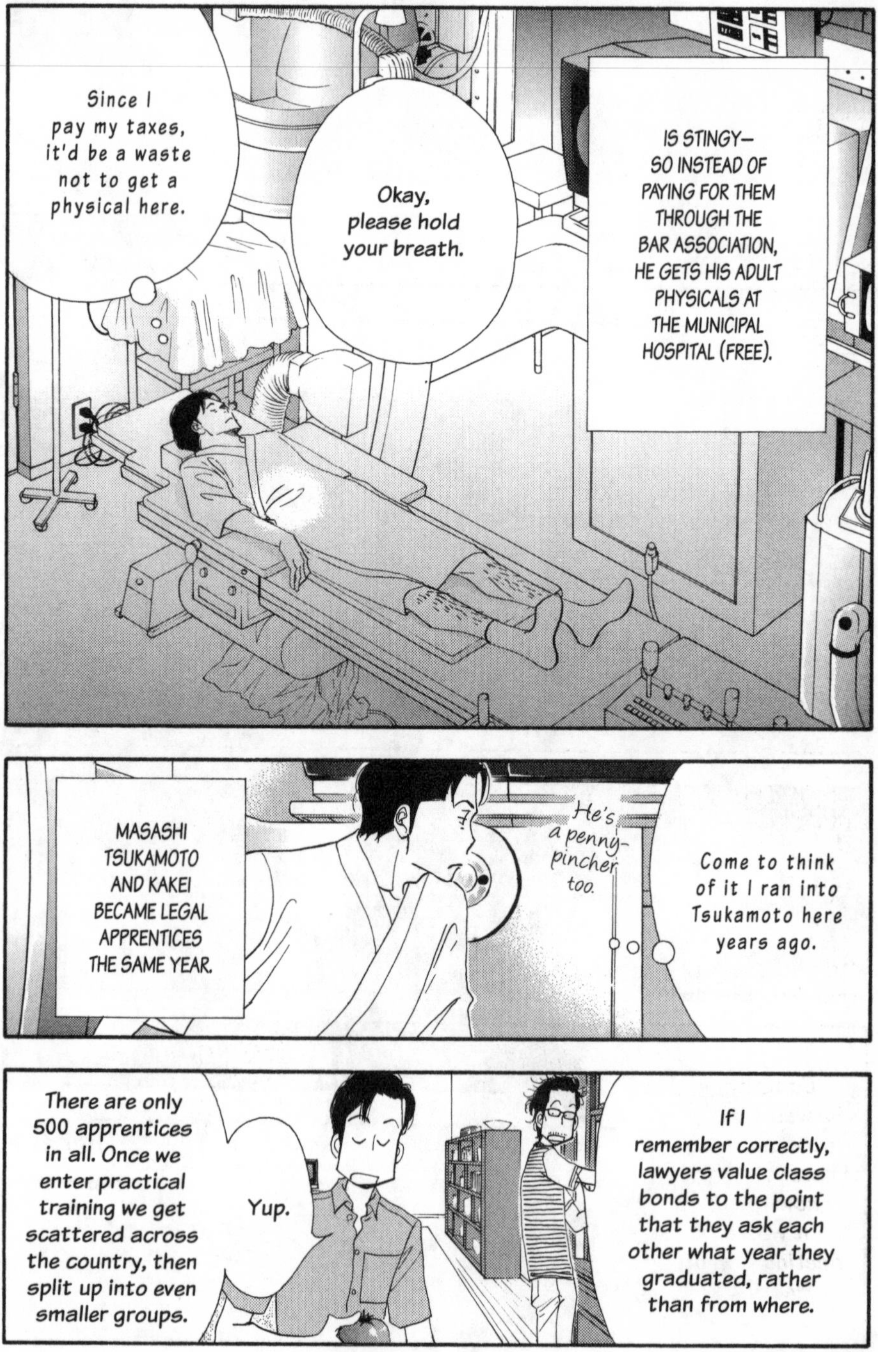
IS STINGY— SO INSTEAD OF PAYING FOR THEM THROUGH THE BAR ASSOCIATION, HE GETS HIS ADULT PHYSICALS AT THE MUNICIPAL HOSPITAL (FREE).
Okay, please hold your breath.
Since I pay my taxes, it'd be a waste not to get a physical here.
Come to think of it I ran into Tsukamoto here years ago.
He's a penny-pincher too.
MASASHI TSUKAMOTO AND KAKEI BECAME LEGAL APPRENTICES THE SAME YEAR.
If I remember correctly, lawyers value class bonds to the point that they ask each other what year they graduated, rather than from where.
Yup.
There are only 500 apprentices in all. Once we enter practical training we get scattered across the country, then split up into even smaller groups.

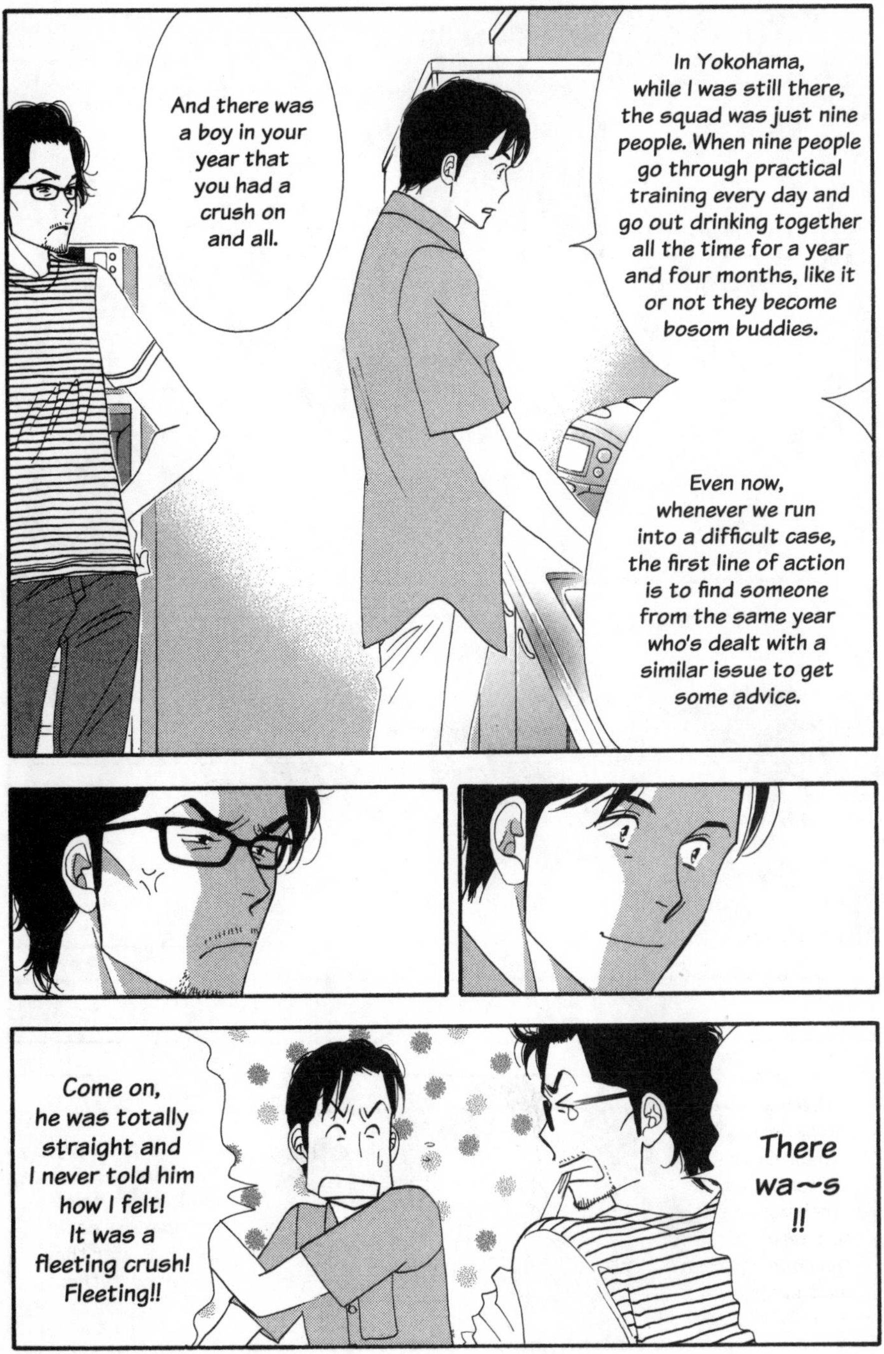
In Yokohama, while I was still there, the squad was just nine people. When nine people go through practical training every day and go out drinking together all the time for a year and four months, like it or not they become bosom buddies.
Even now, whenever we run into a difficult case, the first line of action is to find someone from the same year who's dealt with a similar issue to get some advice.
And there was a boy in your year that you had a crush on and all.
There wa~s !!
Come on, he was totally straight and I never told him how I felt! It was a fleeting crush! Fleeting!!

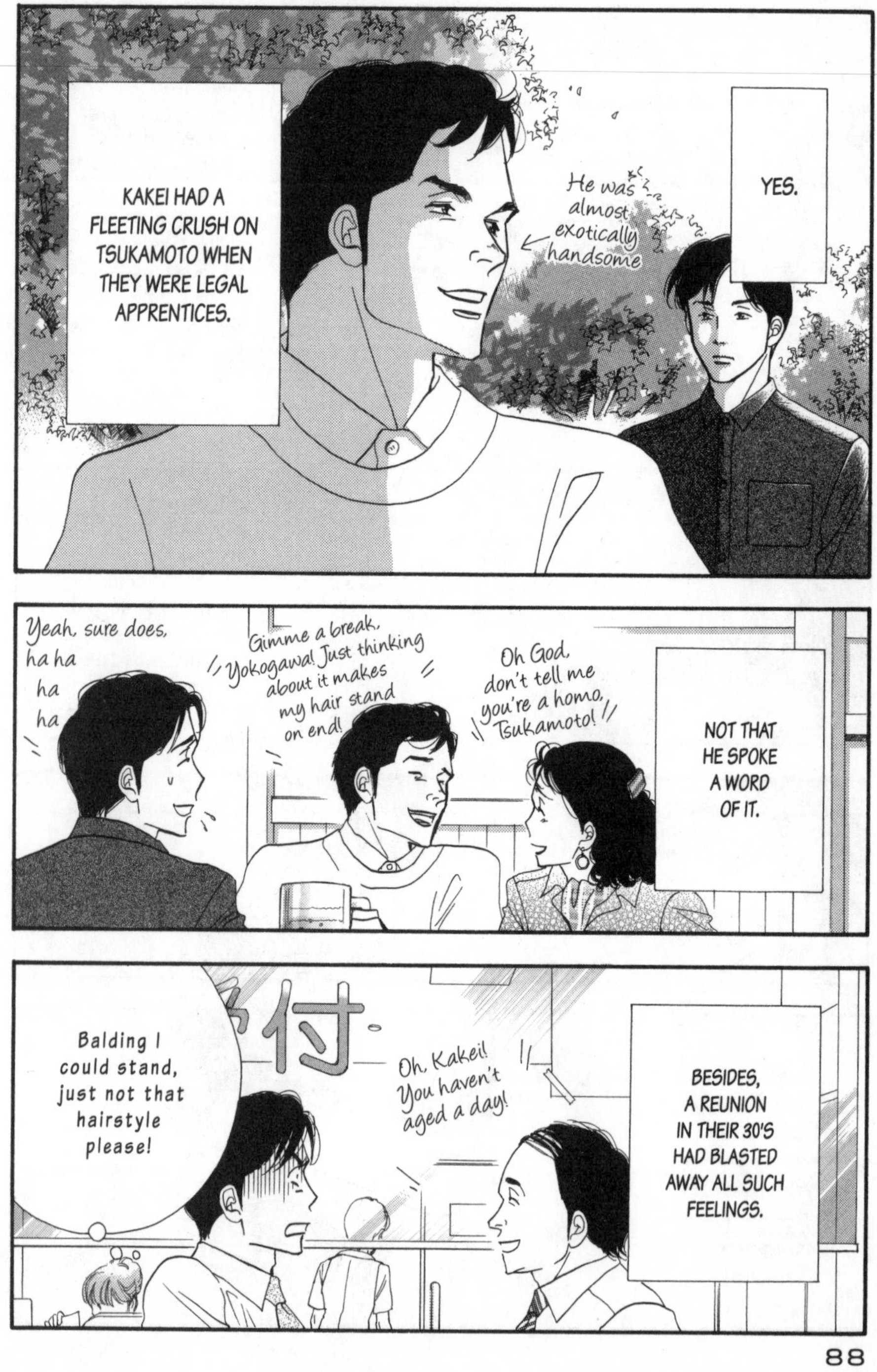
YES.
He was almost exotically handsome
KAKEI HAD A FLEETING CRUSH ON TSUKAMOTO WHEN THEY WERE LEGAL APPRENTICES.
NOT THAT HE SPOKE A WORD OF IT.
Oh God, don't tell me you're a homo, Tsukamoto!
Gimme a break, Yokogawa! Just thinking about it makes my hair stand on end!
Yeah, sure does, ha ha ha ha
BESIDES, A REUNION IN THEIR 30'S HAD BLASTED AWAY ALL SUCH FEELINGS.
Oh, Kakei! You haven't aged a day!
Balding I could stand, just not that hairstyle please!

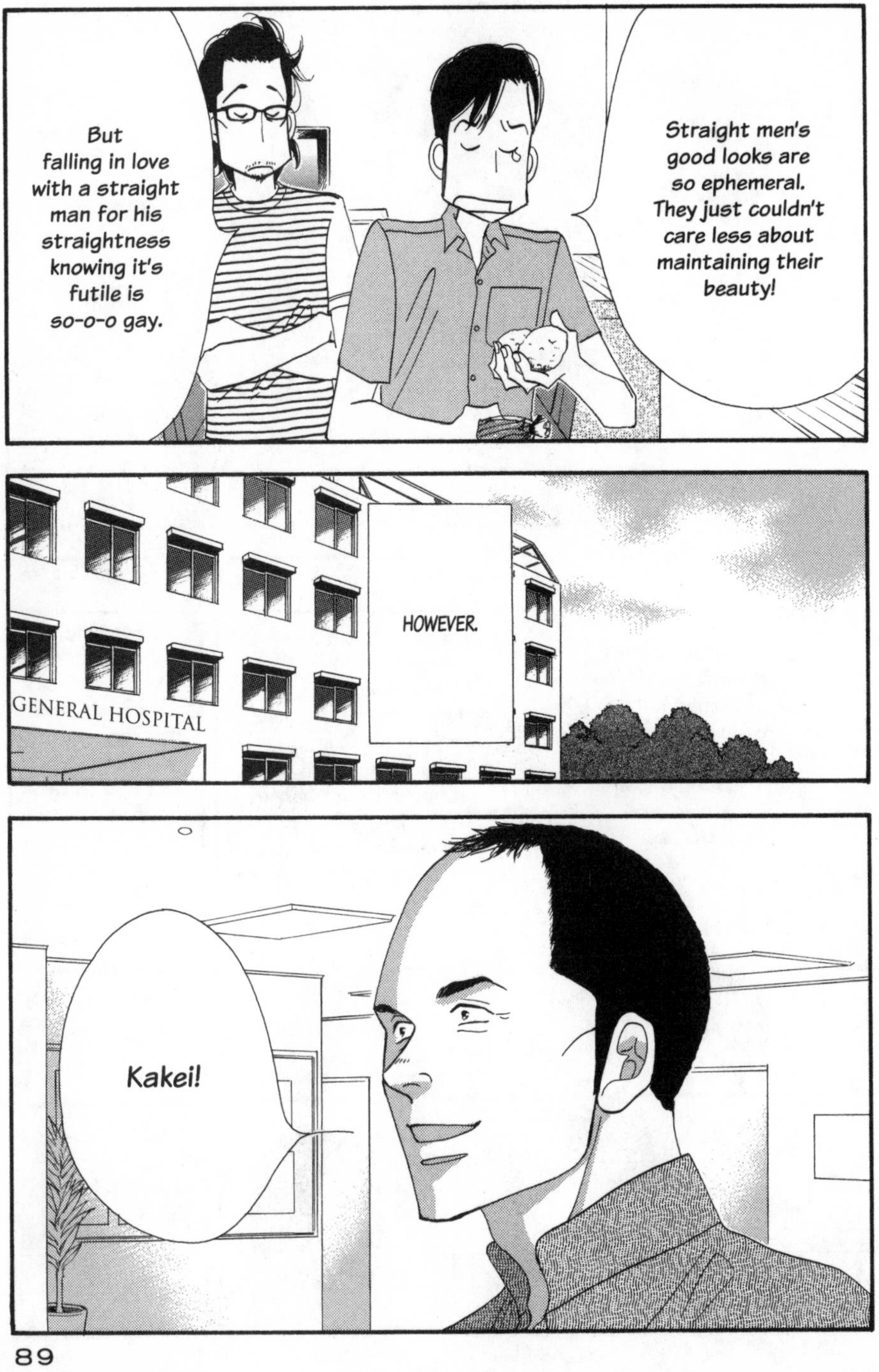
Straight men's good looks are so ephemeral. They just couldn't care less about maintaining their beauty!
But falling in love with a straight man for his straightness knowing it's futile is so-o-o gay.
GENERAL HOSPITAL
HOWEVER.
Kakei!

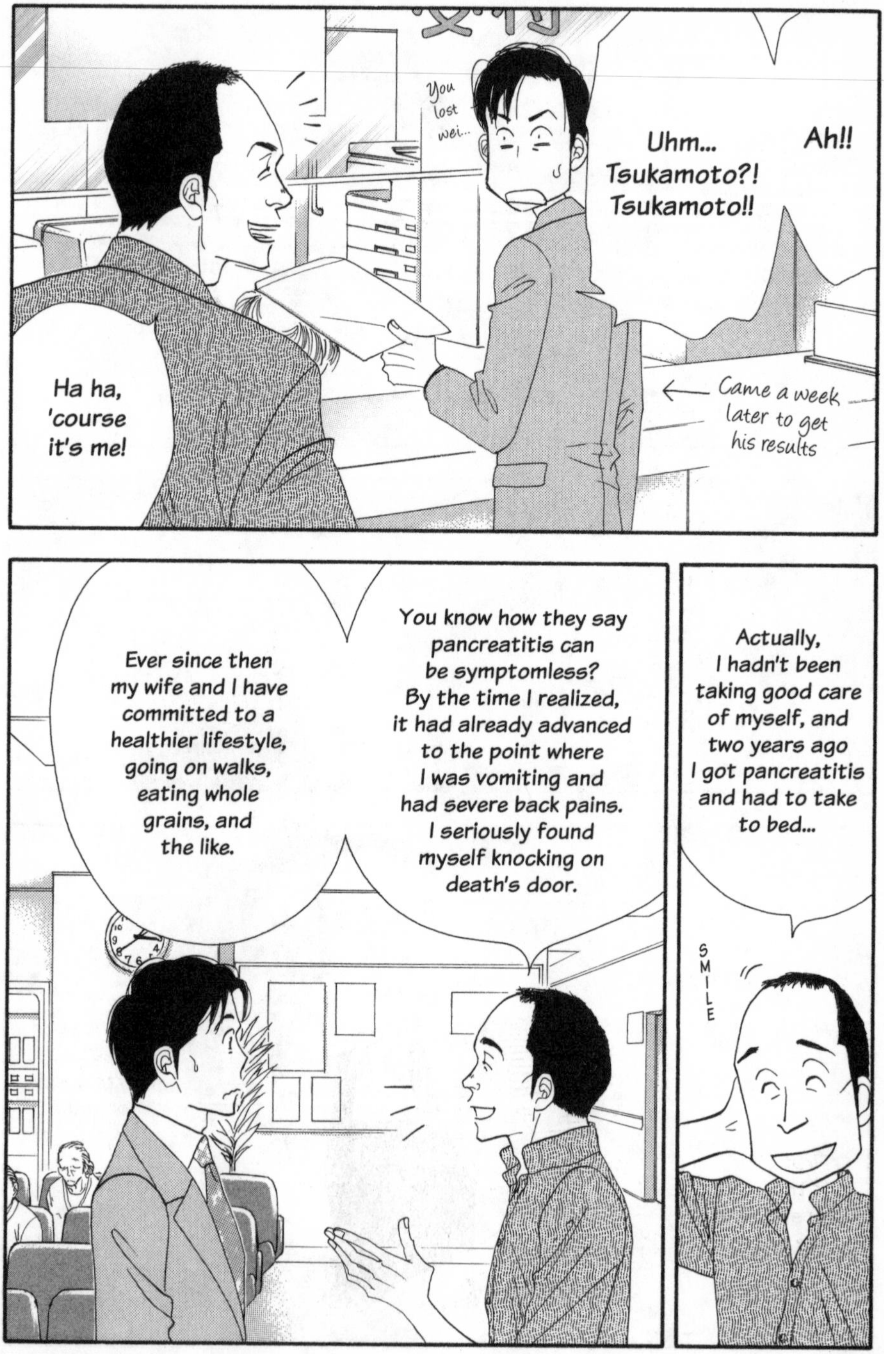
Ah!!
Uhm... Tsukamoto?! Tsukamoto!!
You lost wei...
Came a week later to get his results
Ha ha, 'course it's me!
Actually, I hadn't been taking good care of myself, and two years ago I got pancreatitis and had to take to bed...
SMILE
You know how they say pancreatitis can be symptomless? By the time I realized, it had already advanced to the point where I was vomiting and had severe back pains. I seriously found myself knocking on death's door.
Ever since then my wife and I have committed to a healthier lifestyle, going on walks, eating whole grains, and the like.

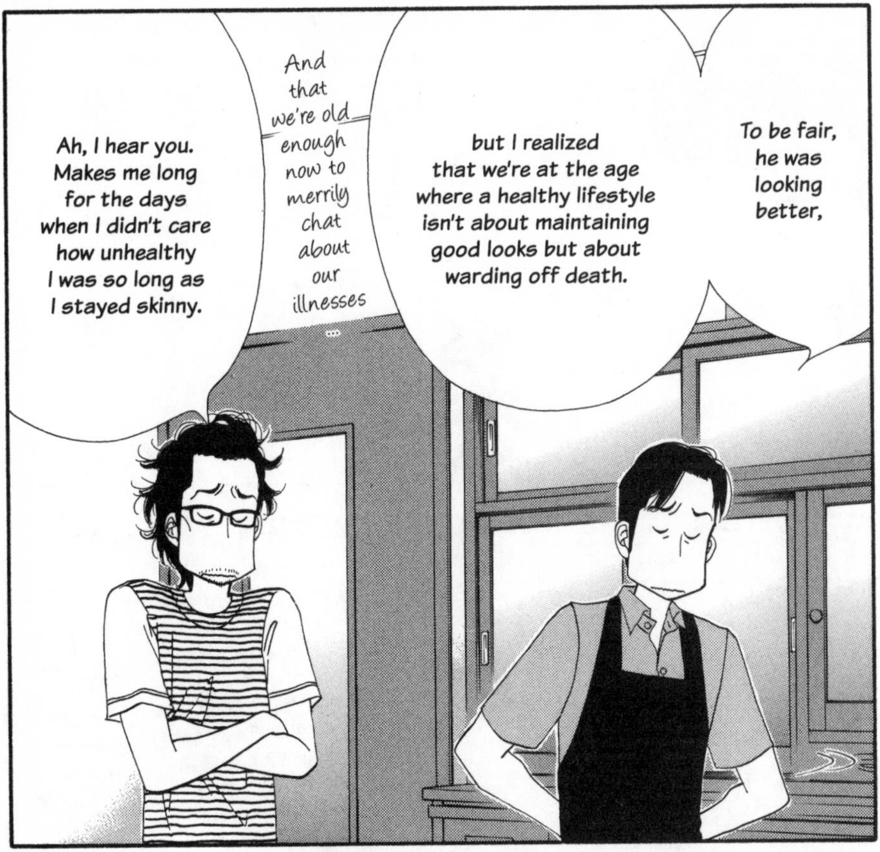
To be fair, he was looking better,
but I realized that we're at the age where a healthy lifestyle isn't about maintaining good looks but about warding off death.
And that we're old enough now to merrily chat about our illnesses ...
Ah, I hear you. Makes me long for the days when I didn't care how unhealthy I was so long as I stayed skinny.
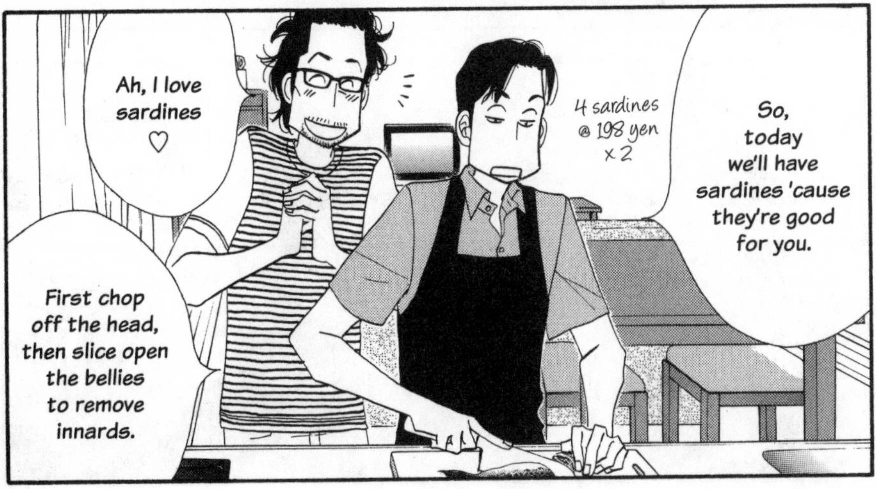
So, today we'll have sardines 'cause they're good for you.
4 sardines @ 198 yen x 2
Ah, I love sardines ♡
First chop off the head, then slice open the bellies to remove innards.

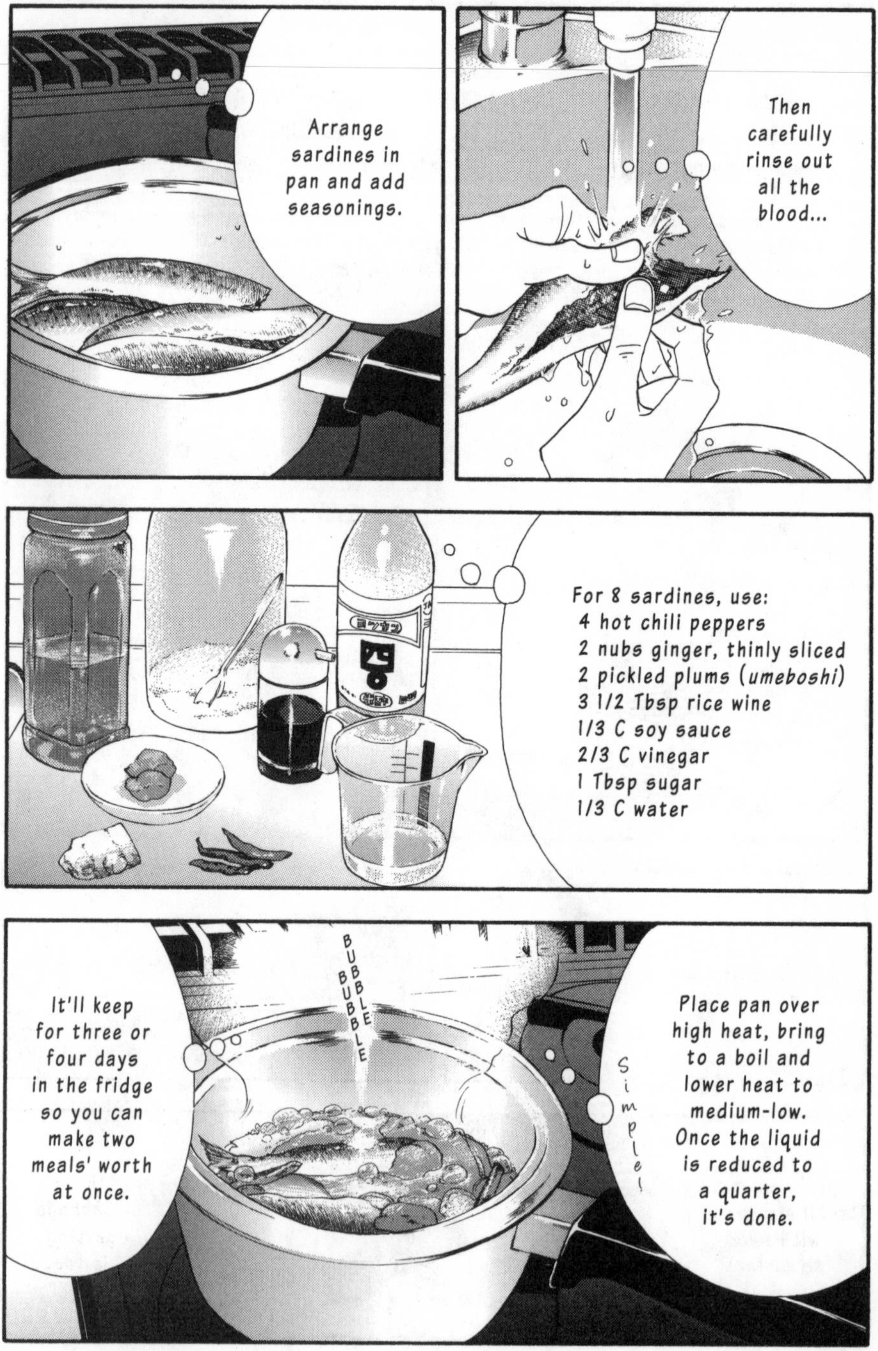
Then carefully rinse out all the blood...
Arrange sardines in pan and add seasonings.
For 8 sardines, use:
4 hot chili peppers
2 nubs ginger, thinly sliced
2 pickled plums (*umeboshi*)
3 1/2 Tbsp rice wine
1/3 C soy sauce
2/3 C vinegar
1 Tbsp sugar
1/3 C water
Place pan over high heat, bring to a boil and lower heat to medium-low. Once the liquid is reduced to a quarter, it's done.
Simple!
BUBBLE BUBBLE
It'll keep for three or four days in the fridge so you can make two meals' worth at once.

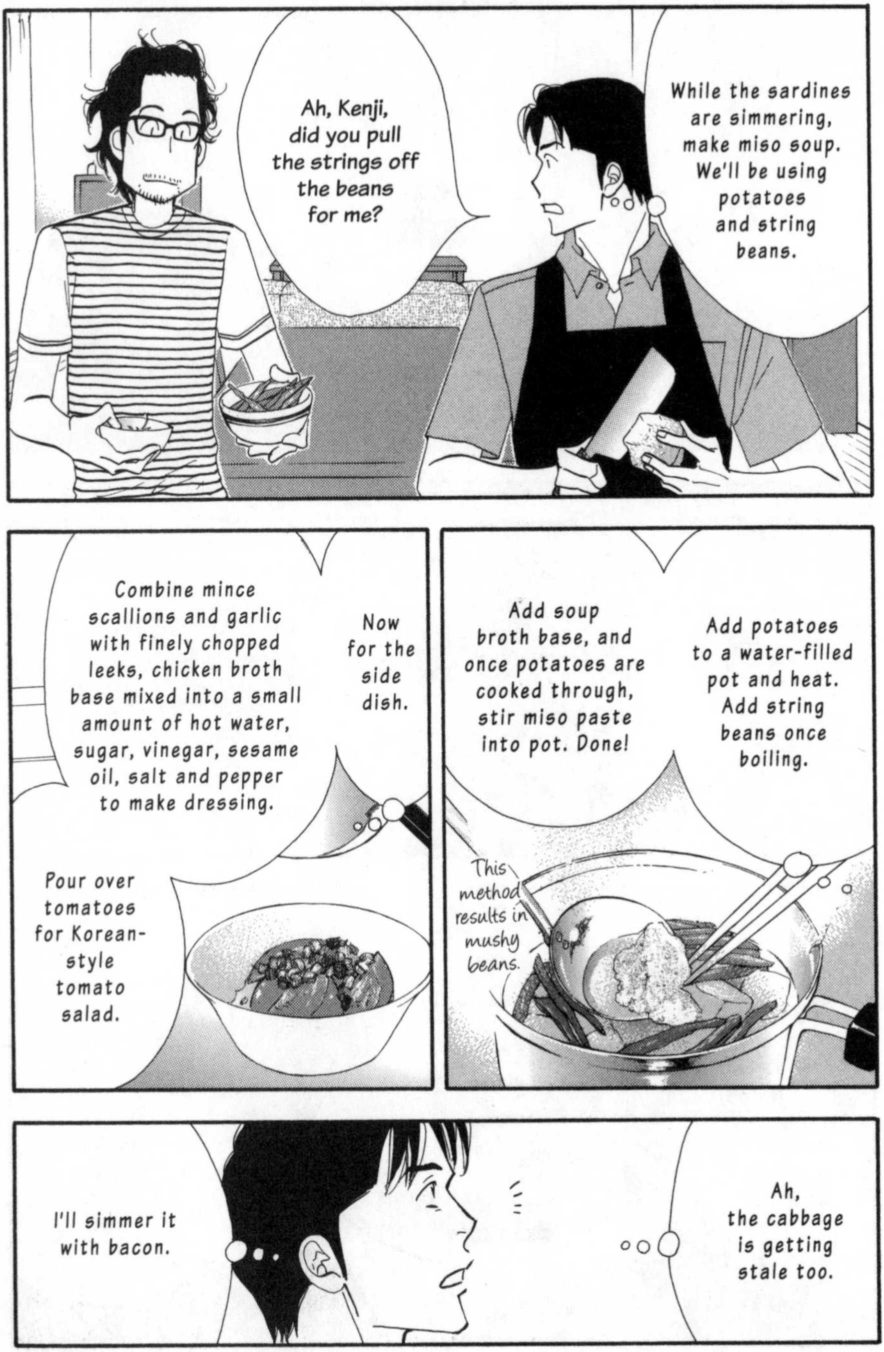
While the sardines are simmering, make miso soup. We'll be using potatoes and string beans.
Ah, Kenji, did you pull the strings off the beans for me?
Add potatoes to a water-filled pot and heat. Add string beans once boiling.
Add soup broth base, and once potatoes are cooked through, stir miso paste into pot. Done!
This method results in mushy beans.
Now for the side dish.
Combine mince scallions and garlic with finely chopped leeks, chicken broth base mixed into a small amount of hot water, sugar, vinegar, sesame oil, salt and pepper to make dressing.
Pour over tomatoes for Korean-style tomato salad.
Ah, the cabbage is getting stale too.
I'll simmer it with bacon.

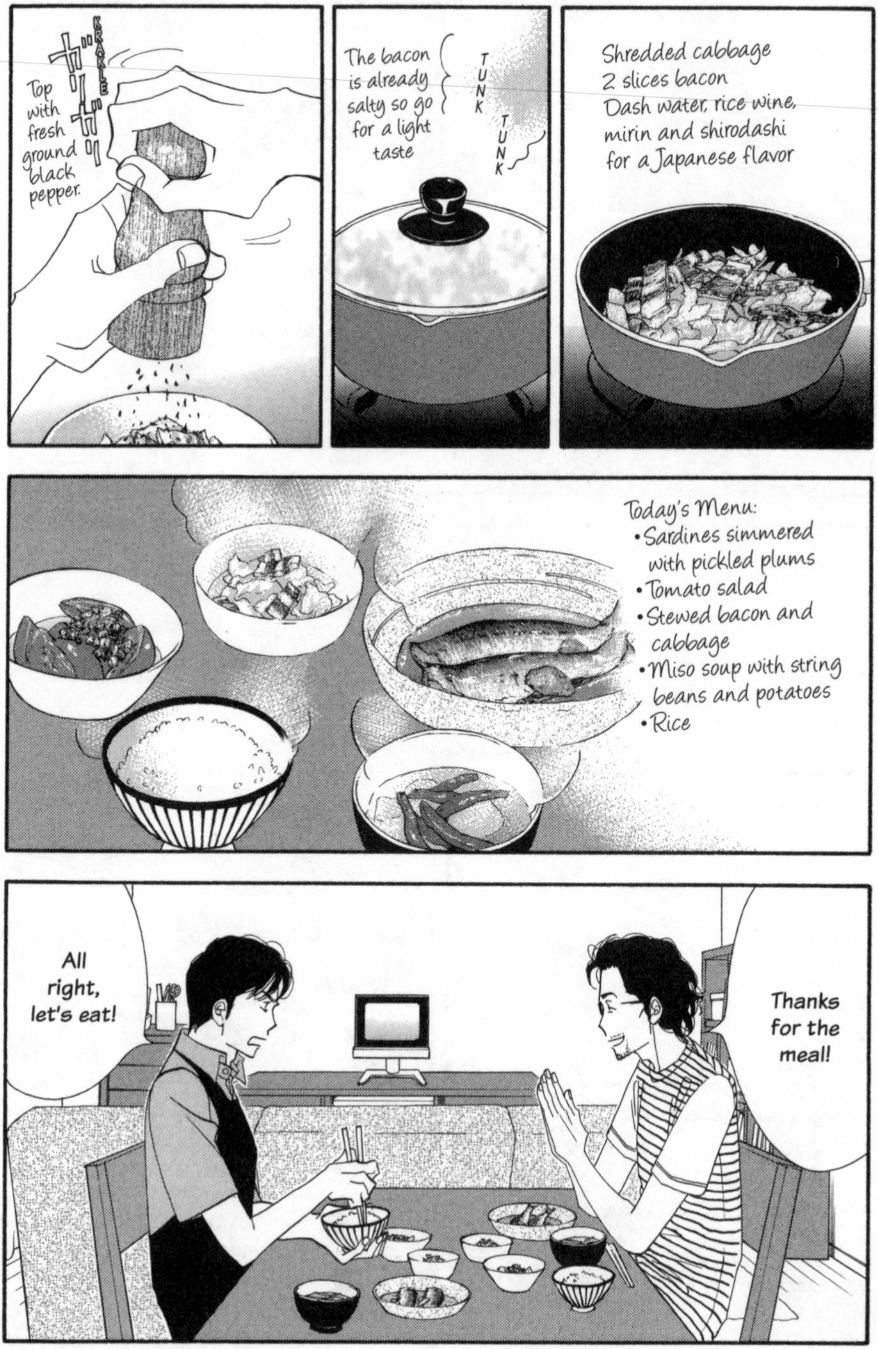

Shredded cabbage
2 slices bacon
Dash water, rice wine, mirin and shirodashi for a Japanese flavor
The bacon is already salty so go for a light taste
TUNK
TUNK
KRAKLE
Top with fresh ground black pepper.
Today's Menu:
• Sardines simmered with pickled plums
• Tomato salad
• Stewed bacon and cabbage
• Miso soup with string beans and potatoes
• Rice
Thanks for the meal!
All right, let's eat!

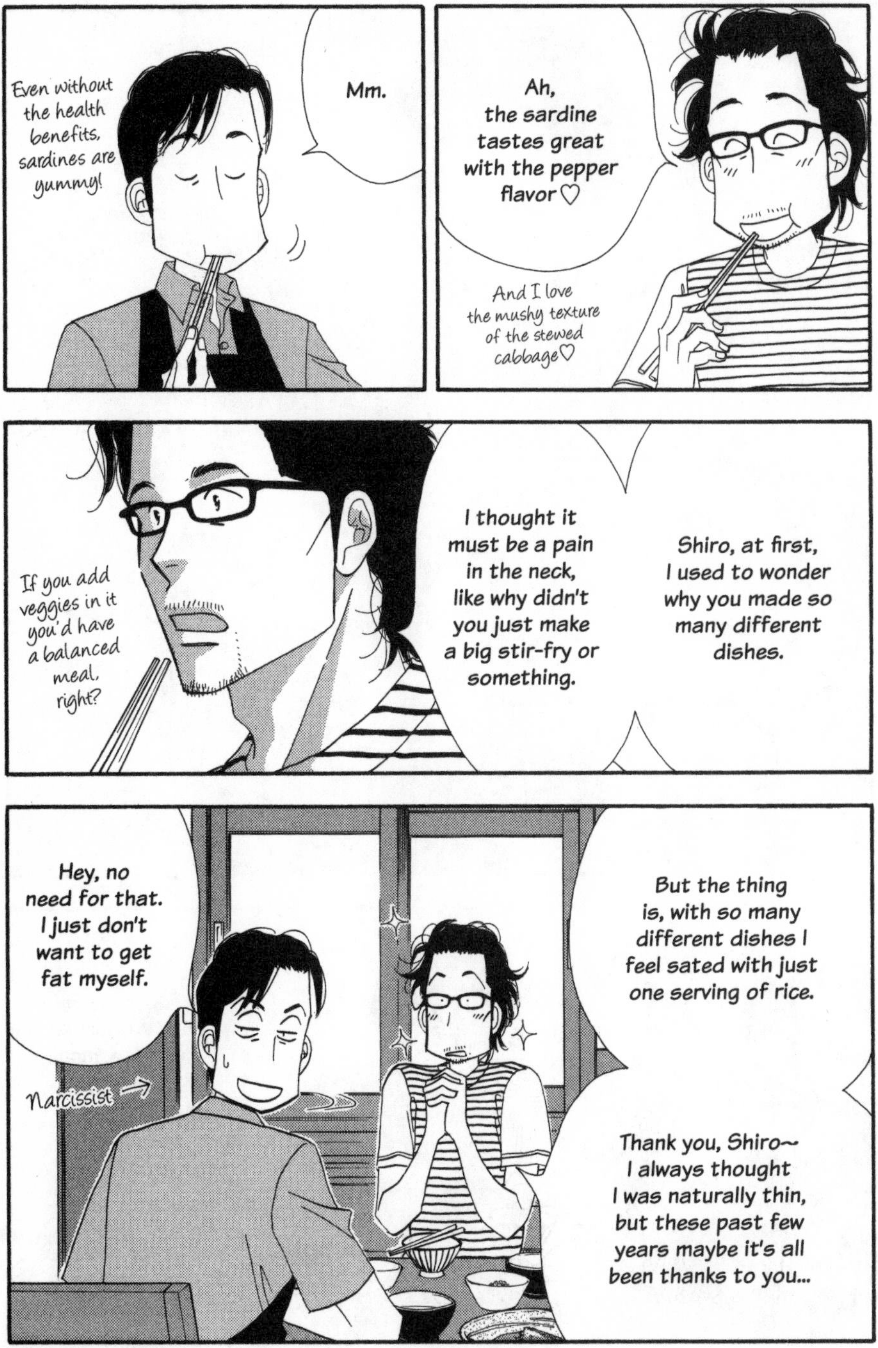

Ah, the sardine tastes great with the pepper flavor♡
And I love the mushy texture of the stewed cabbage♡
Mm.
Even without the health benefits, sardines are yummy!
Shiro, at first, I used to wonder why you made so many different dishes.
I thought it must be a pain in the neck, like why didn't you just make a big stir-fry or something.
If you add veggies in it you'd have a balanced meal, right?
But the thing is, with so many different dishes I feel sated with just one serving of rice.
Thank you, Shiro~ I always thought I was naturally thin, but these past few years maybe it's all been thanks to you...
Hey, no need for that. I just don't want to get fat myself.
Narcissist →

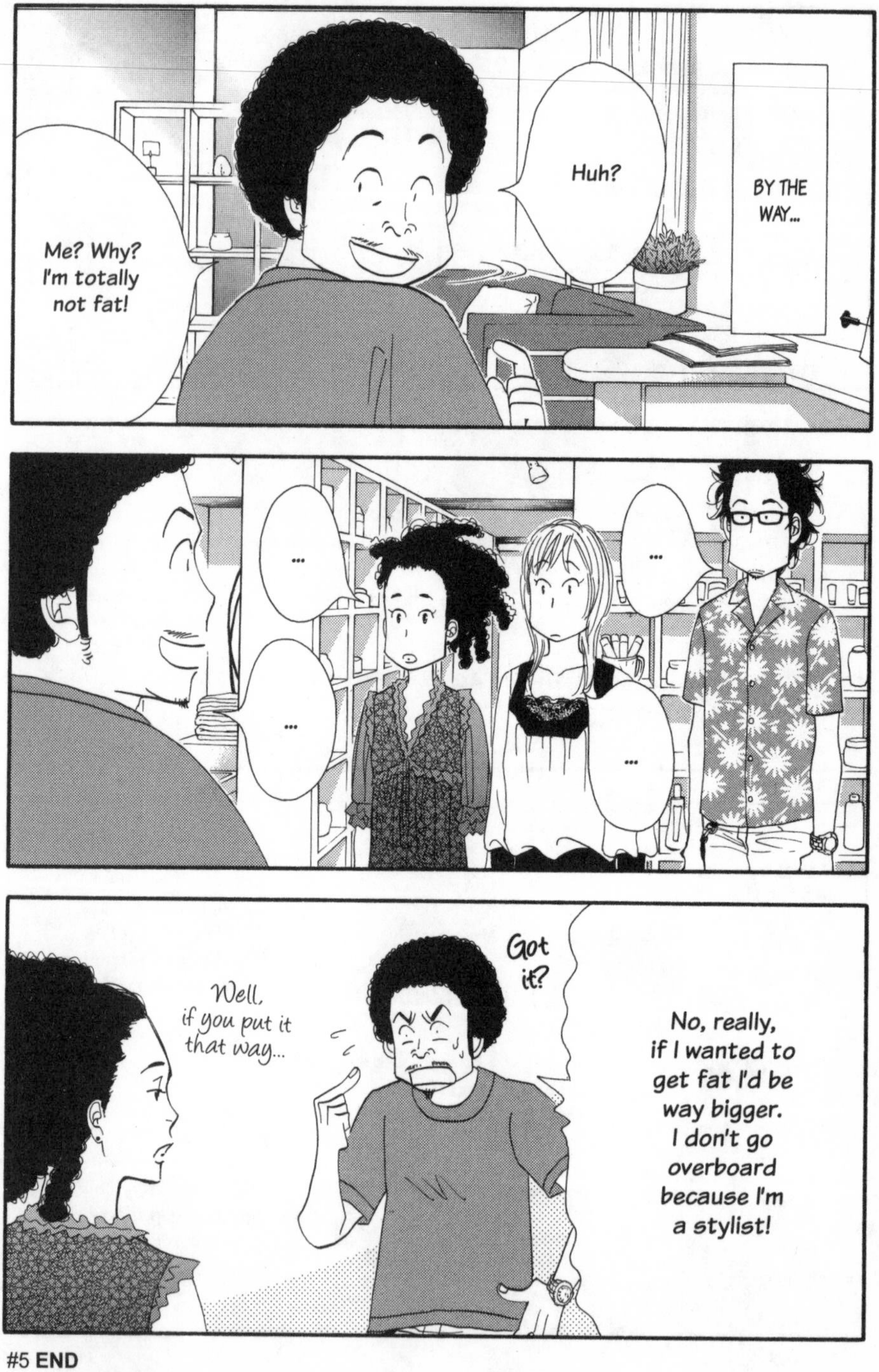
BY THE WAY...
Huh?
Me? Why? I'm totally not fat!
...
...
...
...
No, really, if I wanted to get fat I'd be way bigger. I don't go overboard because I'm a stylist!
Got it?
Well, if you put it that way...

#5 END

Re-using leftover boiled sardines in a different menu

•Sardines boiled with pickled plums
•Miso soup with pumpkin and fried tofu
•Stir-fried asparagus
    Thinly slice asparagus on the bias.
    Mince garlic and ginger and stir-fry in vegetable oil.
    Once fragrant, add raw asparagus.
    Season with chicken broth base, dash sugar, dash rice
    wine, salt and pepper.
    Combine equal parts potato starch and water and add
    to pan to thicken.
•*Hiyayakko*, i.e., cold silken tofu topped with onions,
 myoga ginger buds and bonito flakes

#6

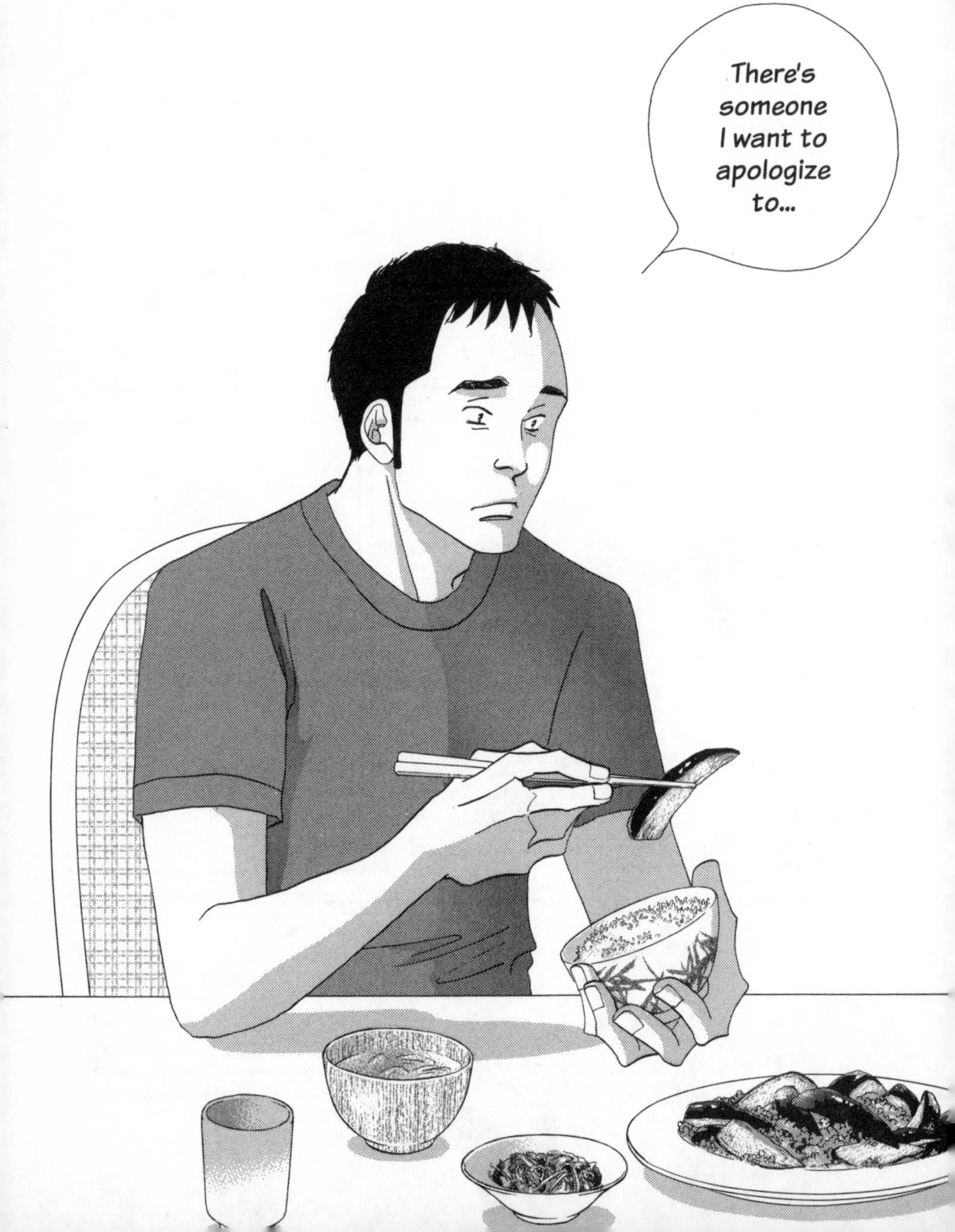
There's someone I want to apologize to...

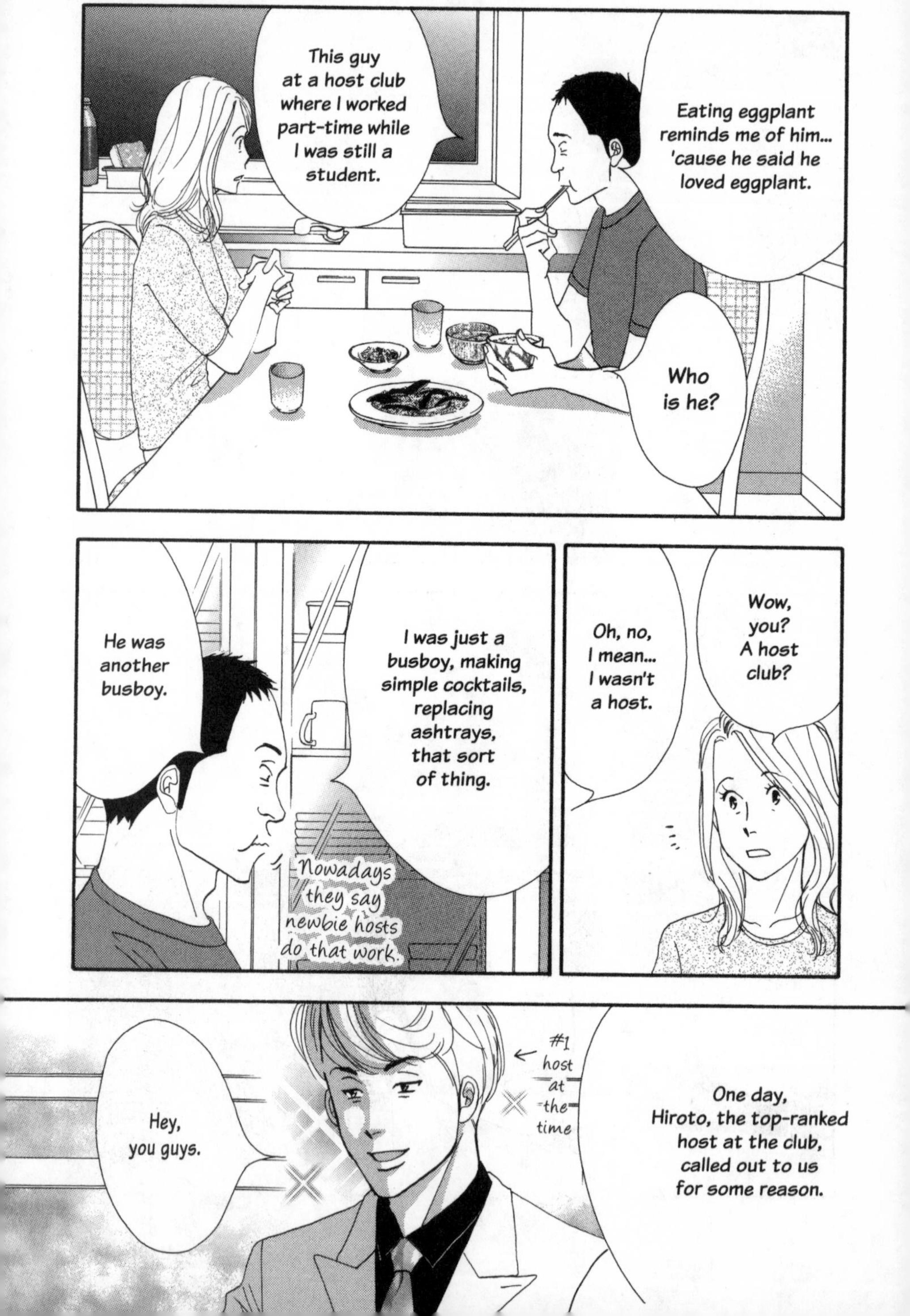
Eating eggplant reminds me of him... 'cause he said he loved eggplant.
Who is he?
This guy at a host club where I worked part-time while I was still a student.
Wow, you? A host club?
Oh, no, I mean... I wasn't a host.
I was just a busboy, making simple cocktails, replacing ashtrays, that sort of thing.
Nowadays they say newbie hosts do that work.
He was another busboy.
One day, Hiroto, the top-ranked host at the club, called out to us for some reason.
#1 host at the time
Hey, you guys.

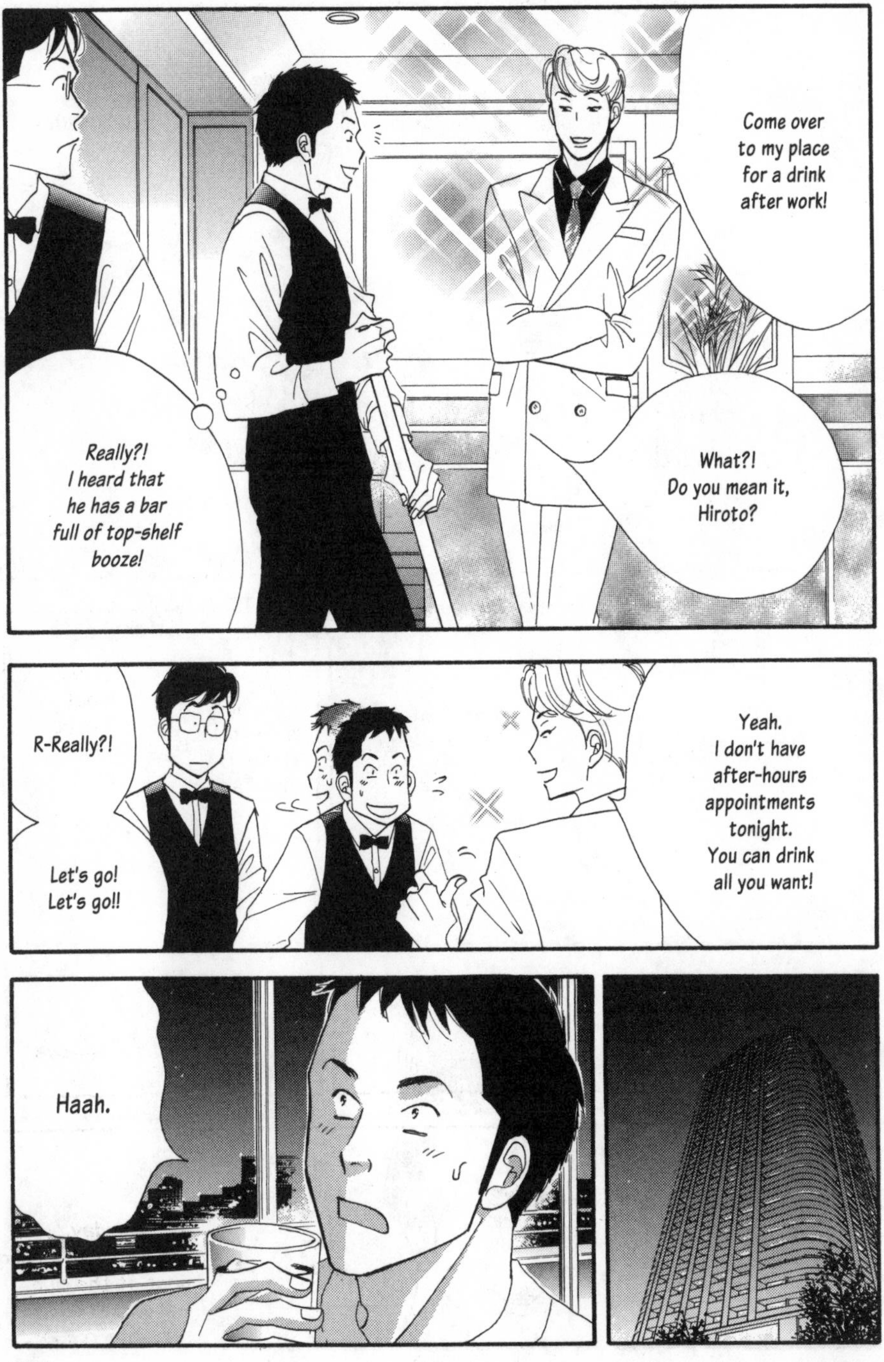
Come over to my place for a drink after work!
What?! Do you mean it, Hiroto?
Really?! I heard that he has a bar full of top-shelf booze!
Yeah. I don't have after-hours appointments tonight. You can drink all you want!
R-Really?!
Let's go! Let's go!!
Haah.

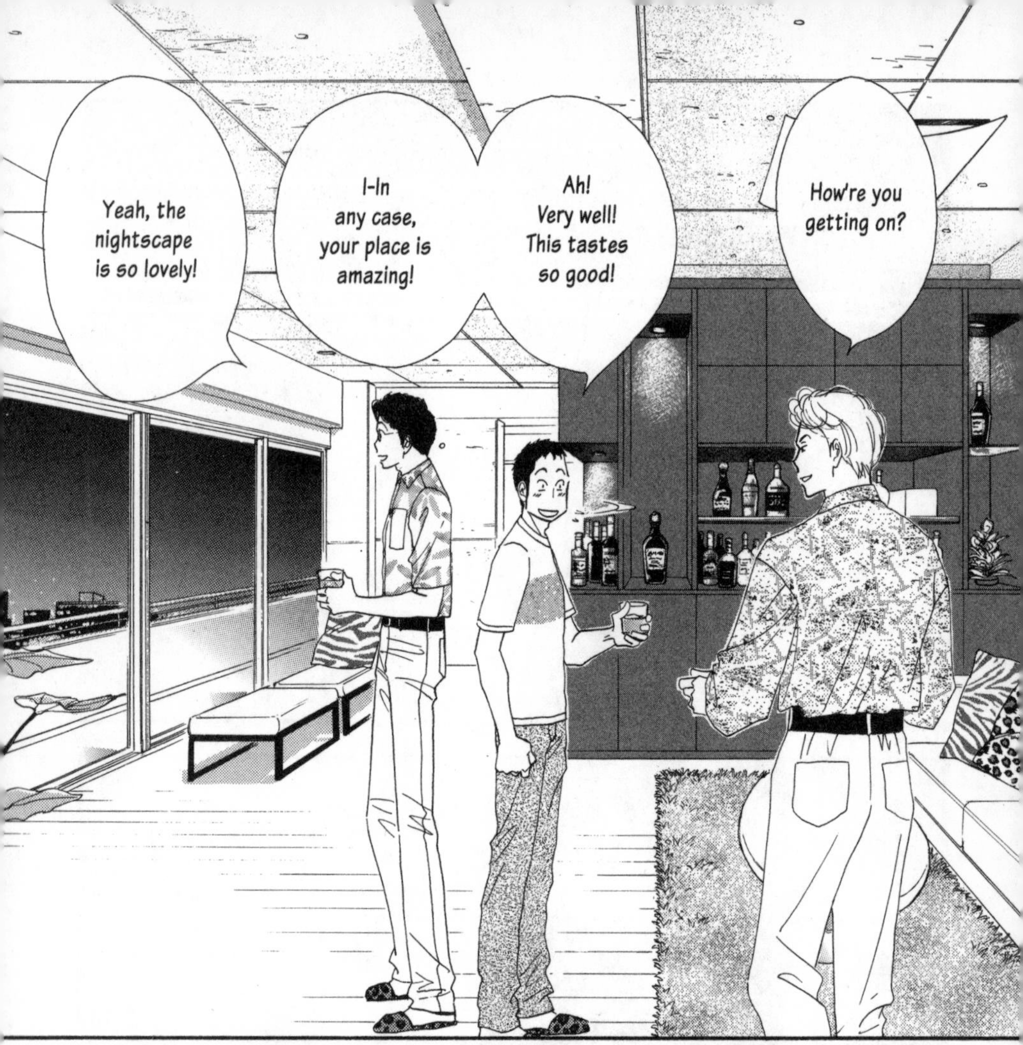
How're you getting on?
Ah! Very well! This tastes so good!
I-In any case, your place is amazing!
Yeah, the nightscape is so lovely!

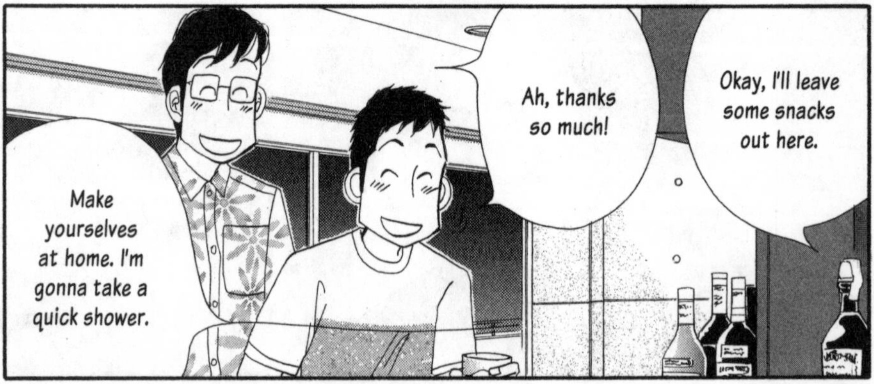
Okay, I'll leave some snacks out here.
Ah, thanks so much!
Make yourselves at home. I'm gonna take a quick shower.

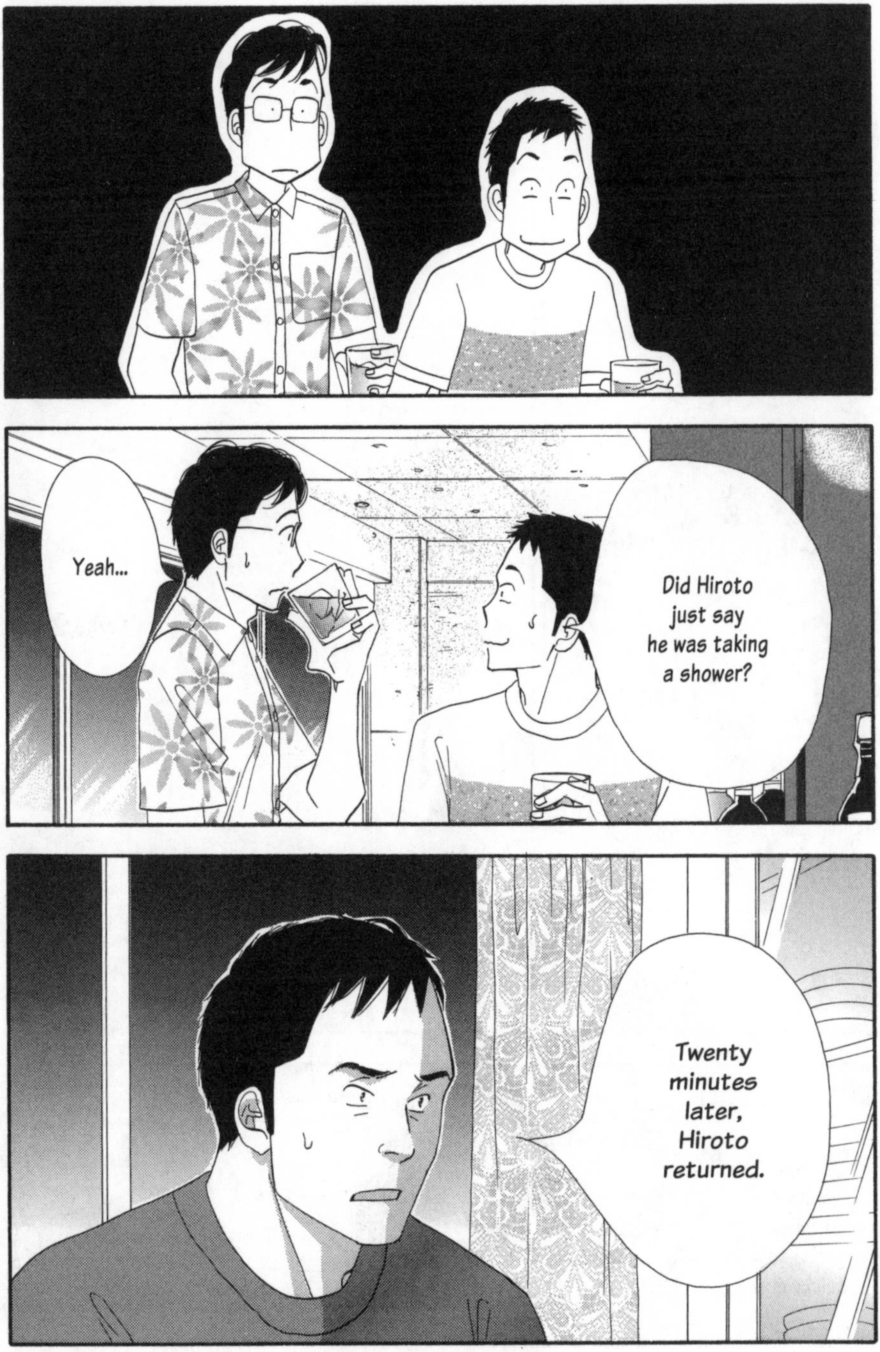
Did Hiroto just say he was taking a shower?
Yeah...
Twenty minutes later, Hiroto returned.

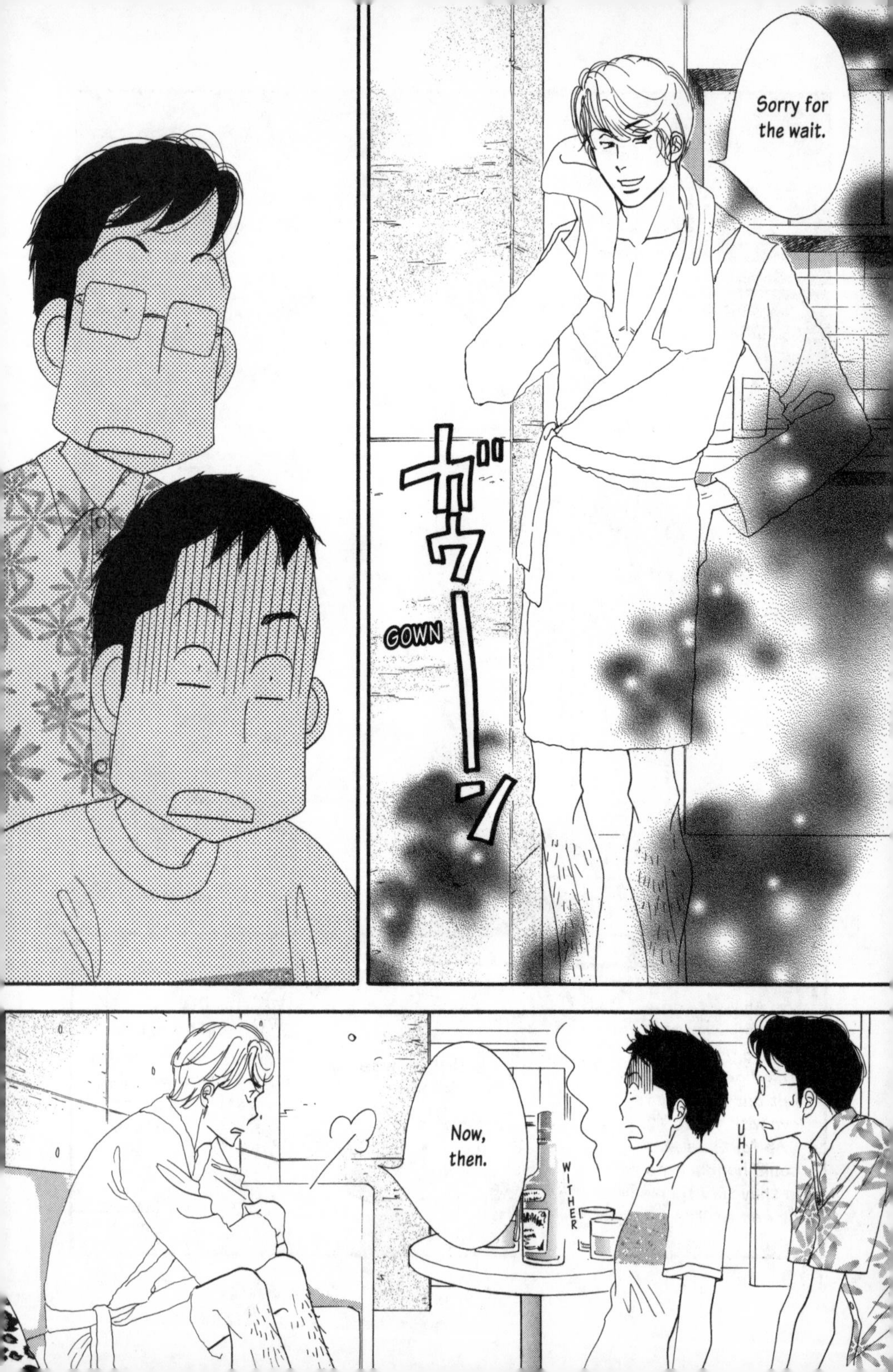

Sorry for the wait.
ガウーン
GOWN
UH...
WITHER
Now, then.

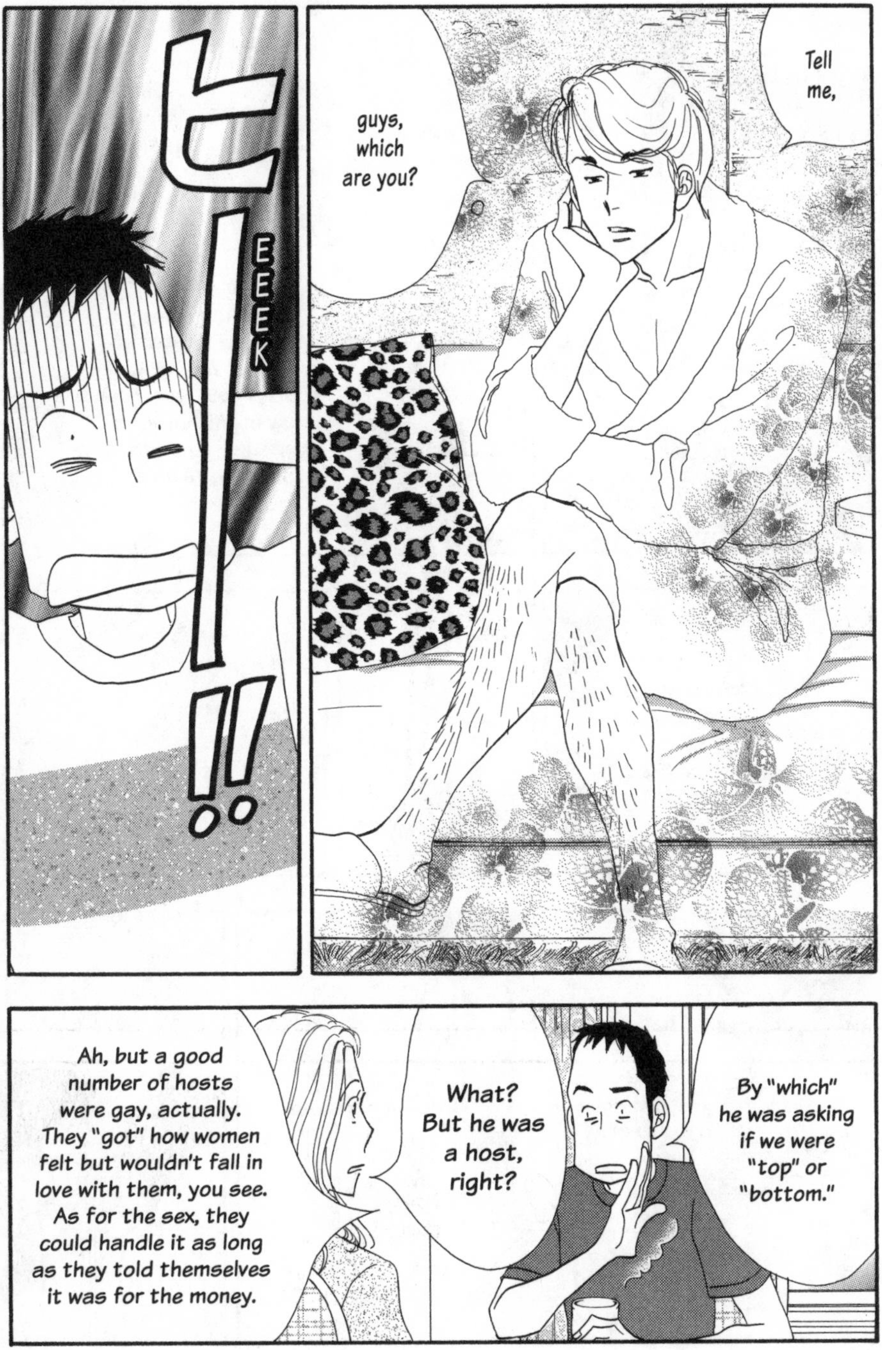
Tell me,
guys, which are you?
ヒー!!
EEEK
By "which" he was asking if we were "top" or "bottom."
What? But he was a host, right?
Ah, but a good number of hosts were gay, actually. They "got" how women felt but wouldn't fall in love with them, you see. As for the sex, they could handle it as long as they told themselves it was for the money.

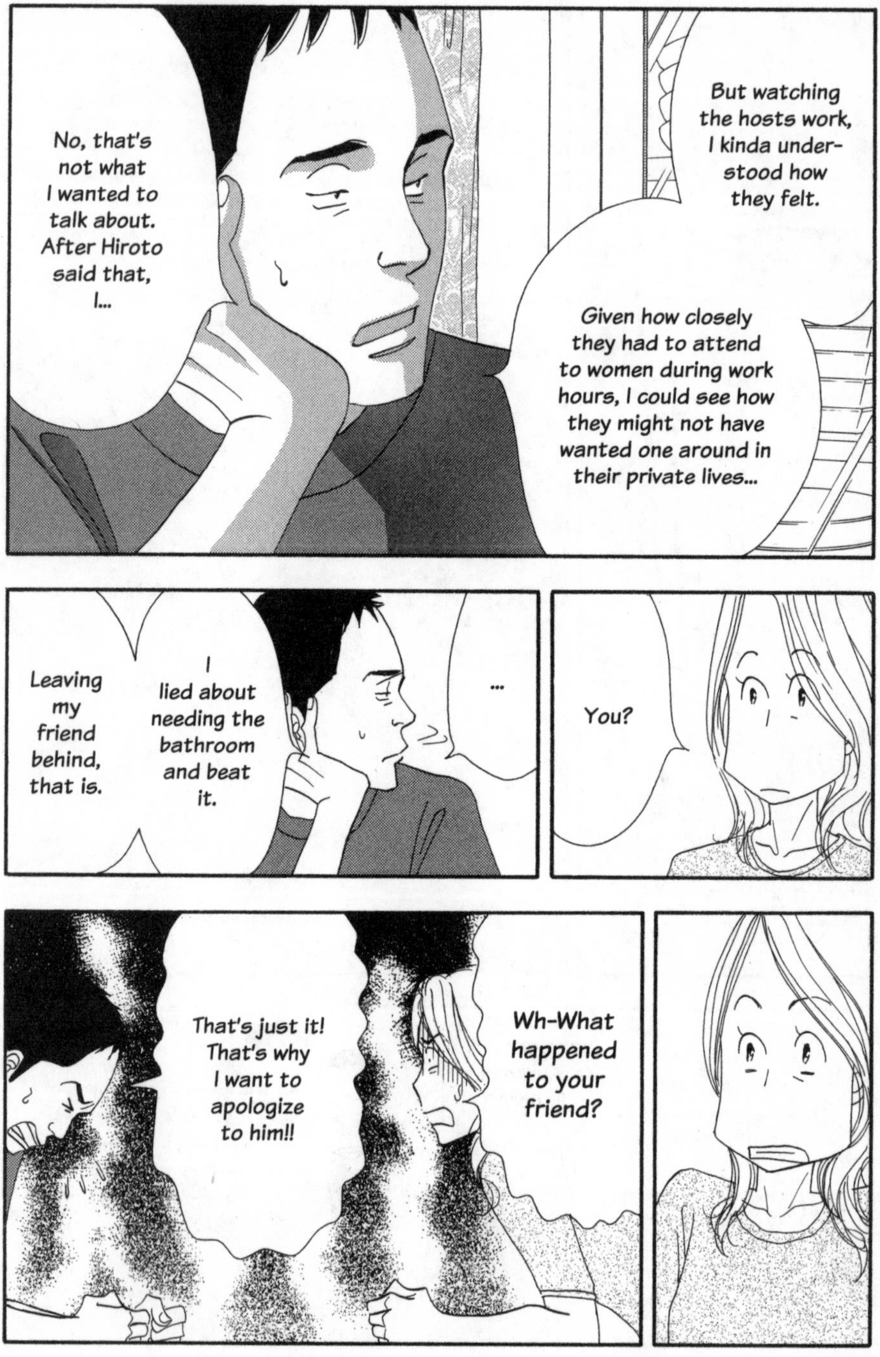
But watching the hosts work, I kinda understood how they felt.
Given how closely they had to attend to women during work hours, I could see how they might not have wanted one around in their private lives...
No, that's not what I wanted to talk about. After Hiroto said that, I...
You?
...
I lied about needing the bathroom and beat it.
Leaving my friend behind, that is.
Wh-What happened to your friend?
That's just it! That's why I want to apologize to him!!

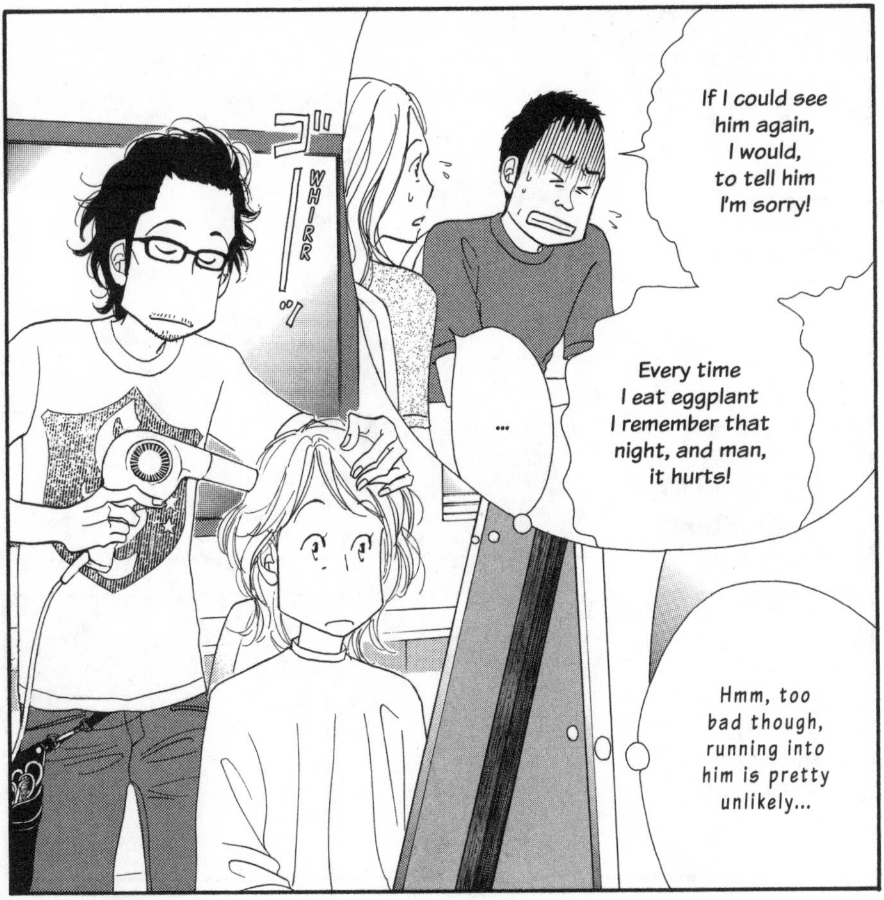
If I could see him again, I would, to tell him I'm sorry!
WHIRR
Every time I eat eggplant I remember that night, and man, it hurts!
...
Hmm, too bad though, running into him is pretty unlikely...

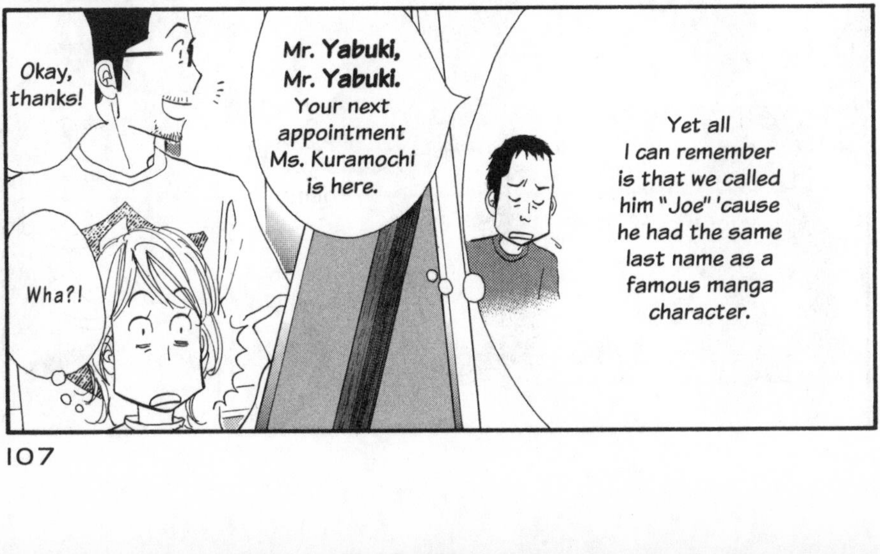
Yet all I can remember is that we called him "Joe" 'cause he had the same last name as a famous manga character.
Mr. **Yabuki**, Mr. **Yabuki**. Your next appointment Ms. Kuramochi is here.
Okay, thanks!
Wha?!

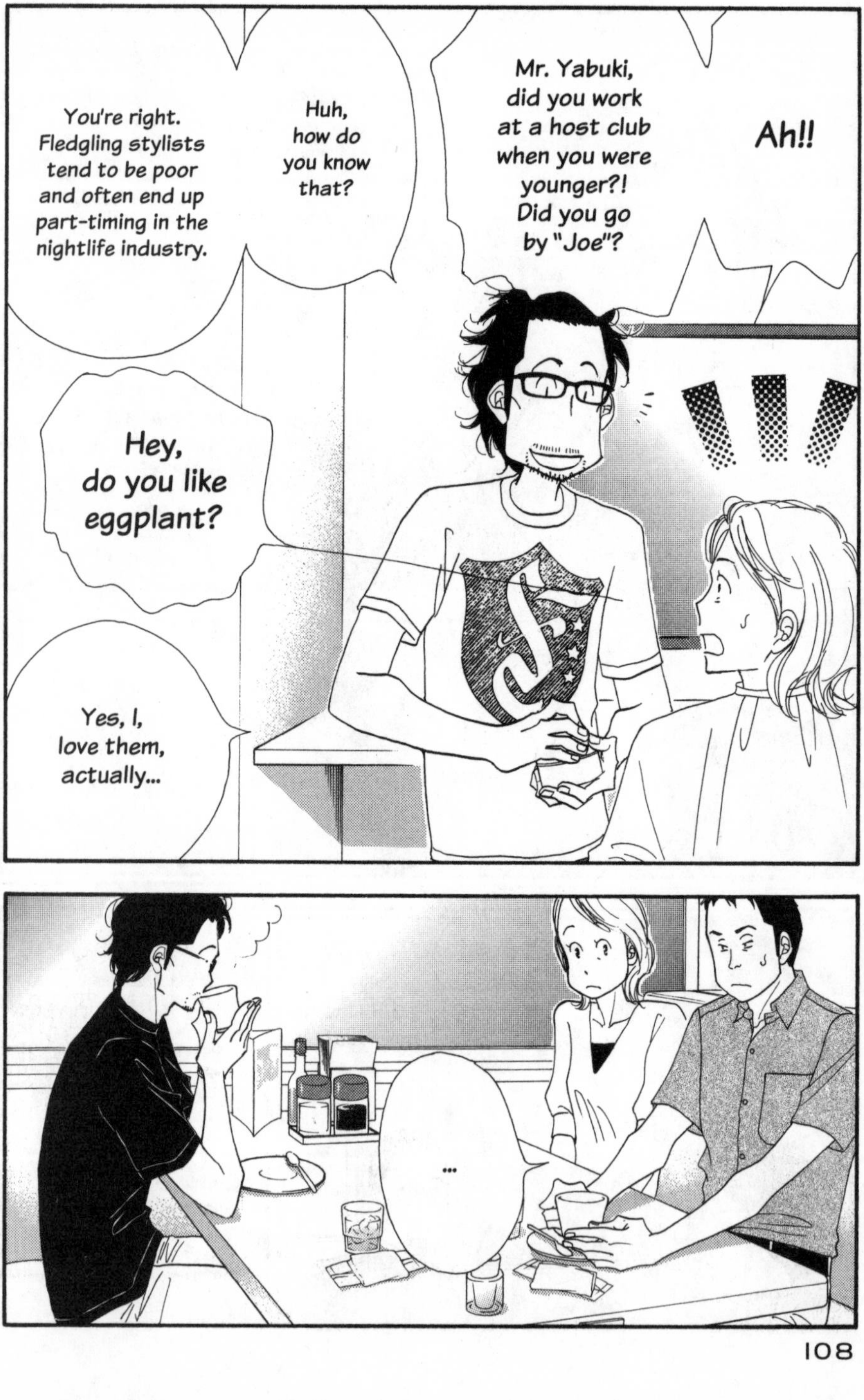

Ah!!
Mr. Yabuki, did you work at a host club when you were younger?! Did you go by "Joe"?
Huh, how do you know that?
You're right. Fledgling stylists tend to be poor and often end up part-timing in the nightlife industry.
Hey, do you like eggplant?
Yes, I, love them, actually...
...

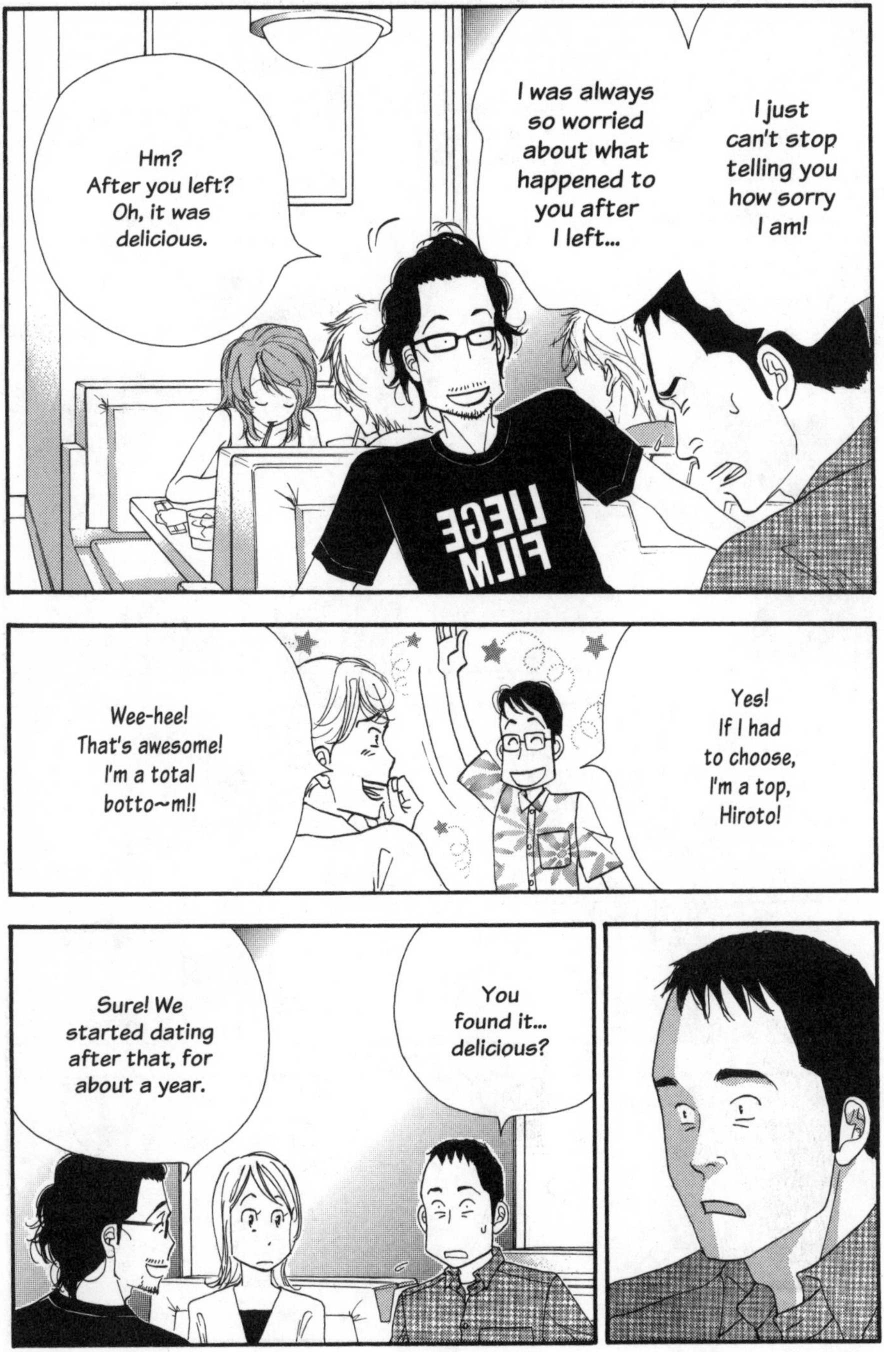
I just can't stop telling you how sorry I am!
I was always so worried about what happened to you after I left...
Hm? After you left? Oh, it was delicious.
Yes! If I had to choose, I'm a top, Hiroto!
Wee-hee! That's awesome! I'm a total botto~m!!
You found it... delicious?
Sure! We started dating after that, for about a year.

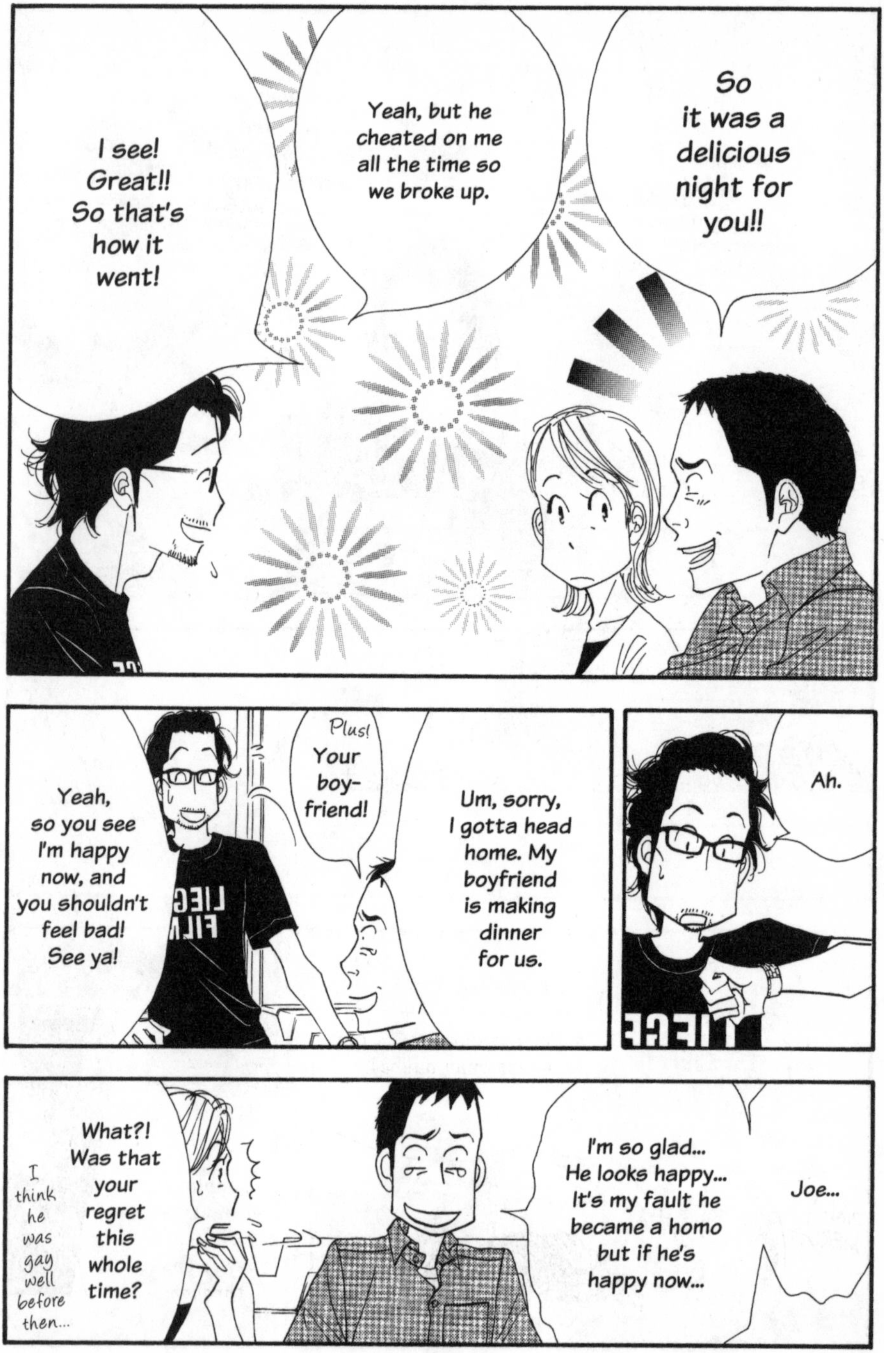
So it was a delicious night for you!!
Yeah, but he cheated on me all the time so we broke up.
I see! Great!! So that's how it went!
Ah.
Um, sorry, I gotta head home. My boyfriend is making dinner for us.
Plus! Your boy-friend!
Yeah, so you see I'm happy now, and you shouldn't feel bad! See ya!
Joe...
I'm so glad... He looks happy... It's my fault he became a homo but if he's happy now...
What?! Was that your regret this whole time?
I think he was gay well before then...

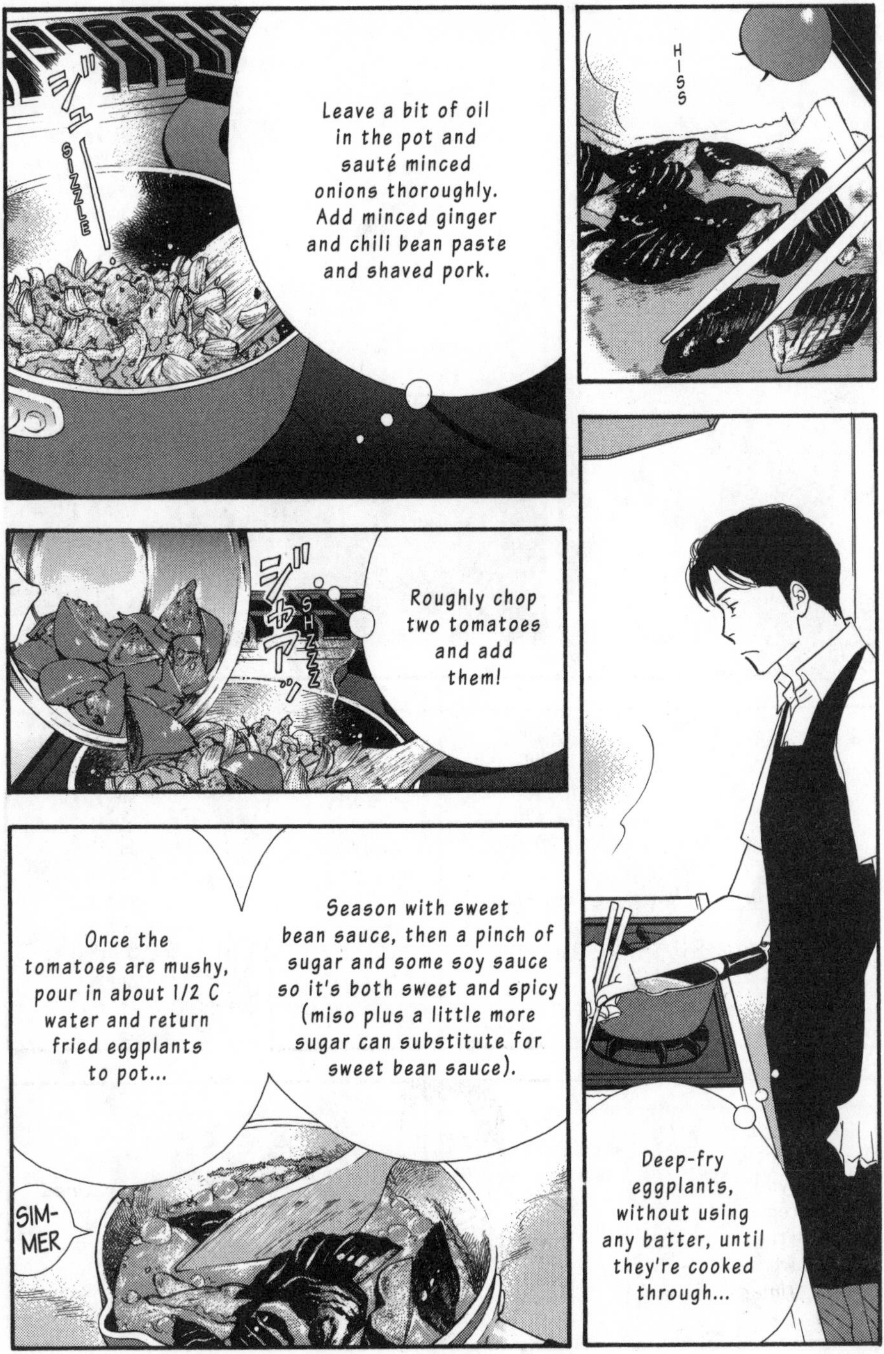
HISS
Leave a bit of oil in the pot and sauté minced onions thoroughly. Add minced ginger and chili bean paste and shaved pork.
SIZZLE
Deep-fry eggplants, without using any batter, until they're cooked through...
Roughly chop two tomatoes and add them!
SHZZZ
Season with sweet bean sauce, then a pinch of sugar and some soy sauce so it's both sweet and spicy (miso plus a little more sugar can substitute for sweet bean sauce).
Once the tomatoes are mushy, pour in about 1/2 C water and return fried eggplants to pot...
SIM-MER

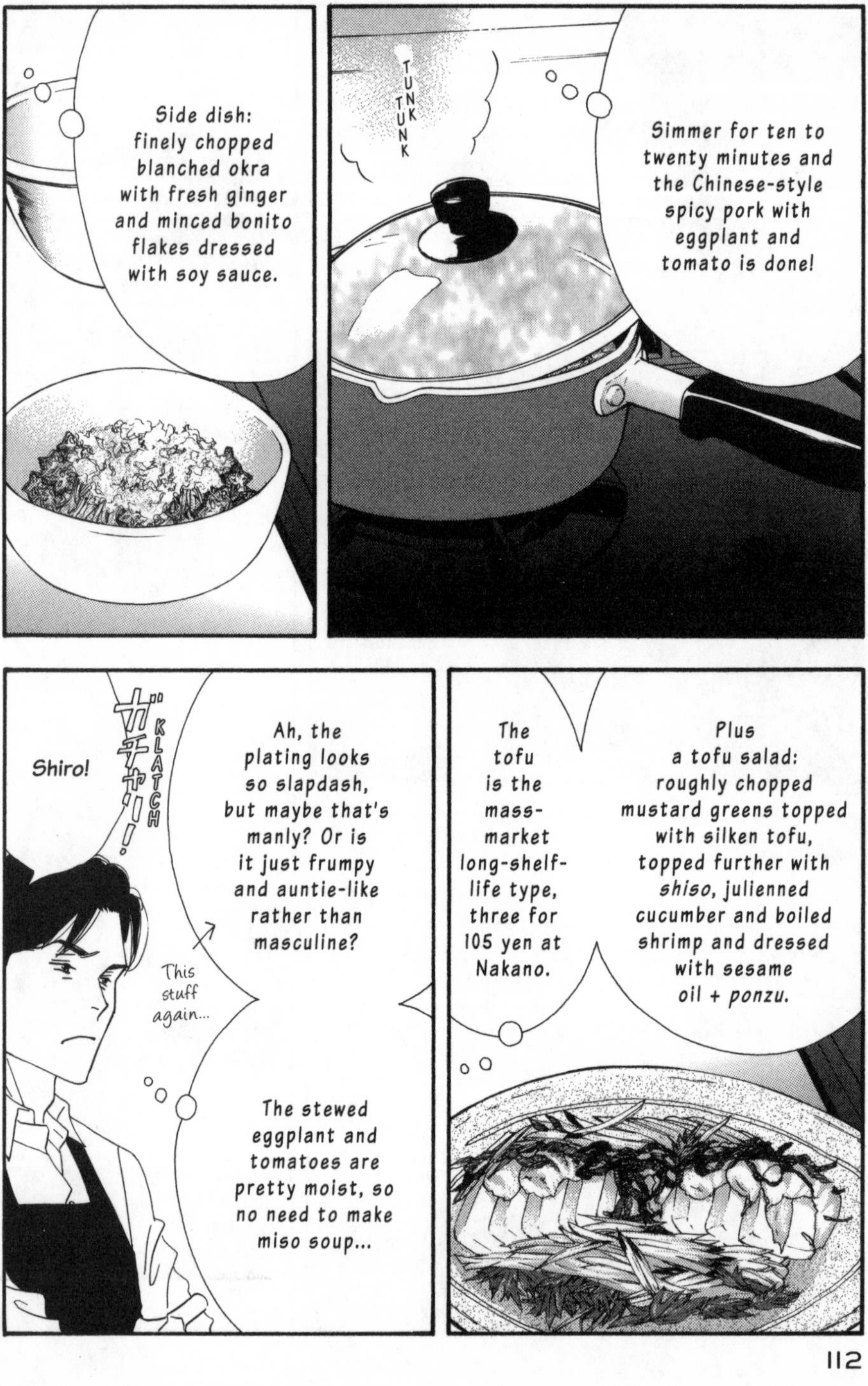
TUNK TUNK
Simmer for ten to twenty minutes and the Chinese-style spicy pork with eggplant and tomato is done!
Side dish: finely chopped blanched okra with fresh ginger and minced bonito flakes dressed with soy sauce.
Plus a tofu salad: roughly chopped mustard greens topped with silken tofu, topped further with *shiso*, julienned cucumber and boiled shrimp and dressed with sesame oil + *ponzu*.
The tofu is the mass-market long-shelf-life type, three for 105 yen at Nakano.
Ah, the plating looks so slapdash, but maybe that's manly? Or is it just frumpy and auntie-like rather than masculine?
ガチャ!! KLATCH
Shiro!
This stuff again...
The stewed eggplant and tomatoes are pretty moist, so no need to make miso soup...

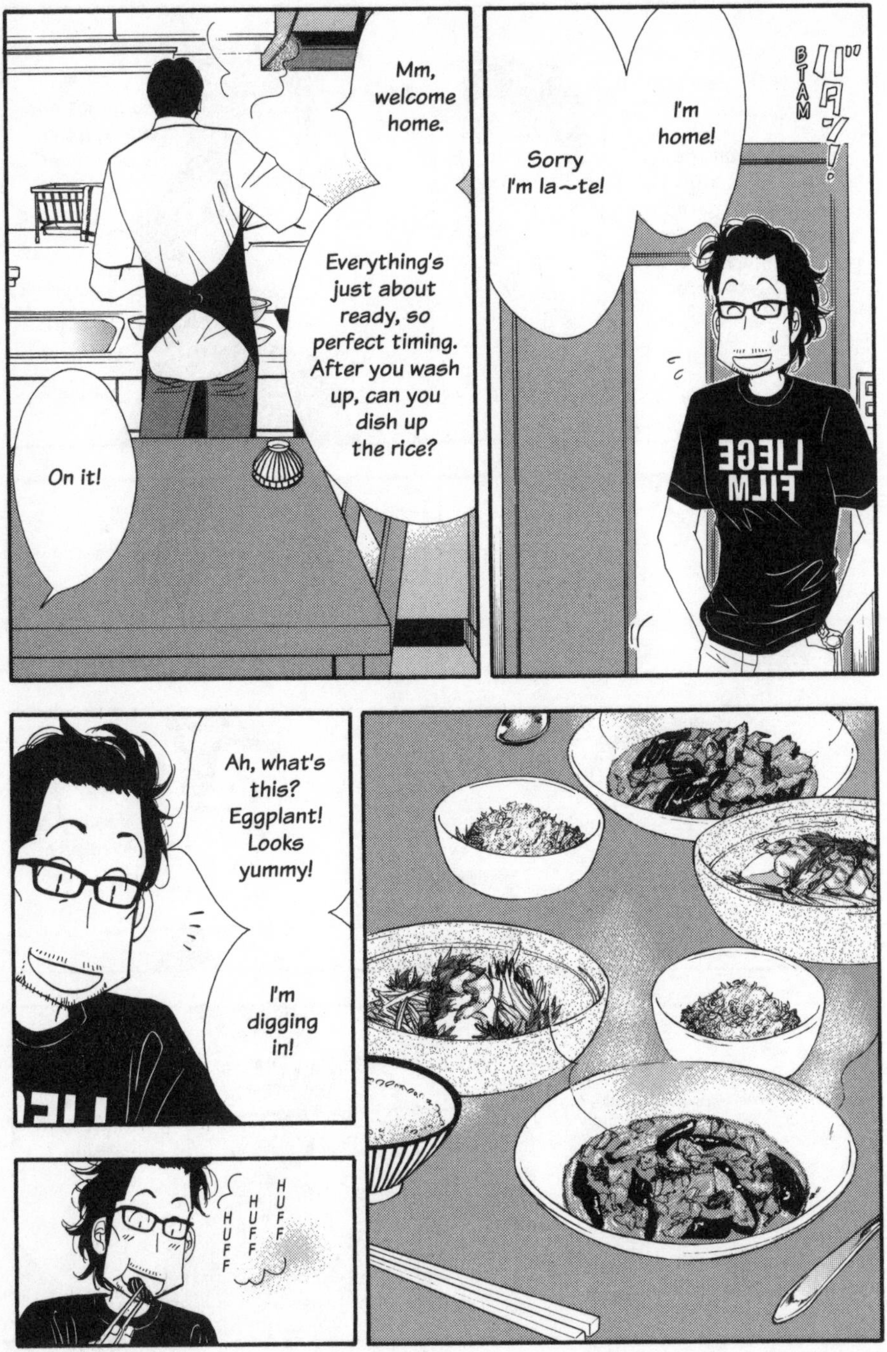
BTAM
I'm home!
Sorry I'm la~te!
Mm, welcome home.
Everything's just about ready, so perfect timing. After you wash up, can you dish up the rice?
On it!
Ah, what's this? Eggplant! Looks yummy!
I'm digging in!
HUFF HUFF HUFF

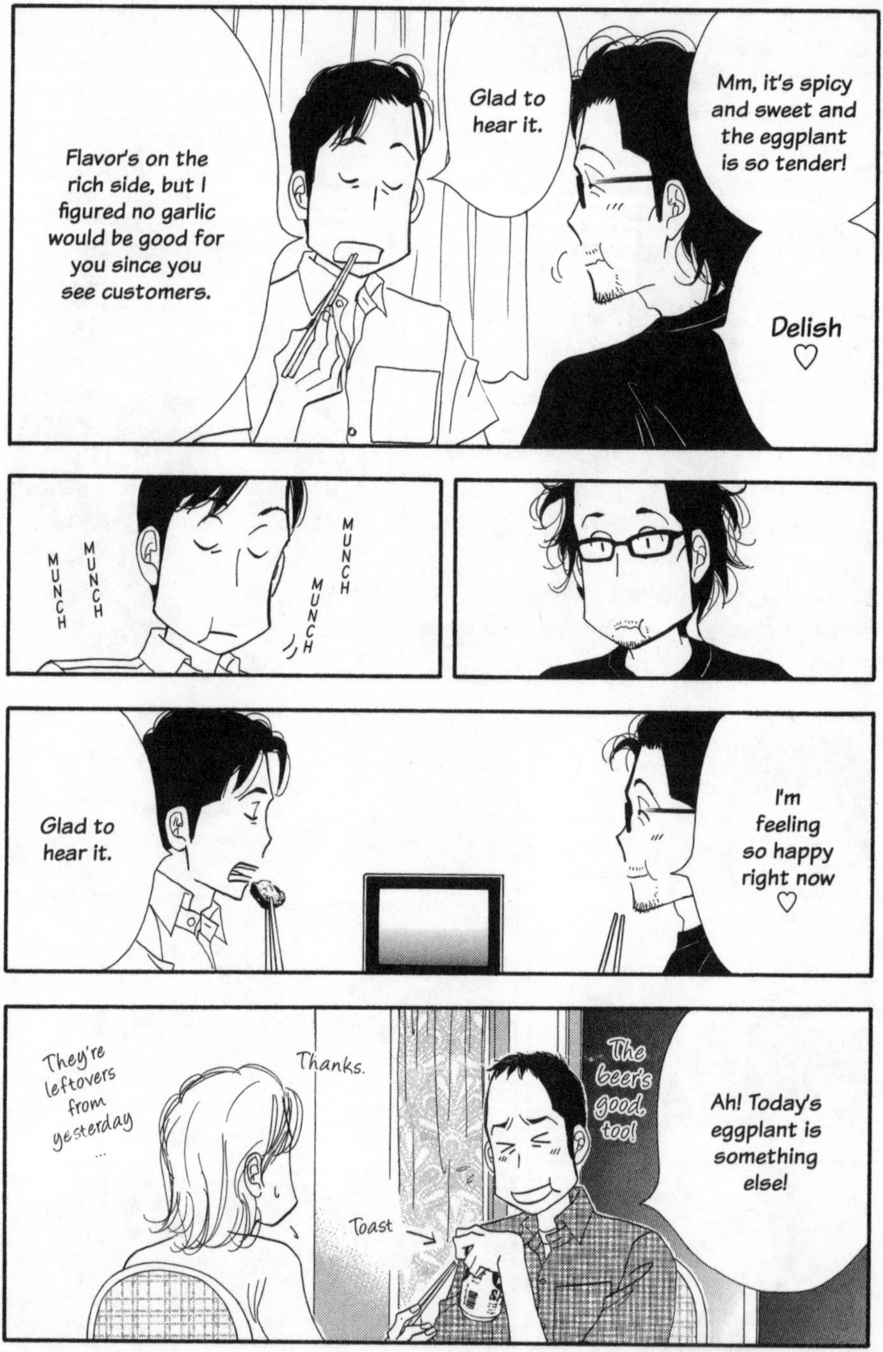

Mm, it's spicy and sweet and the eggplant is so tender!
Delish ♡
Glad to hear it.
Flavor's on the rich side, but I figured no garlic would be good for you since you see customers.
MUNCH
MUNCH
MUNCH
MUNCH
I'm feeling so happy right now ♡
Glad to hear it.
Ah! Today's eggplant is something else!
The beer's good, too!
Thanks.
Toast
They're leftovers from yesterday ...

#6 END

General bottomed-out prices:

Eggplant	1 bag of 5	100 yen
Tomato	1 pack of 4	100 yen
Onion	1 bag of 4	100 yen
Shaved pork	3 1/2 oz	50 yen
Okra	2 bags (7 each)	130 yen
Myoga ginger	1 pack of 3	100 yen
Whiteleg shrimp	20	350 yen
Cucumber	1 pack of 4	100 yen
Shiso leaves	2 bunches	100 yen
Bonito flakes	Pack of 20	198 yen

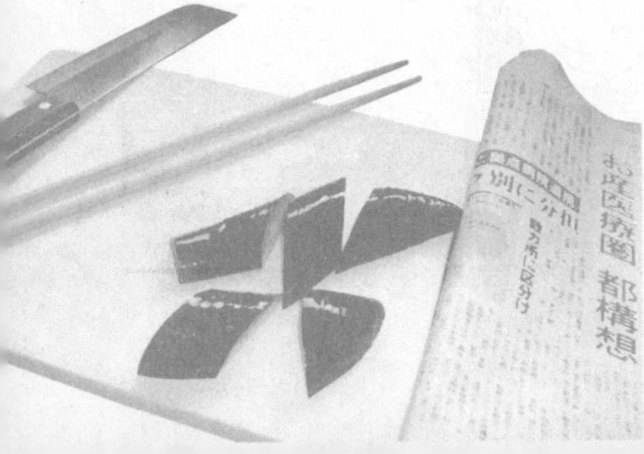
都構想

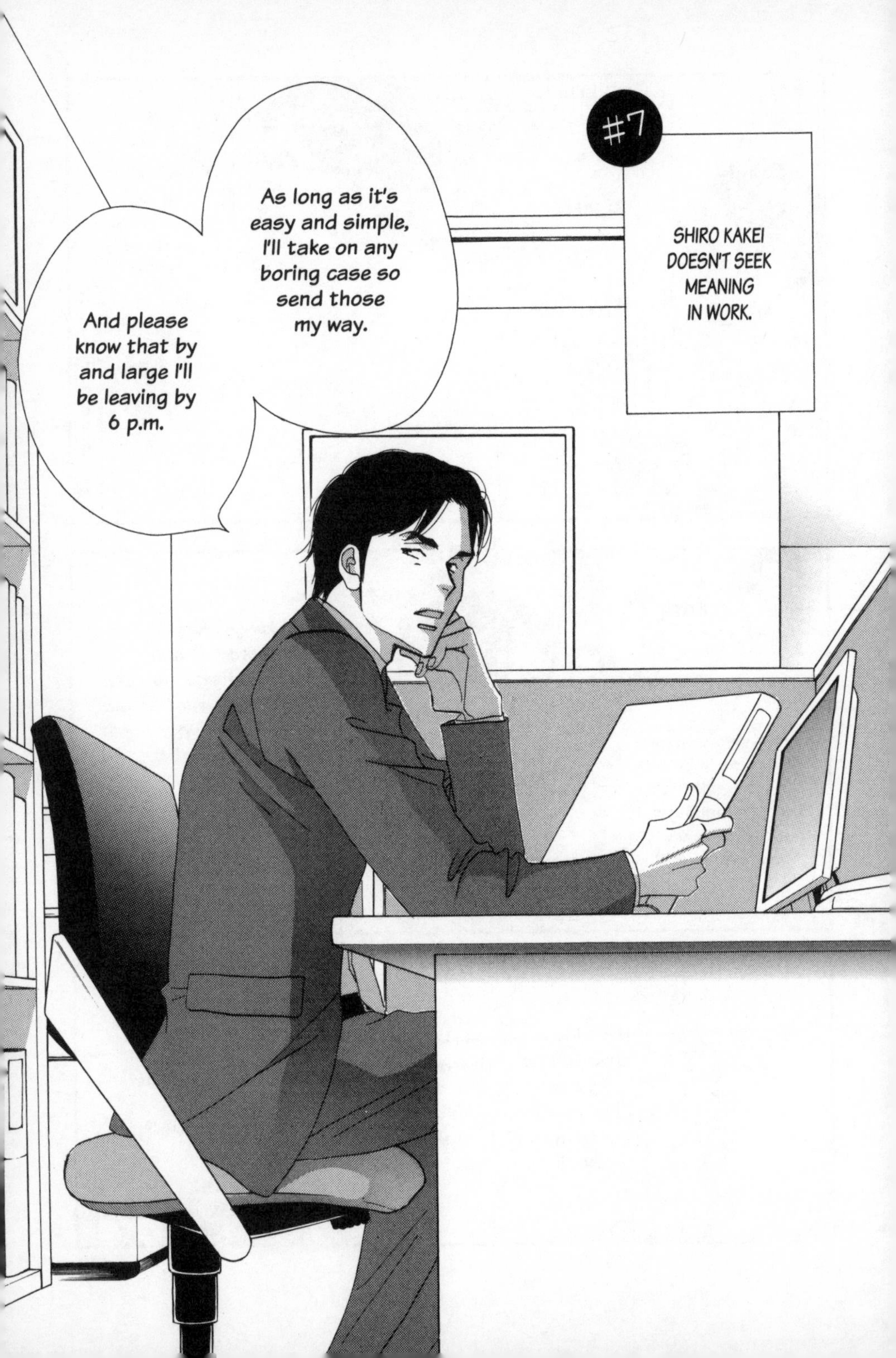
#7
SHIRO KAKEI DOESN'T SEEK MEANING IN WORK.
As long as it's easy and simple, I'll take on any boring case so send those my way.
And please know that by and large I'll be leaving by 6 p.m.

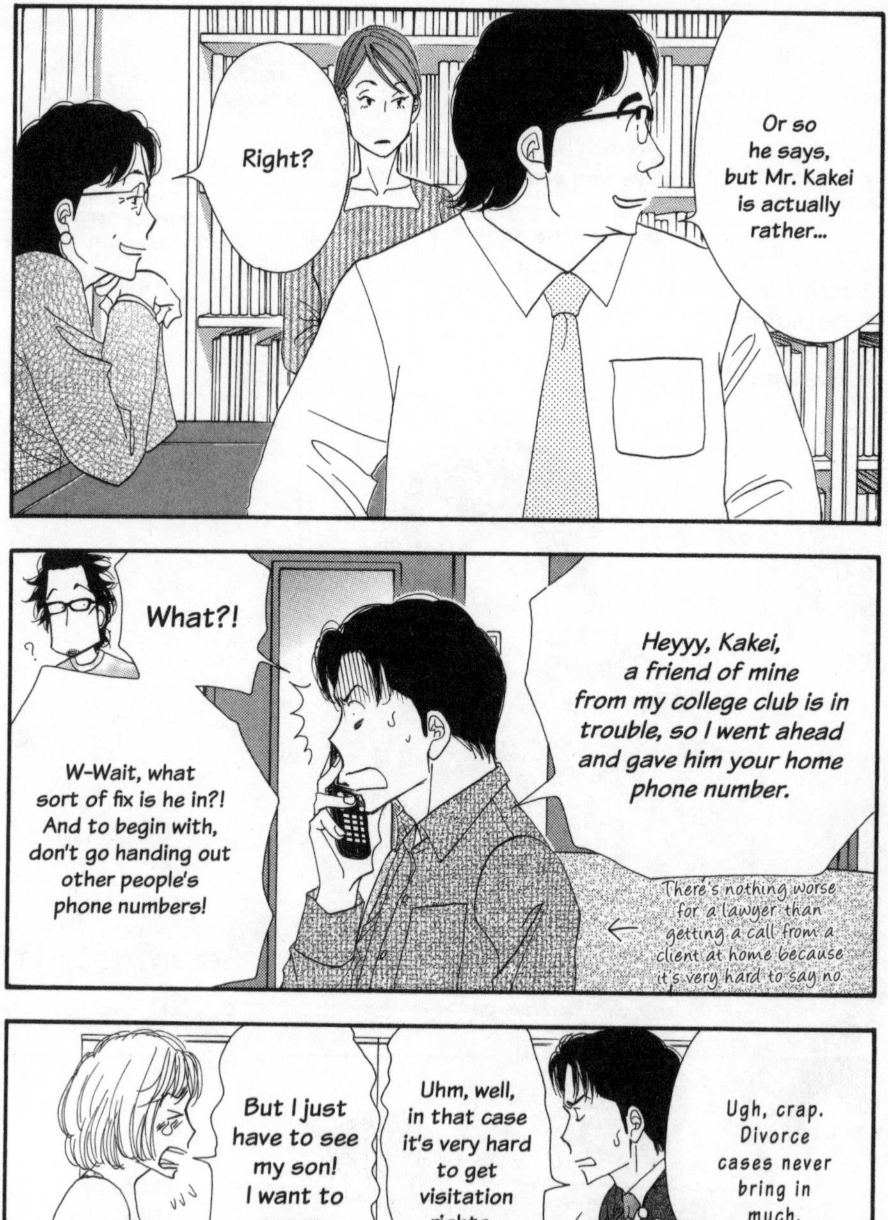

Or so he says, but Mr. Kakei is actually rather...
Right?
Heyyy, Kakei, a friend of mine from my college club is in trouble, so I went ahead and gave him your home phone number.
There's nothing worse for a lawyer than getting a call from a client at home because it's very hard to say no
What?!
W-Wait, what sort of fix is he in?! And to begin with, don't go handing out other people's phone numbers!
Ugh, crap. Divorce cases never bring in much.
Uhm, well, in that case it's very hard to get visitation rights...
But I just have to see my son! I want to see my son!!

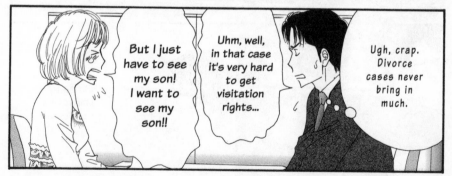

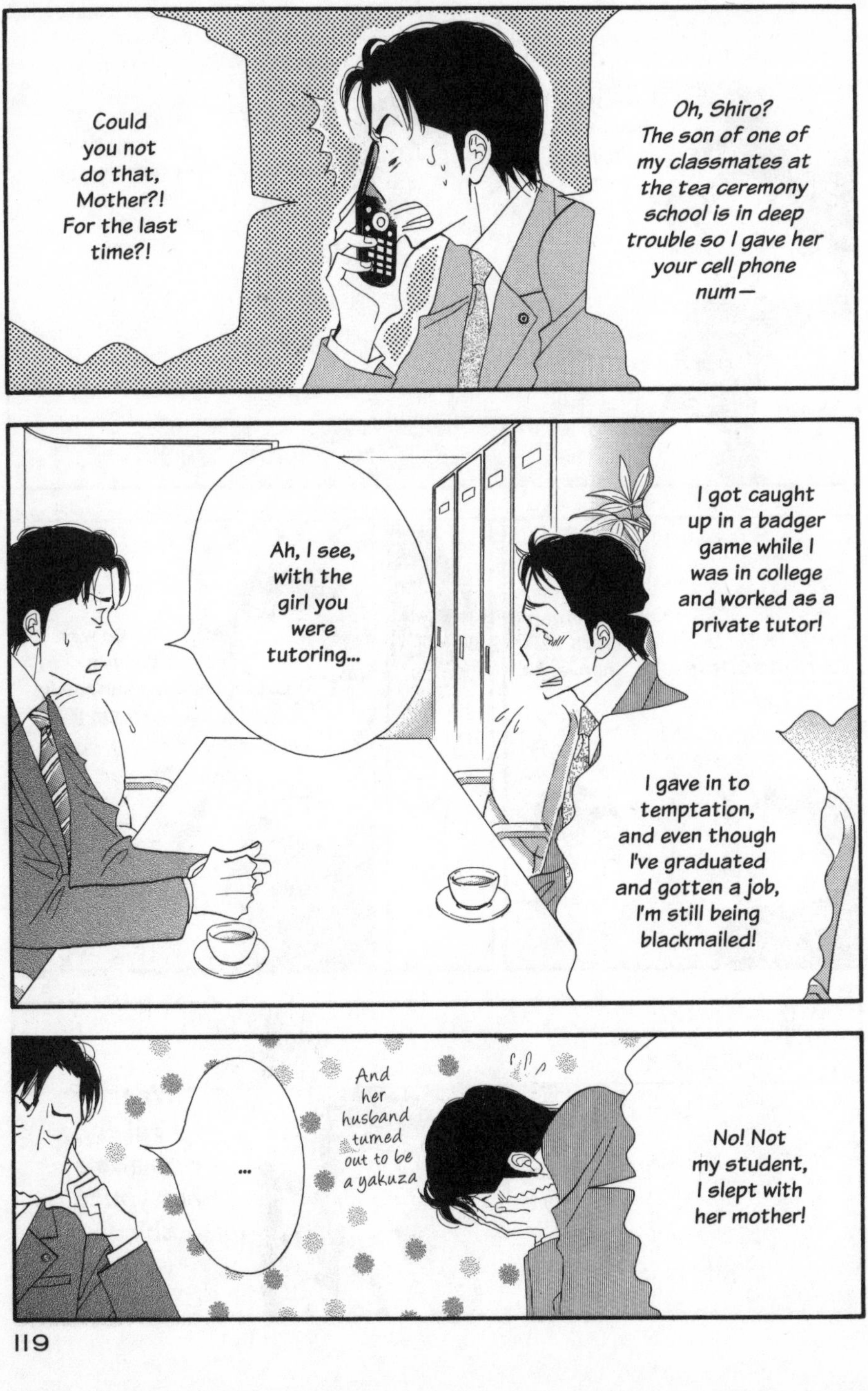
Oh, Shiro? The son of one of my classmates at the tea ceremony school is in deep trouble so I gave her your cell phone num—
Could you not do that, Mother?! For the last time?!
I got caught up in a badger game while I was in college and worked as a private tutor!
Ah, I see, with the girl you were tutoring...
I gave in to temptation, and even though I've graduated and gotten a job, I'm still being blackmailed!
No! Not my student, I slept with her mother!
And her husband turned out to be a yakuza
...

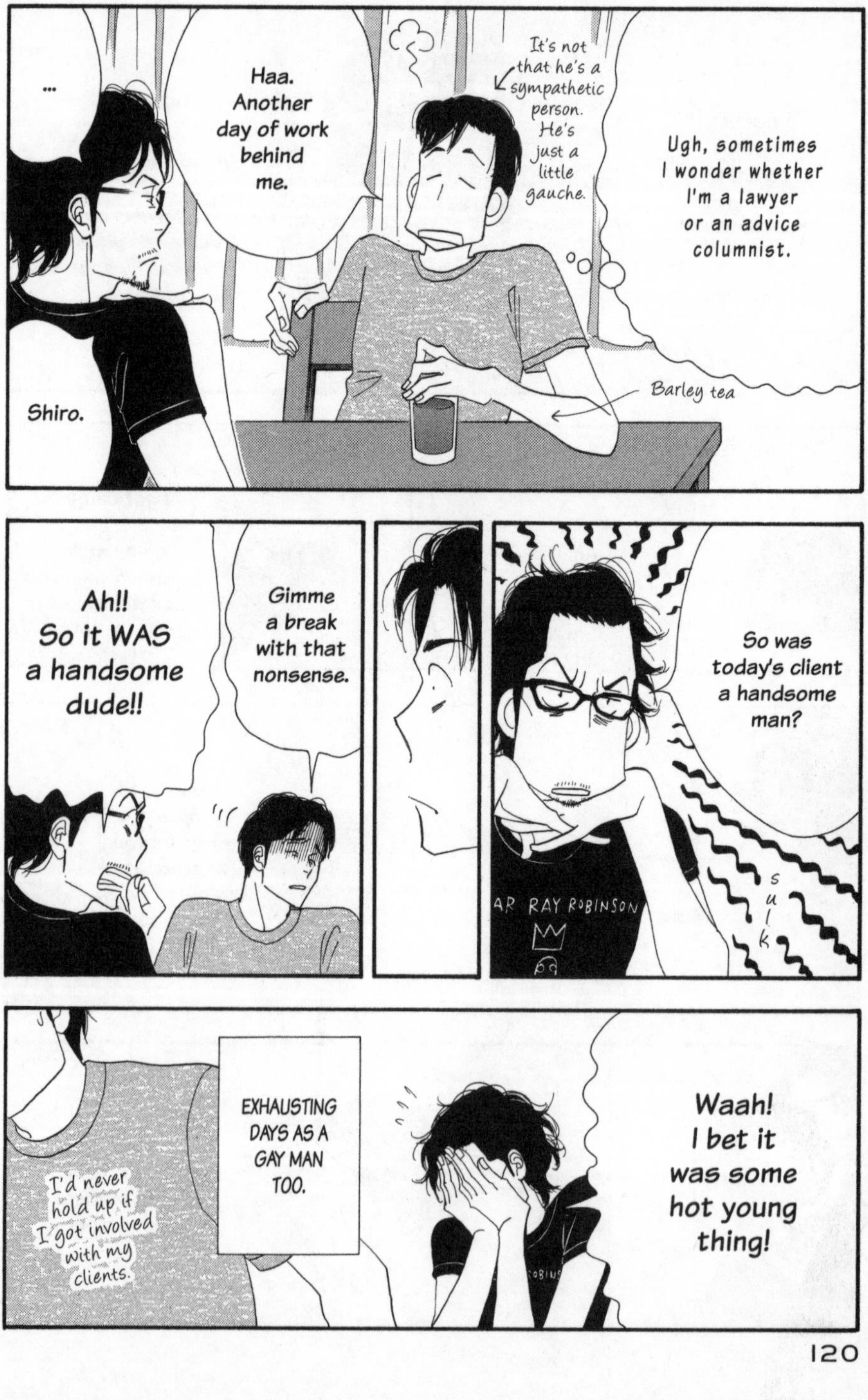

Ugh, sometimes I wonder whether I'm a lawyer or an advice columnist.
It's not that he's a sympathetic person. He's just a little gauche.
Haa. Another day of work behind me.
...
Barley tea
Shiro.
So was today's client a handsome man?
sulk
Gimme a break with that nonsense.
Ah!! So it WAS a handsome dude!!
Waah! I bet it was some hot young thing!
EXHAUSTING DAYS AS A GAY MAN TOO.
I'd never hold up if I got involved with my clients.

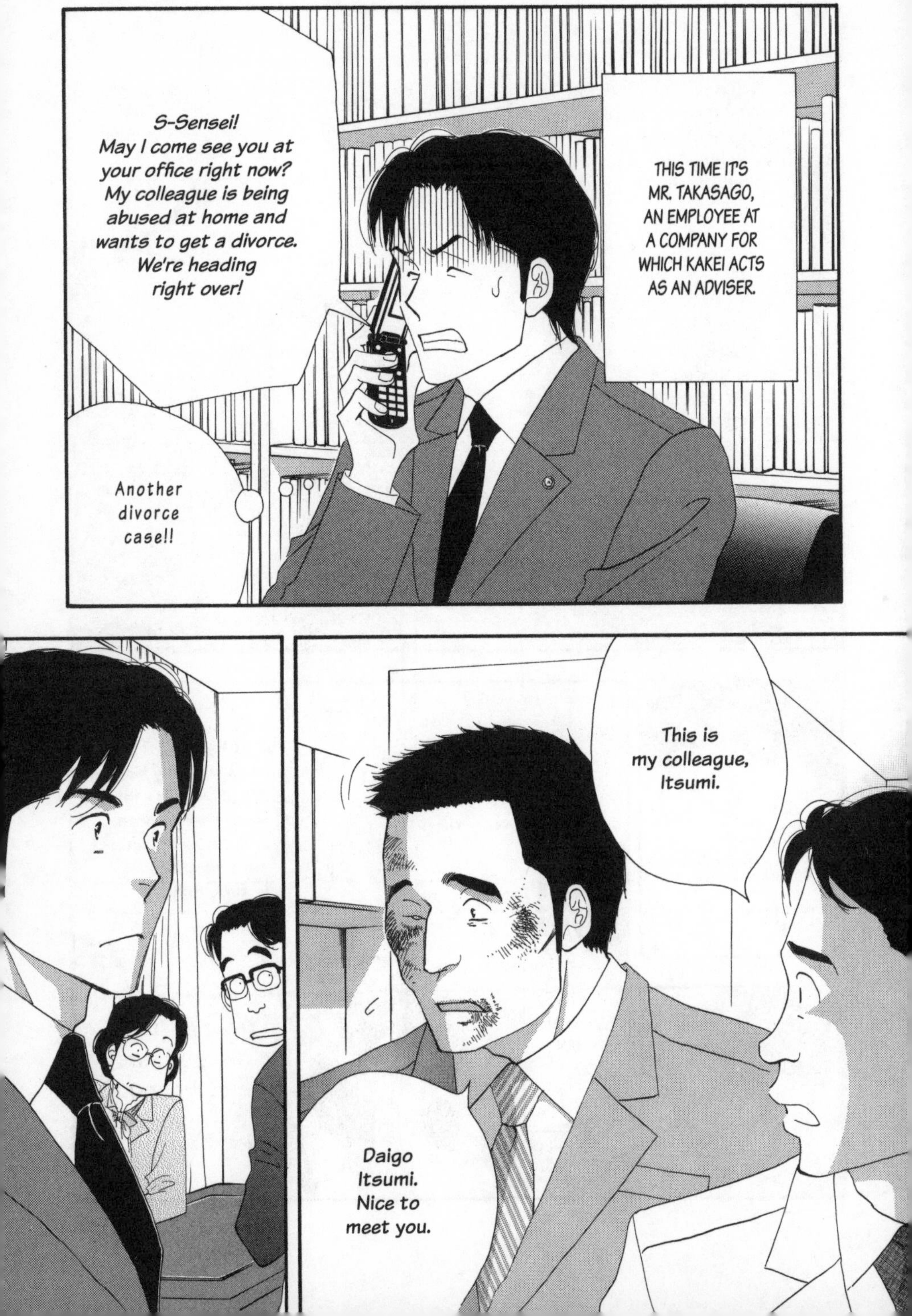
THIS TIME IT'S MR. TAKASAGO, AN EMPLOYEE AT A COMPANY FOR WHICH KAKEI ACTS AS AN ADVISER.
S-Sensei! May I come see you at your office right now? My colleague is being abused at home and wants to get a divorce. We're heading right over!
Another divorce case!!
This is my colleague, Itsumi.
Daigo Itsumi. Nice to meet you.

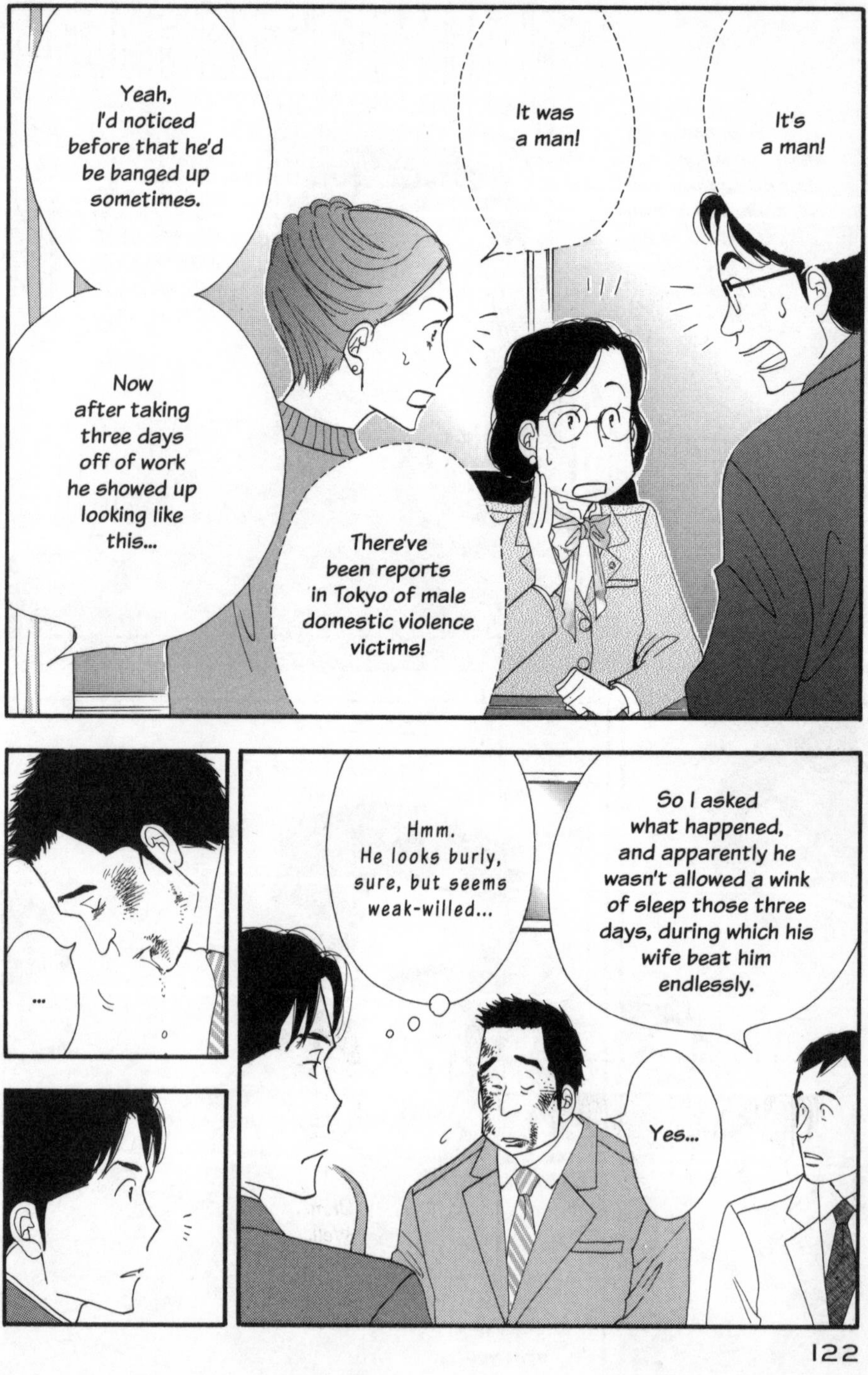
It's a man!
It was a man!
Yeah, I'd noticed before that he'd be banged up sometimes.
Now after taking three days off of work he showed up looking like this...
There've been reports in Tokyo of male domestic violence victims!
So I asked what happened, and apparently he wasn't allowed a wink of sleep those three days, during which his wife beat him endlessly.
Hmm. He looks burly, sure, but seems weak-willed...
Yes...
...

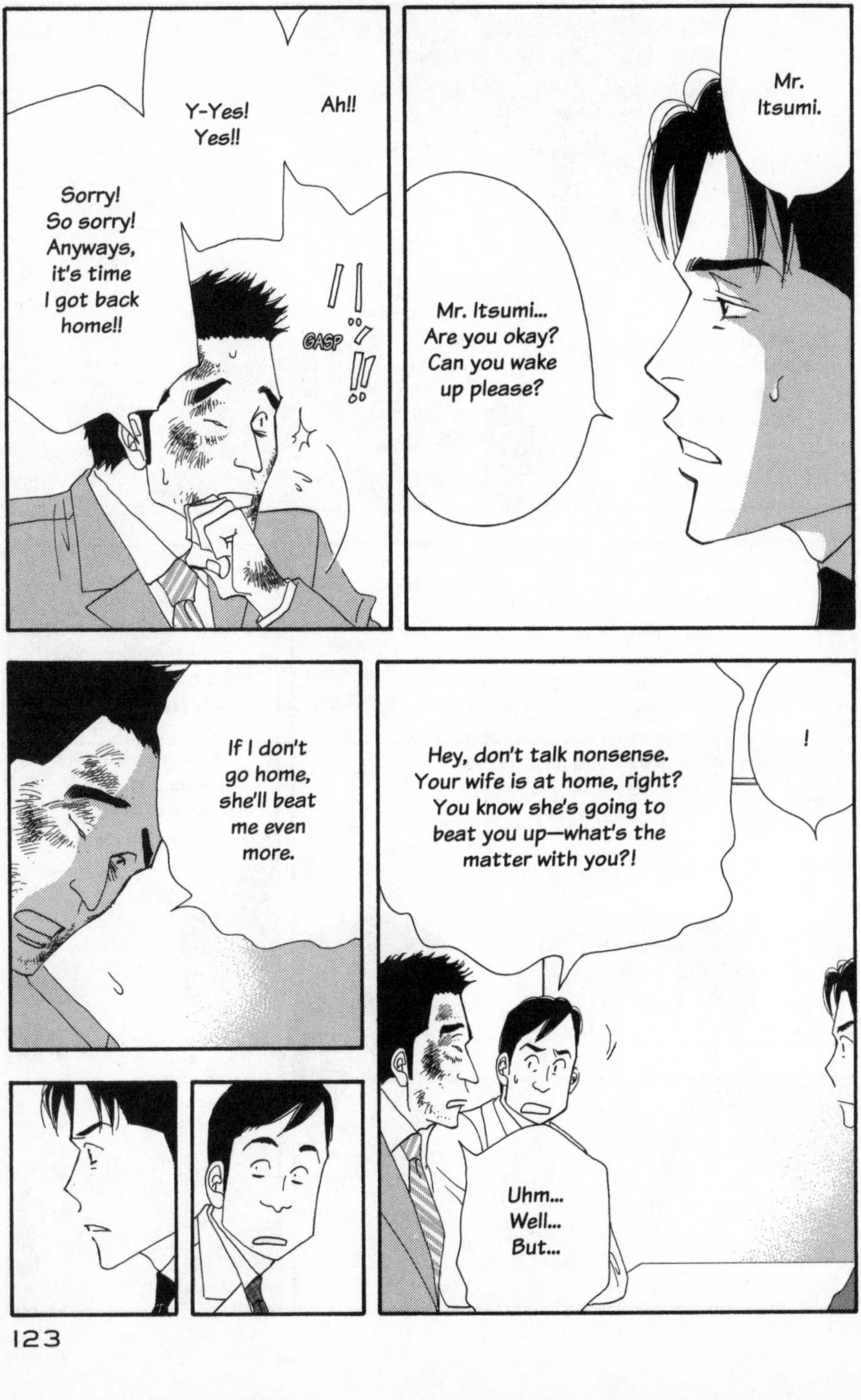
Mr. Itsumi.
Mr. Itsumi... Are you okay? Can you wake up please?
Ah!!
Y-Yes! Yes!!
GASP
Sorry! So sorry! Anyways, it's time I got back home!!
!
Hey, don't talk nonsense. Your wife is at home, right? You know she's going to beat you up—what's the matter with you?!
Uhm... Well... But...
If I don't go home, she'll beat me even more.

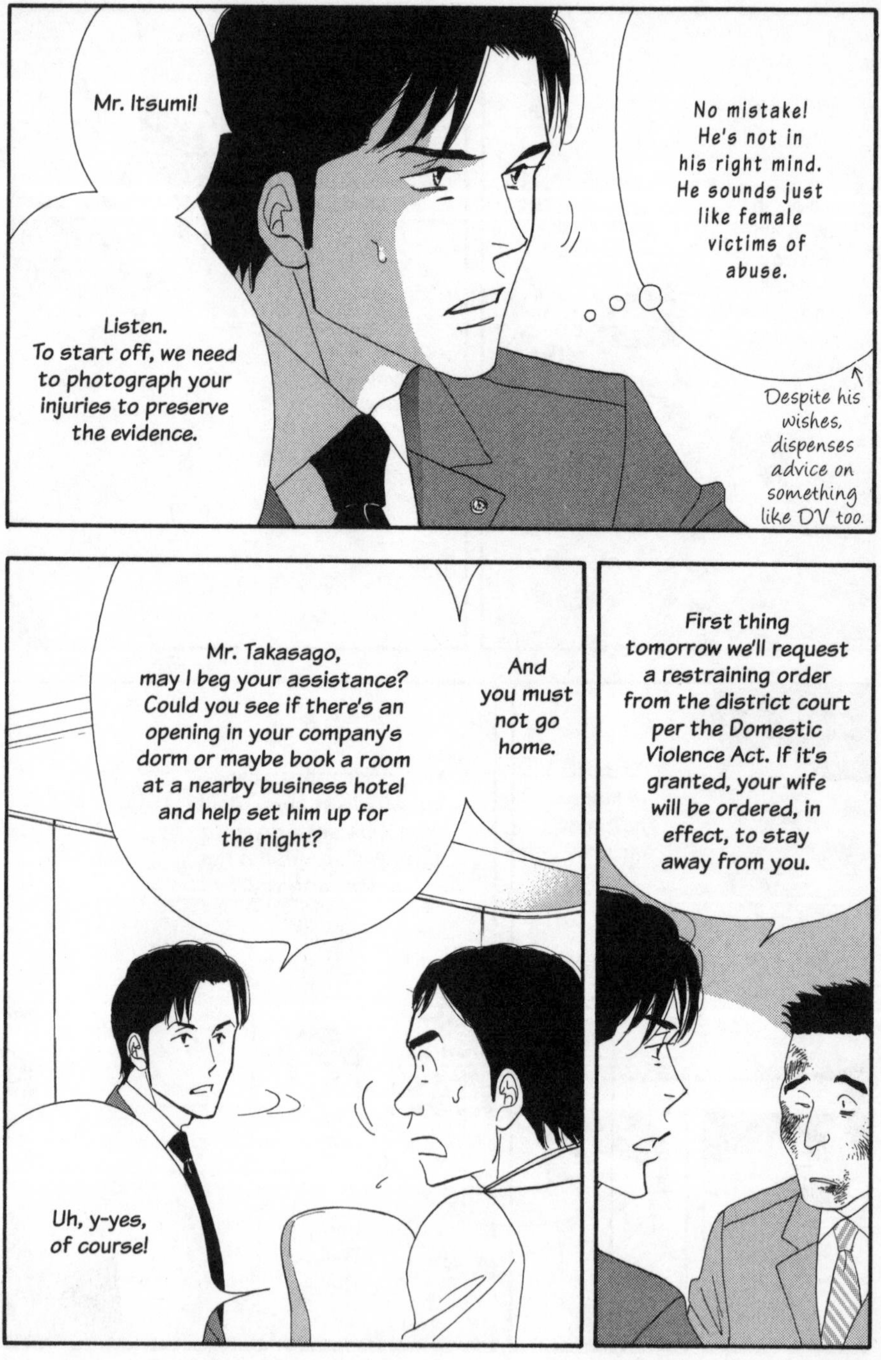
No mistake! He's not in his right mind. He sounds just like female victims of abuse.
Mr. Itsumi!
Listen. To start off, we need to photograph your injuries to preserve the evidence.
Despite his wishes, dispenses advice on something like DV too.
First thing tomorrow we'll request a restraining order from the district court per the Domestic Violence Act. If it's granted, your wife will be ordered, in effect, to stay away from you.
And you must not go home.
Mr. Takasago, may I beg your assistance? Could you see if there's an opening in your company's dorm or maybe book a room at a nearby business hotel and help set him up for the night?
Uh, y-yes, of course!

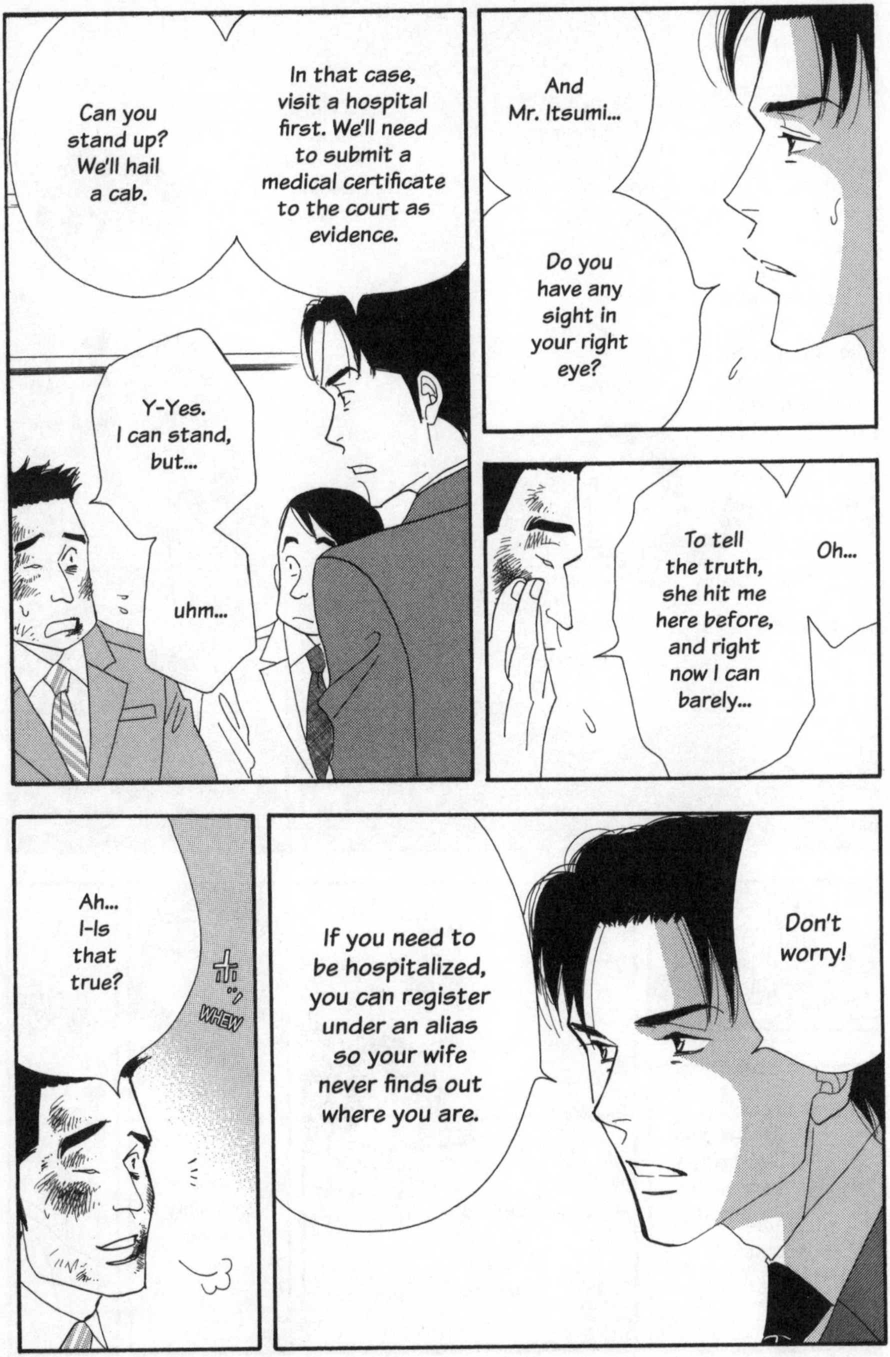
And Mr. Itsumi...
Do you have any sight in your right eye?
Oh...
To tell the truth, she hit me here before, and right now I can barely...
In that case, visit a hospital first. We'll need to submit a medical certificate to the court as evidence.
Can you stand up? We'll hail a cab.
Y-Yes. I can stand, but...
uhm...
Don't worry!
If you need to be hospitalized, you can register under an alias so your wife never finds out where you are.
Ah... I-Is that true?
WHEW

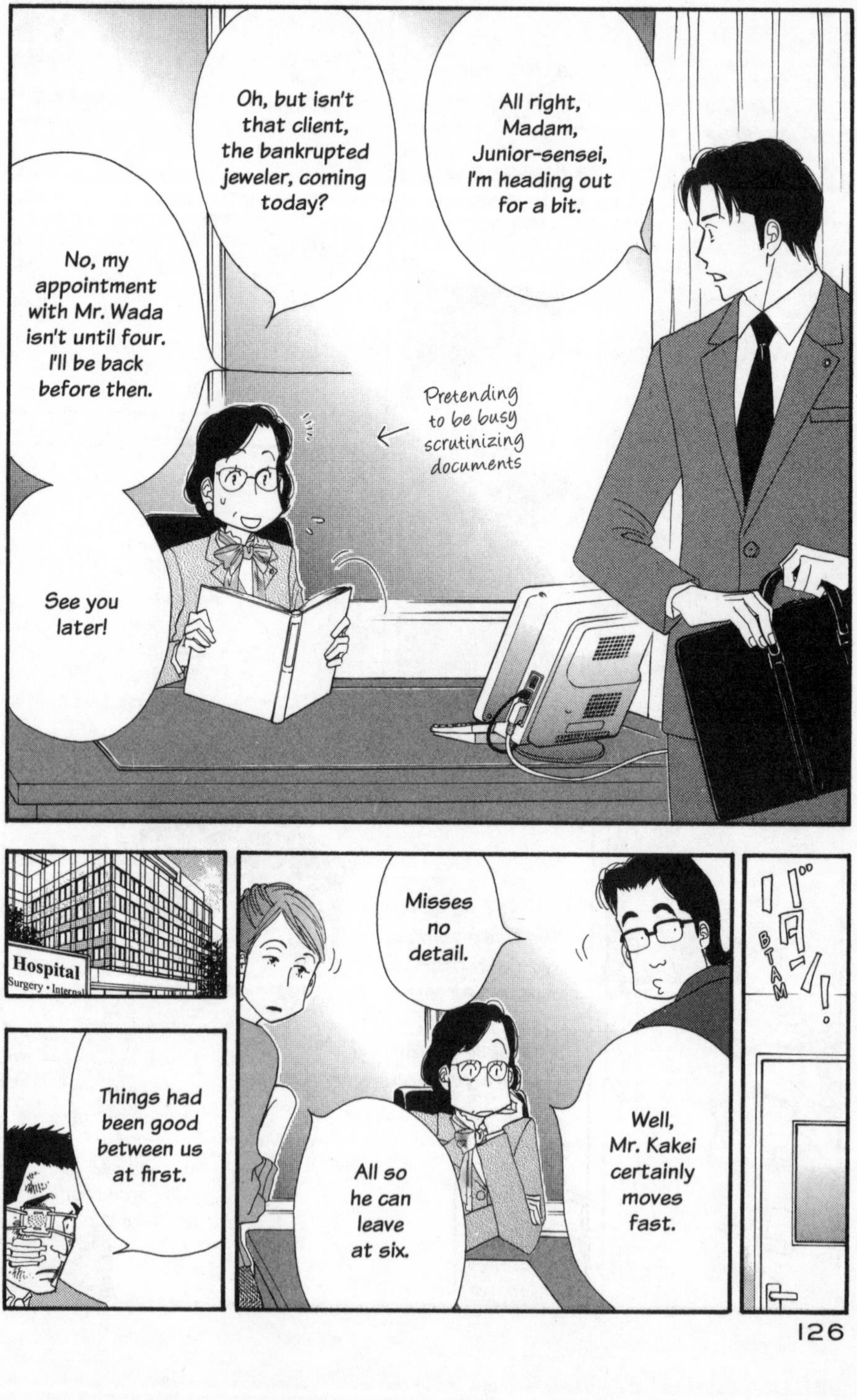
All right, Madam, Junior-sensei, I'm heading out for a bit.
Oh, but isn't that client, the bankrupted jeweler, coming today?
No, my appointment with Mr. Wada isn't until four. I'll be back before then.
Pretending to be busy scrutinizing documents
See you later!
BTAM
Well, Mr. Kakei certainly moves fast.
Misses no detail.
All so he can leave at six.
Hospital
Surgery • Internal
Things had been good between us at first.

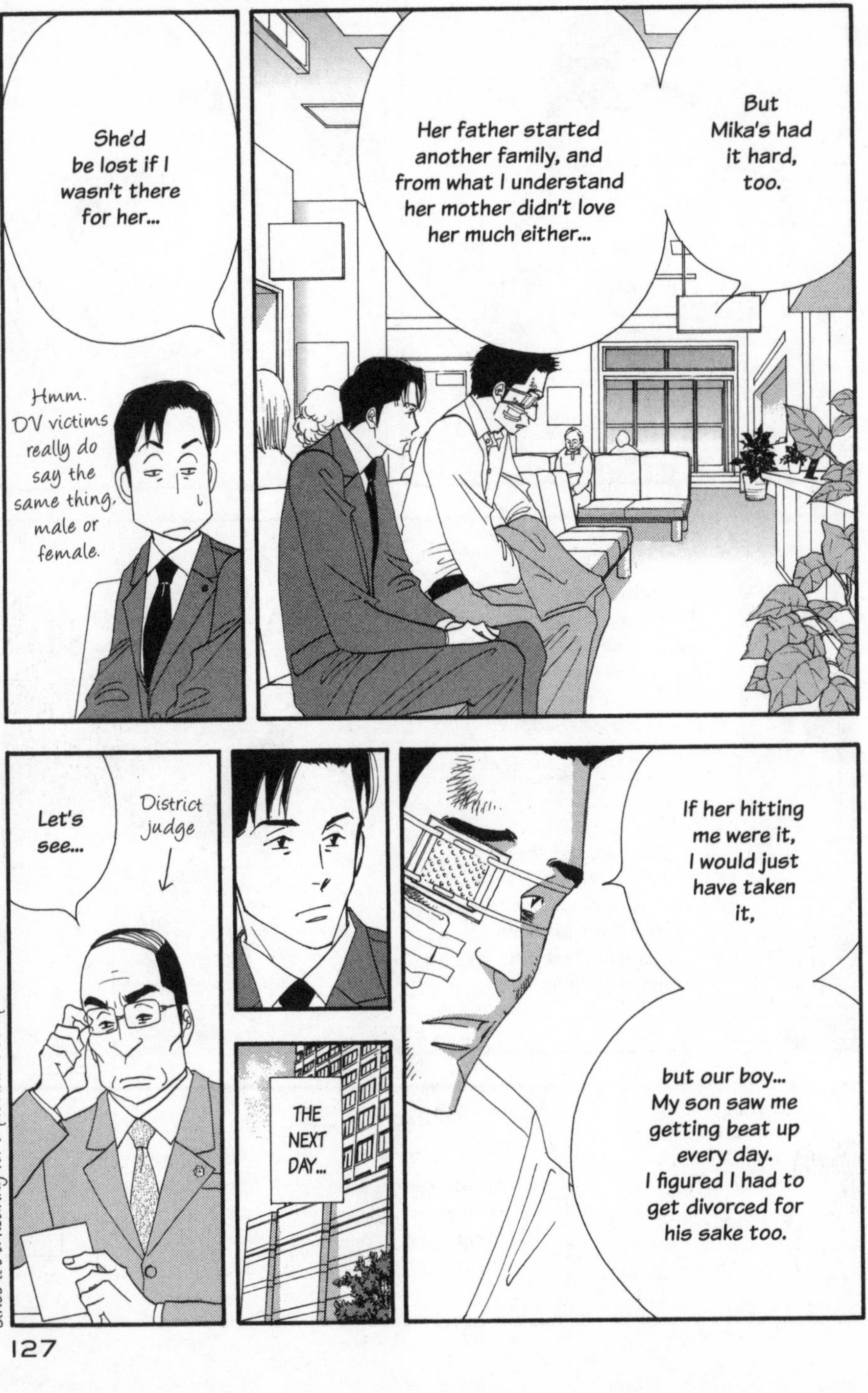
But Mika's had it hard, too.
Her father started another family, and from what I understand her mother didn't love her much either...
She'd be lost if I wasn't there for her...
Hmm. DV victims really do say the same thing, male or female.
If her hitting me were it, I would just have taken it,
but our boy... My son saw me getting beat up every day. I figured I had to get divorced for his sake too.
THE NEXT DAY...
Let's see...
District judge

Since it's a hearing for a provisional disposition, he's not in formal robes.

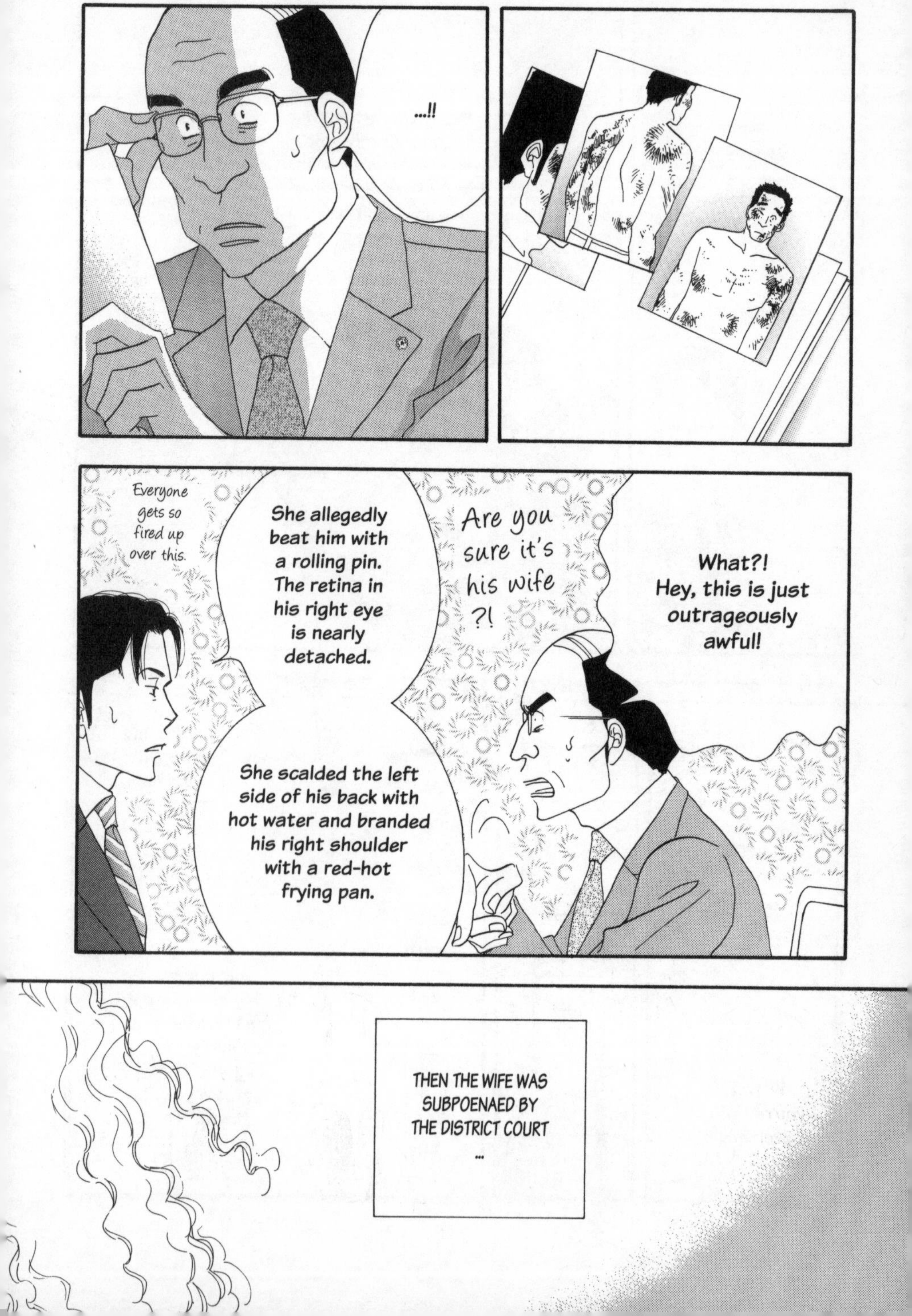
...!!
What?! Hey, this is just outrageously awful!
Are you sure it's his wife ?!
She allegedly beat him with a rolling pin. The retina in his right eye is nearly detached.
She scalded the left side of his back with hot water and branded his right shoulder with a red-hot frying pan.
Everyone gets so fired up over this.
THEN THE WIFE WAS SUBPOENAED BY THE DISTRICT COURT ...

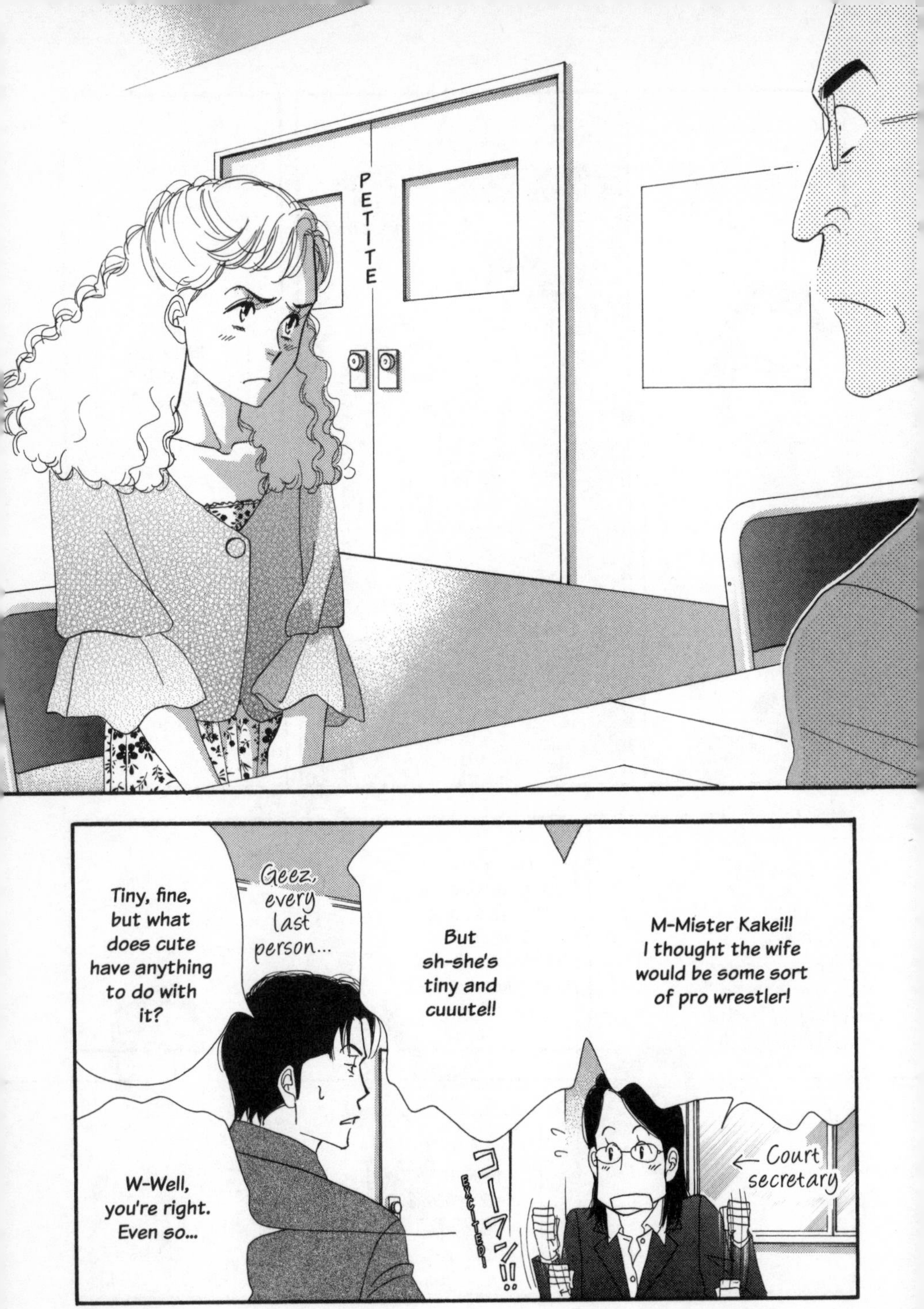
PETITE
M-Mister Kakei!! I thought the wife would be some sort of pro wrestler!
Court secretary
But sh-she's tiny and cuuute!!
コーフン!!
EXCITED!
Geez, every last person...
Tiny, fine, but what does cute have anything to do with it?
W-Well, you're right. Even so...

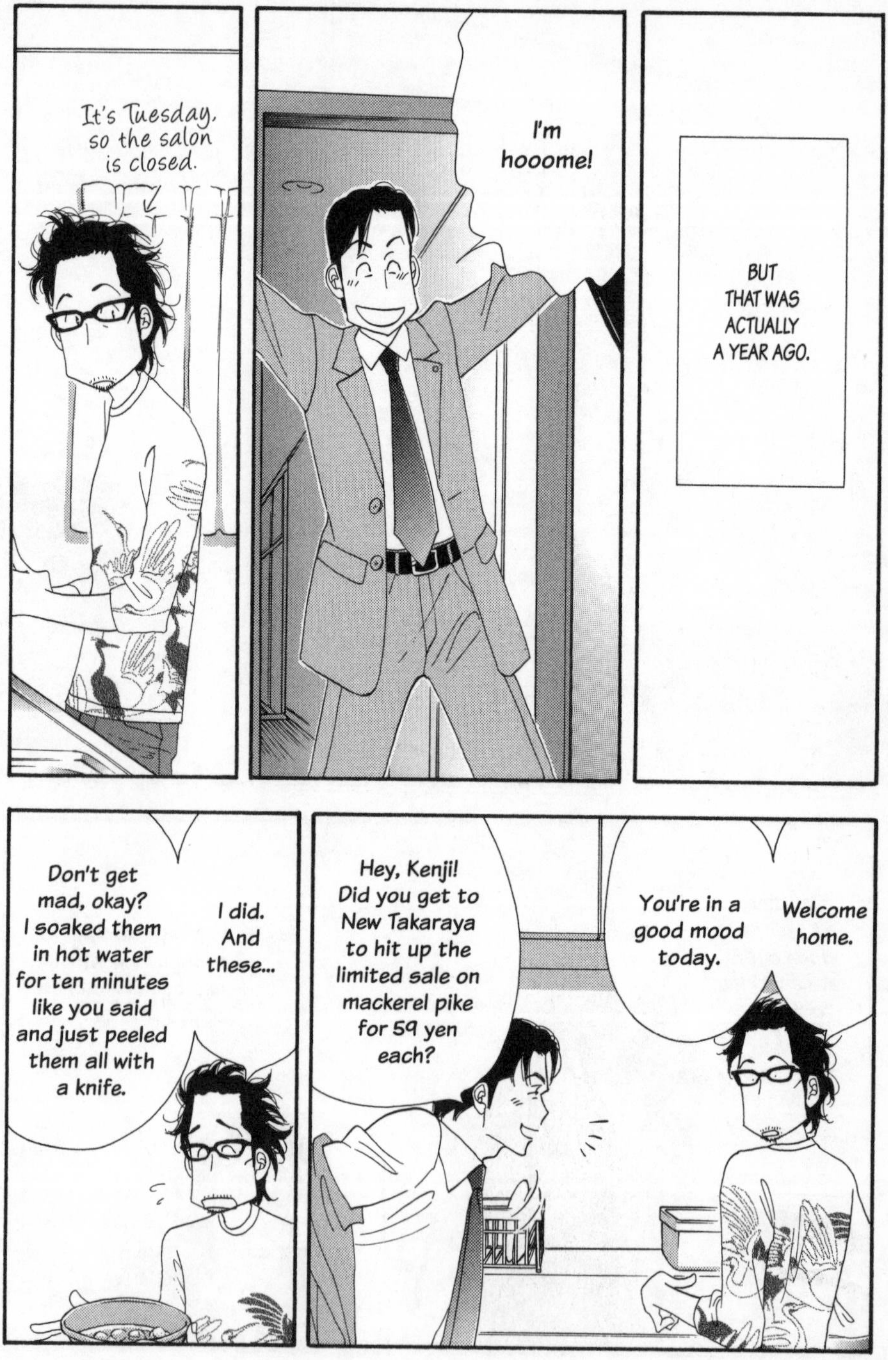
BUT THAT WAS ACTUALLY A YEAR AGO.
I'm hooome!
It's Tuesday, so the salon is closed.
Welcome home.
You're in a good mood today.
Hey, Kenji! Did you get to New Takaraya to hit up the limited sale on mackerel pike for 59 yen each?
I did. And these...
Don't get mad, okay? I soaked them in hot water for ten minutes like you said and just peeled them all with a knife.

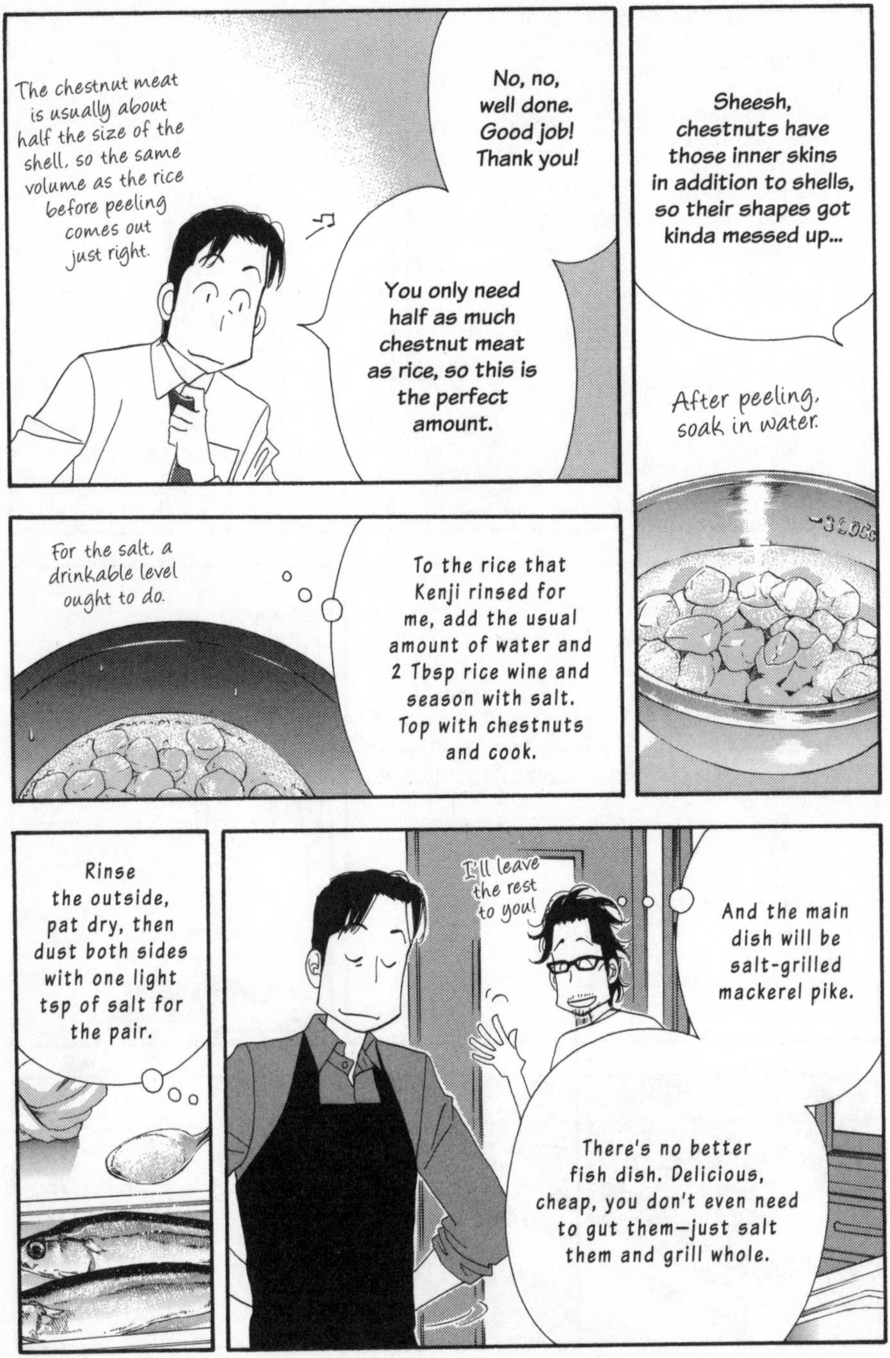

Sheesh, chestnuts have those inner skins in addition to shells, so their shapes got kinda messed up...
After peeling, soak in water.
No, no, well done. Good job! Thank you!
You only need half as much chestnut meat as rice, so this is the perfect amount.
The chestnut meat is usually about half the size of the shell, so the same volume as the rice before peeling comes out just right.
To the rice that Kenji rinsed for me, add the usual amount of water and 2 Tbsp rice wine and season with salt. Top with chestnuts and cook.
For the salt, a drinkable level ought to do.
And the main dish will be salt-grilled mackerel pike.
I'll leave the rest to you!
There's no better fish dish. Delicious, cheap, you don't even need to gut them—just salt them and grill whole.
Rinse the outside, pat dry, then dust both sides with one light tsp of salt for the pair.

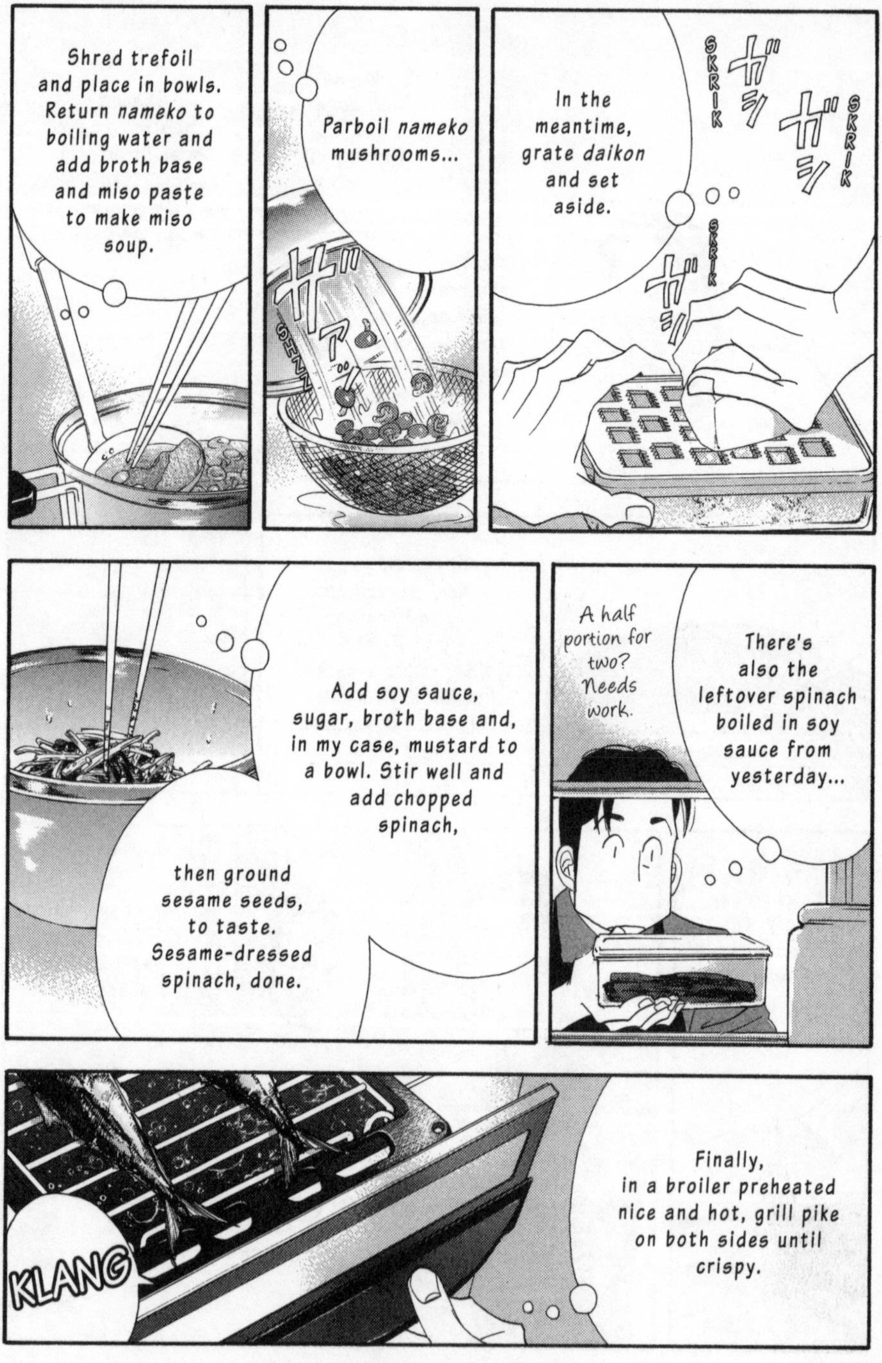

SKRIK
SKRIK
In the meantime, grate *daikon* and set aside.
SKRIK
Parboil *nameko* mushrooms...
SHZZ
Shred trefoil and place in bowls. Return *nameko* to boiling water and add broth base and miso paste to make miso soup.
There's also the leftover spinach boiled in soy sauce from yesterday...
A half portion for two? Needs work.
Add soy sauce, sugar, broth base and, in my case, mustard to a bowl. Stir well and add chopped spinach,
then ground sesame seeds, to taste. Sesame-dressed spinach, done.
Finally, in a broiler preheated nice and hot, grill pike on both sides until crispy.
KLANG

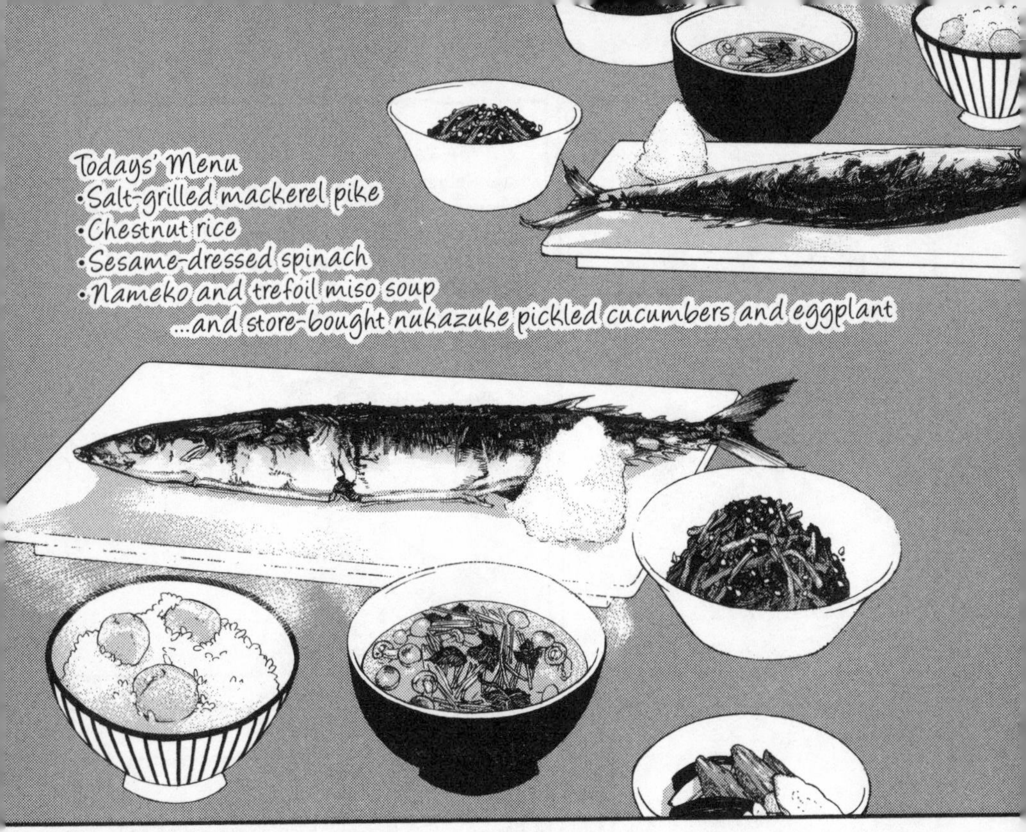
Todays' Menu
•Salt-grilled mackerel pike
•Chestnut rice
•Sesame-dressed spinach
•Nameko and trefoil miso soup
...and store-bought nukazuke pickled cucumbers and eggplant

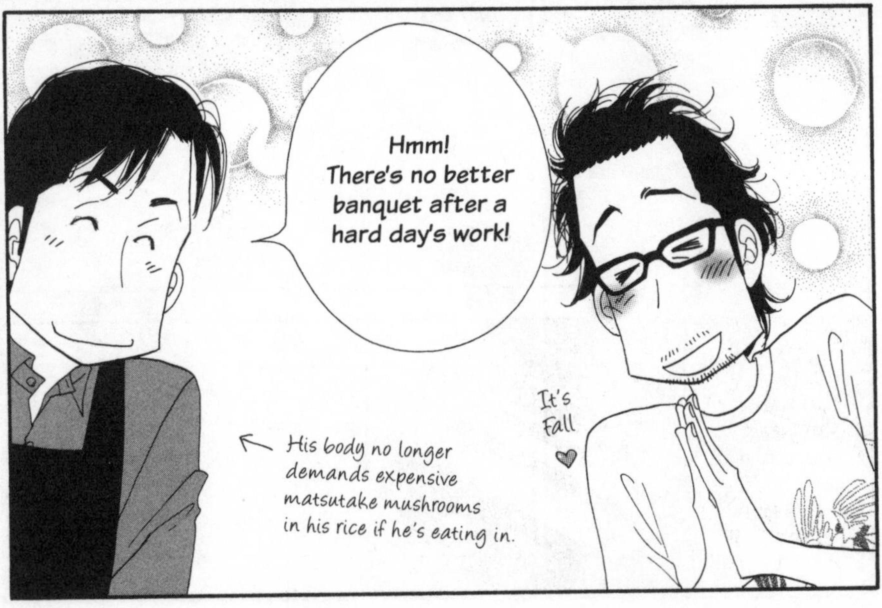
Hmm! There's no better banquet after a hard day's work!
It's Fall ♥
His body no longer demands expensive matsutake mushrooms in his rice if he's eating in.

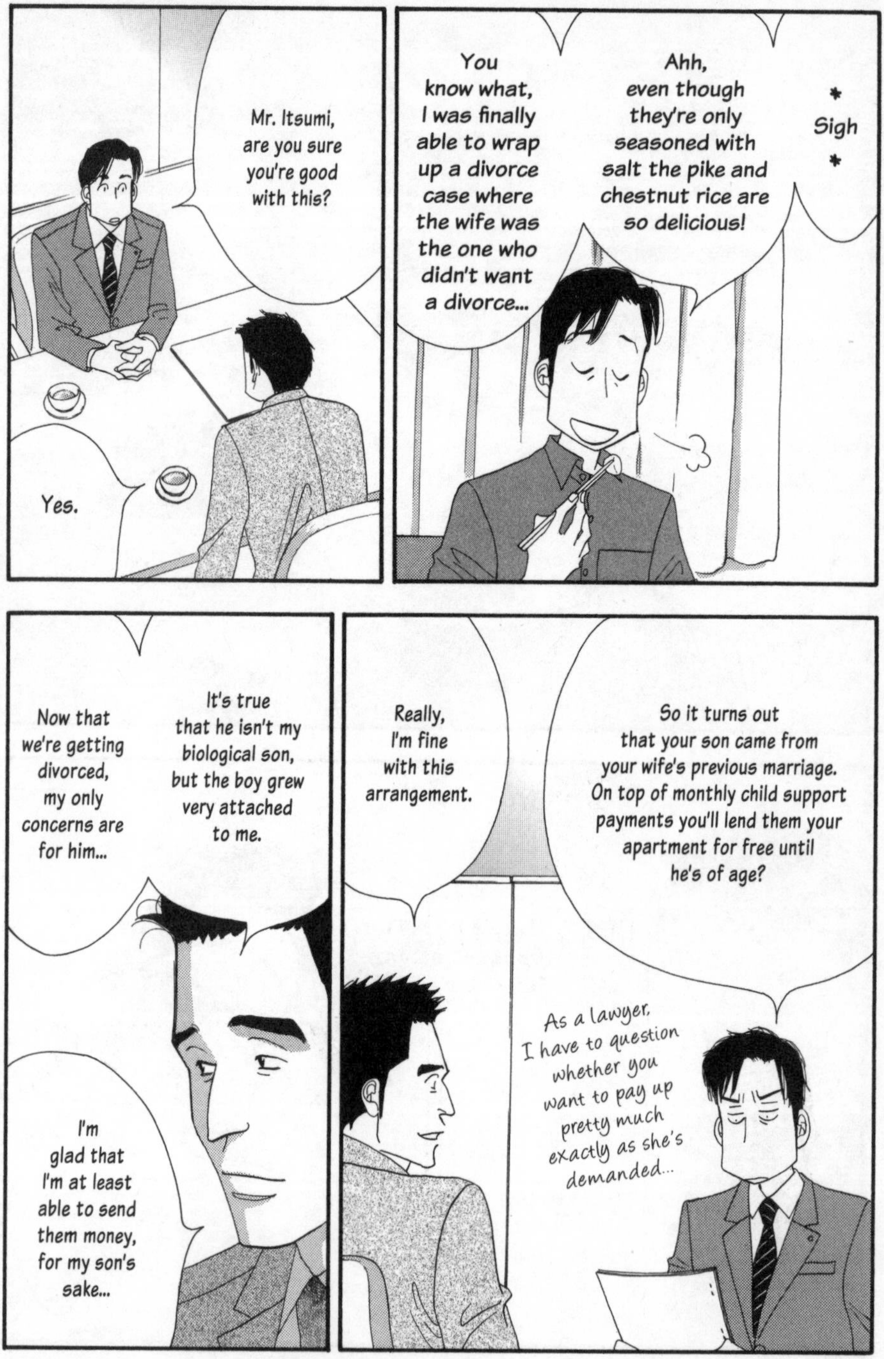
* Sigh *
Ahh, even though they're only seasoned with salt the pike and chestnut rice are so delicious!
You know what, I was finally able to wrap up a divorce case where the wife was the one who didn't want a divorce...
Mr. Itsumi, are you sure you're good with this?
Yes.
So it turns out that your son came from your wife's previous marriage. On top of monthly child support payments you'll lend them your apartment for free until he's of age?
As a lawyer, I have to question whether you want to pay up pretty much exactly as she's demanded...
Really, I'm fine with this arrangement.
It's true that he isn't my biological son, but the boy grew very attached to me.
Now that we're getting divorced, my only concerns are for him...
I'm glad that I'm at least able to send them money, for my son's sake...

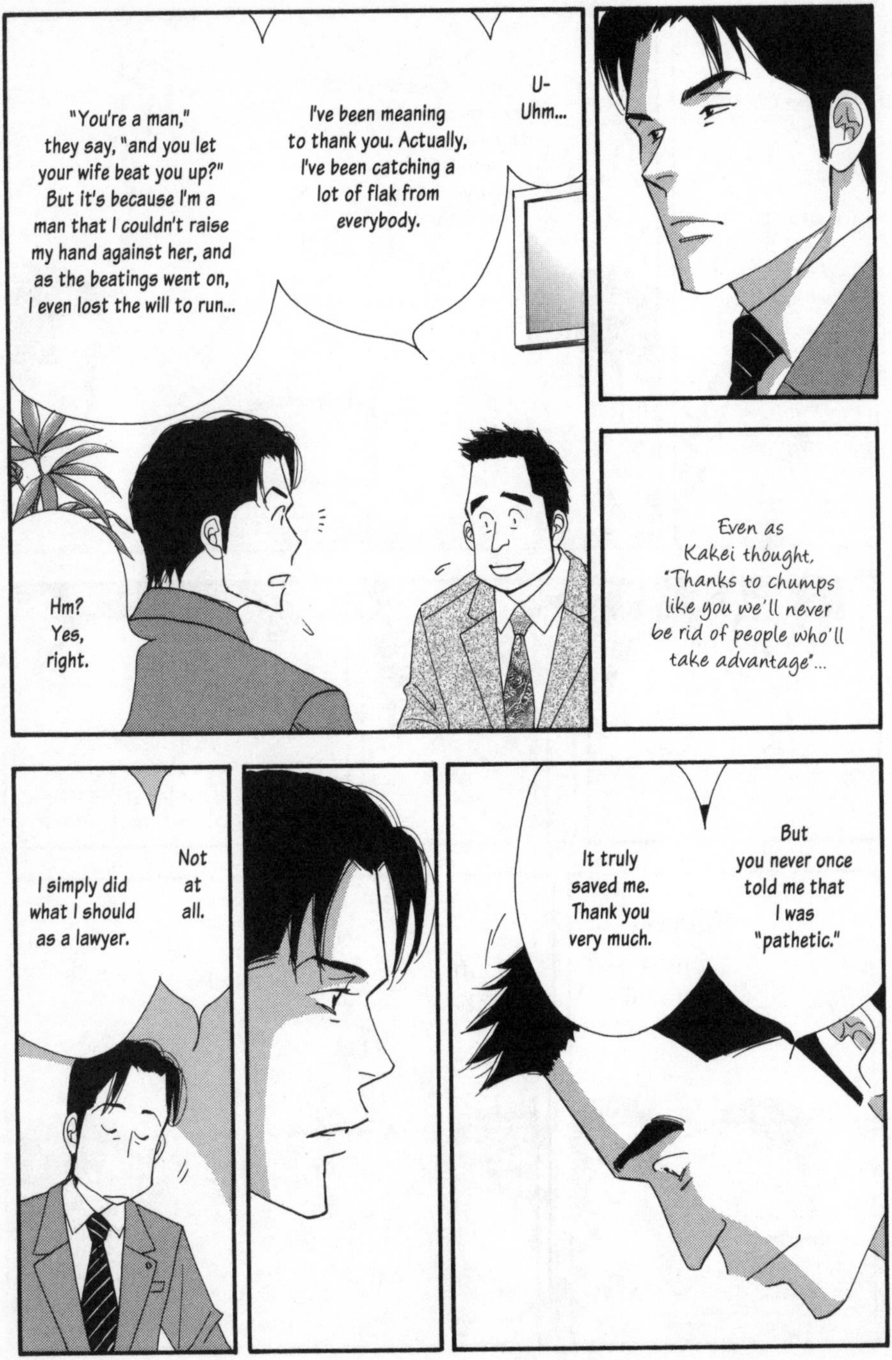
Even as Kakei thought, "Thanks to chumps like you we'll never be rid of people who'll take advantage"...
U- Uhm...
I've been meaning to thank you. Actually, I've been catching a lot of flak from everybody.
"You're a man," they say, "and you let your wife beat you up?" But it's because I'm a man that I couldn't raise my hand against her, and as the beatings went on, I even lost the will to run...
Hm? Yes, right.
But you never once told me that I was "pathetic."
It truly saved me. Thank you very much.
Not at all.
I simply did what I should as a lawyer.

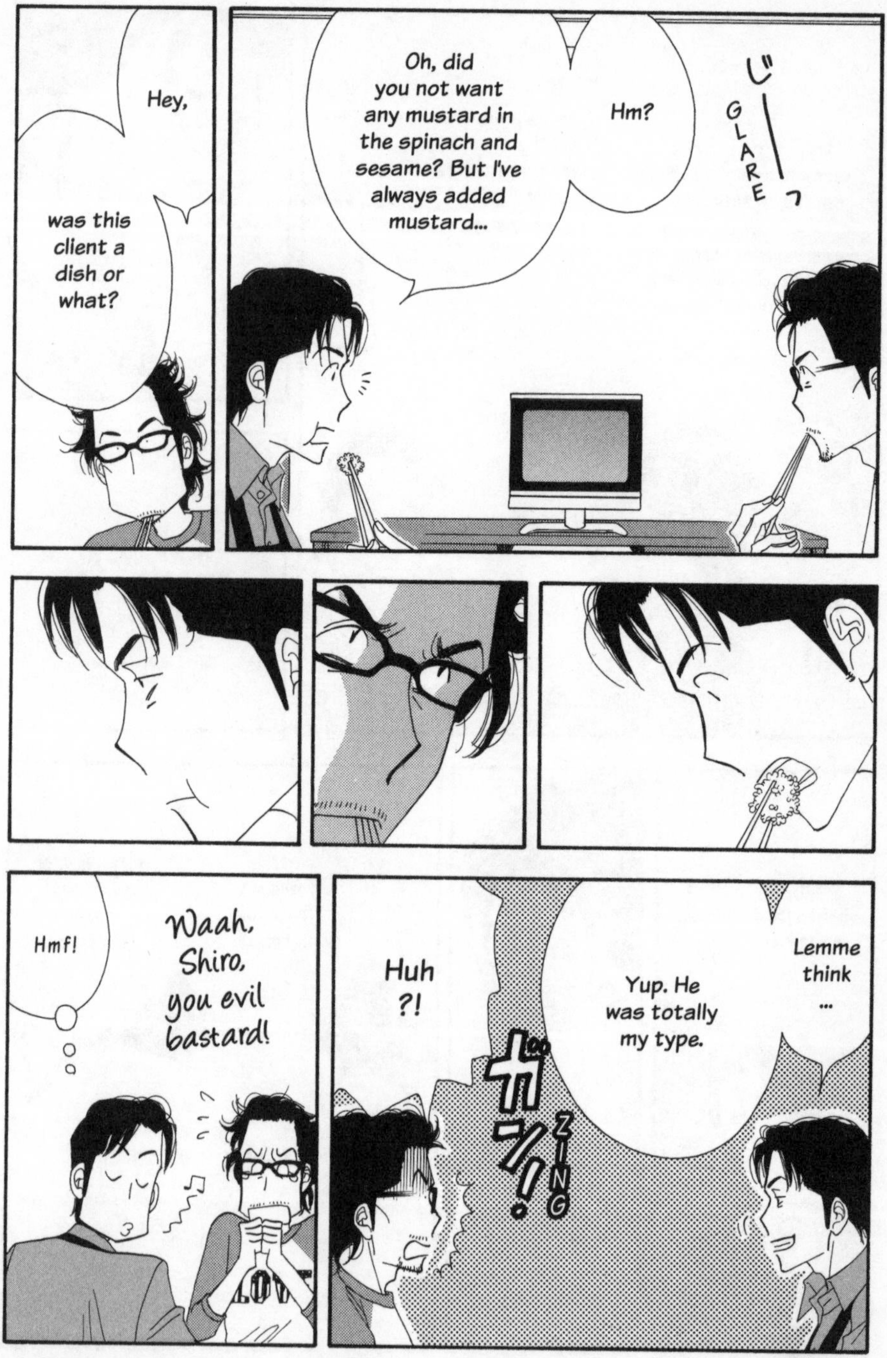
GLARE
Hm?
Oh, did you not want any mustard in the spinach and sesame? But I've always added mustard...
Hey,
was this client a dish or what?
Lemme think ...
Yup. He was totally my type.
ZING
Huh ?!
Waah, Shiro, you evil bastard!
Hmf!

#7 END

Application: Mackerel Pike Rice

Mackerel pike (*sanma*)   1
Rice   1 1/2 C
Rice wine, soy sauce, ginger, white roasted sesame seeds,
scallions

Gut pike, sprinkle with salt and grill.
Rinse rice, season with rice wine and soy sauce then cook.
Remove head and bones from pike, shred meat, mix with
julienned ginger and stir into cooked rice.
Garnish with sesame seeds and minced scallions
before serving.

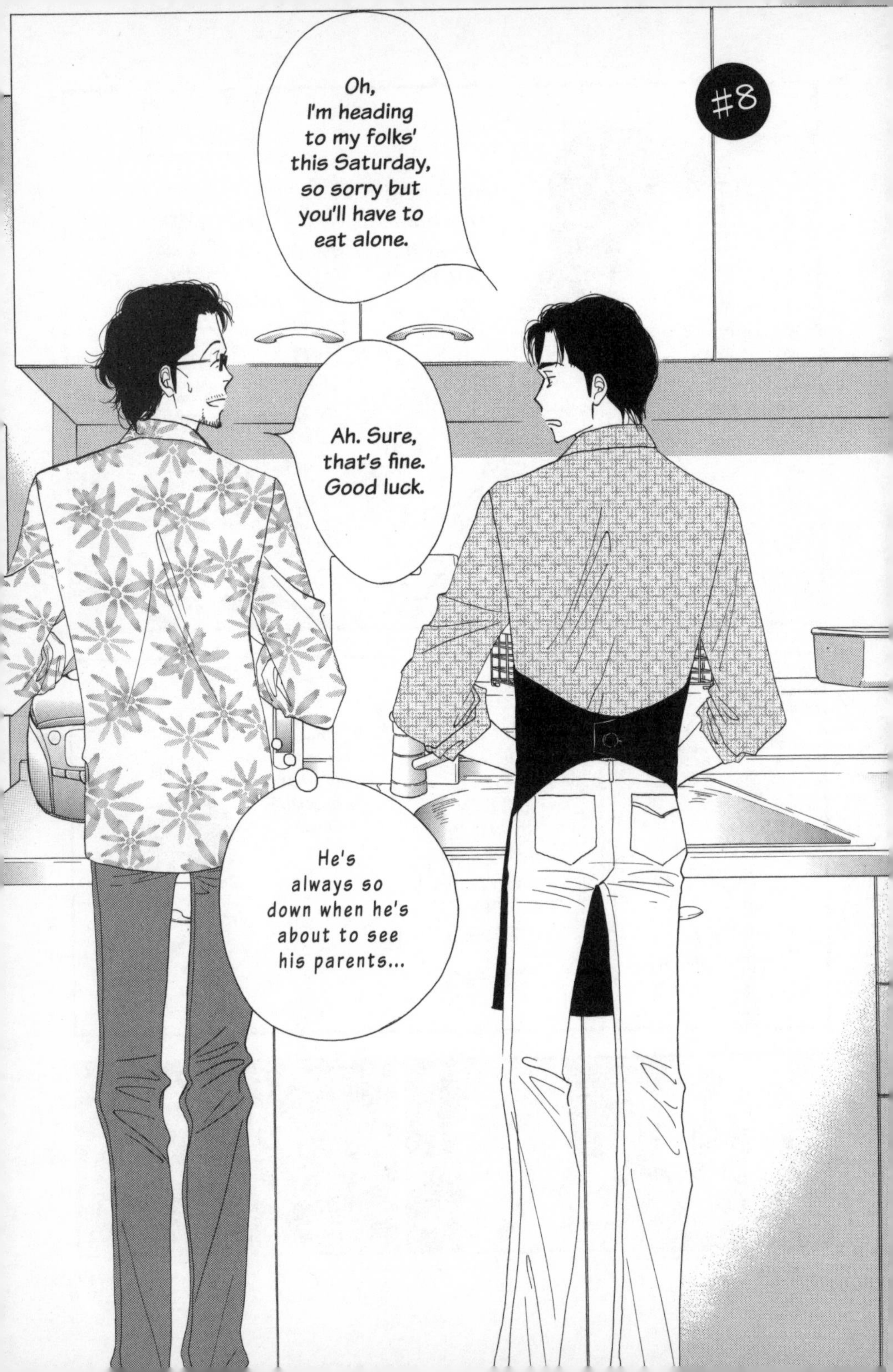
#8
Oh, I'm heading to my folks' this Saturday, so sorry but you'll have to eat alone.
Ah. Sure, that's fine. Good luck.
He's always so down when he's about to see his parents...

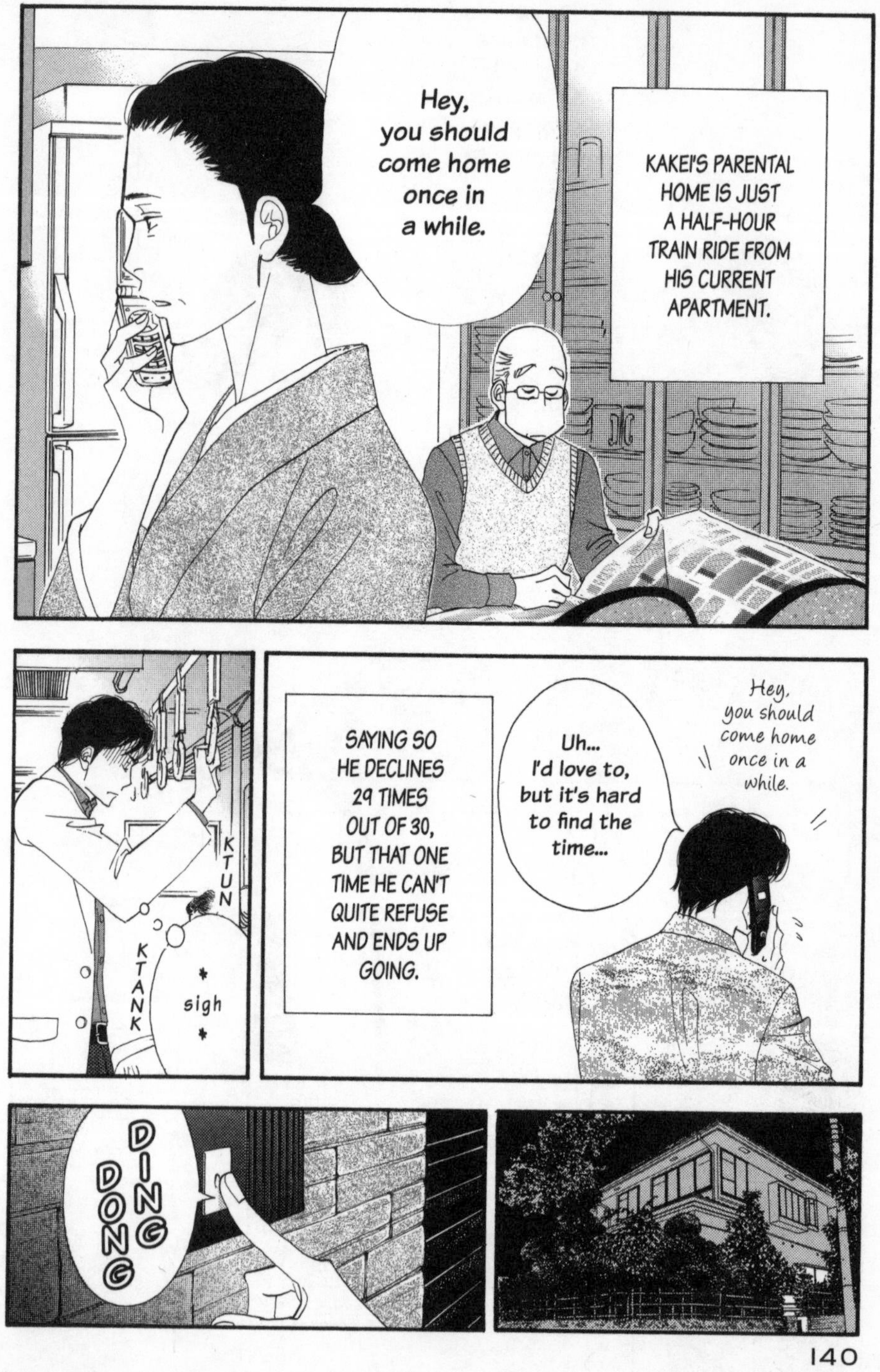
Hey, you should come home once in a while.
KAKEI'S PARENTAL HOME IS JUST A HALF-HOUR TRAIN RIDE FROM HIS CURRENT APARTMENT.
Hey, you should come home once in a while.
Uh... I'd love to, but it's hard to find the time...
SAYING SO HE DECLINES 29 TIMES OUT OF 30, BUT THAT ONE TIME HE CAN'T QUITE REFUSE AND ENDS UP GOING.
KTUN
KTANK
* sigh *
DING DONG

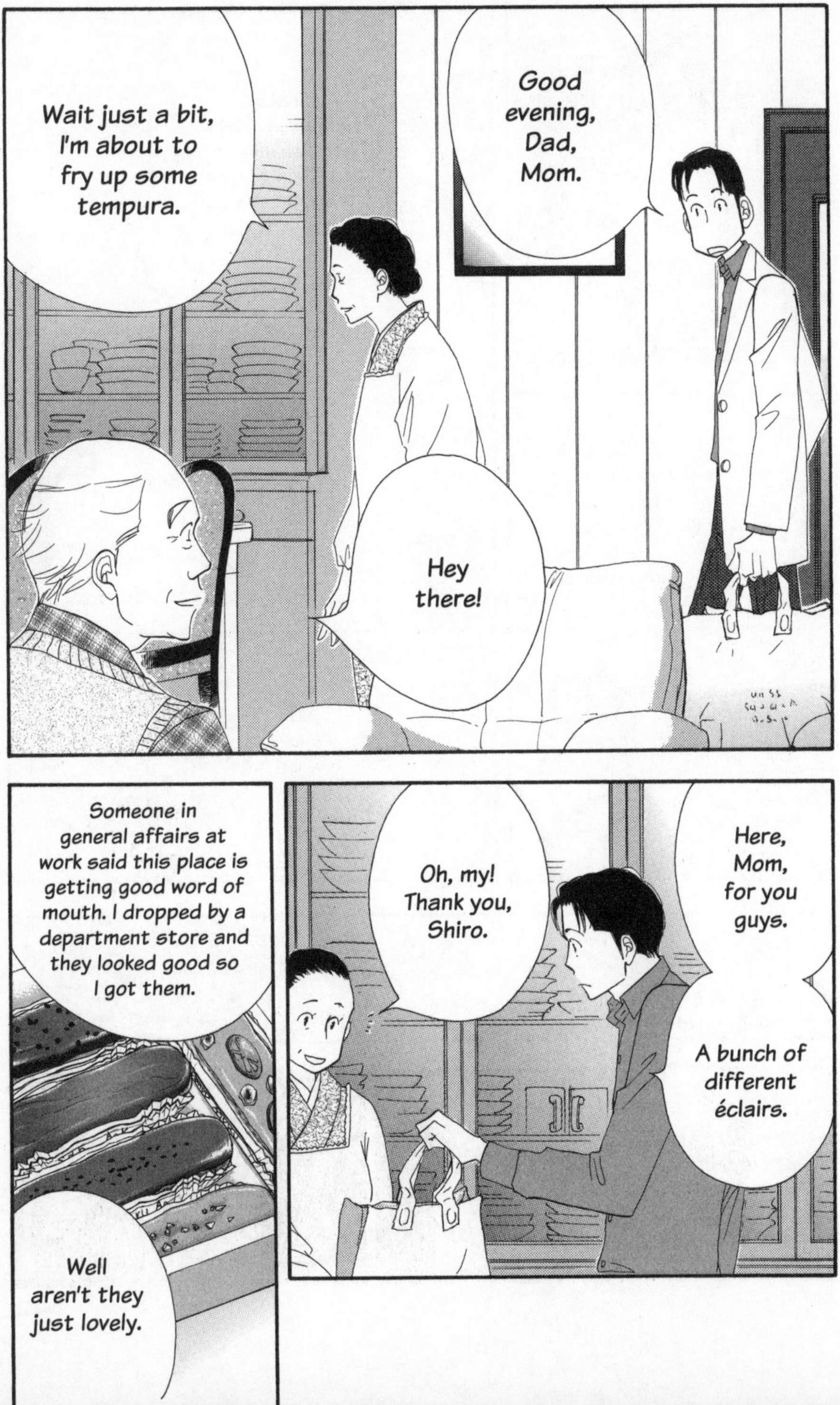
Good evening, Dad, Mom.
Wait just a bit, I'm about to fry up some tempura.
Hey there!
Here, Mom, for you guys.
A bunch of different éclairs.
Oh, my! Thank you, Shiro.
Someone in general affairs at work said this place is getting good word of mouth. I dropped by a department store and they looked good so I got them.
Well aren't they just lovely.

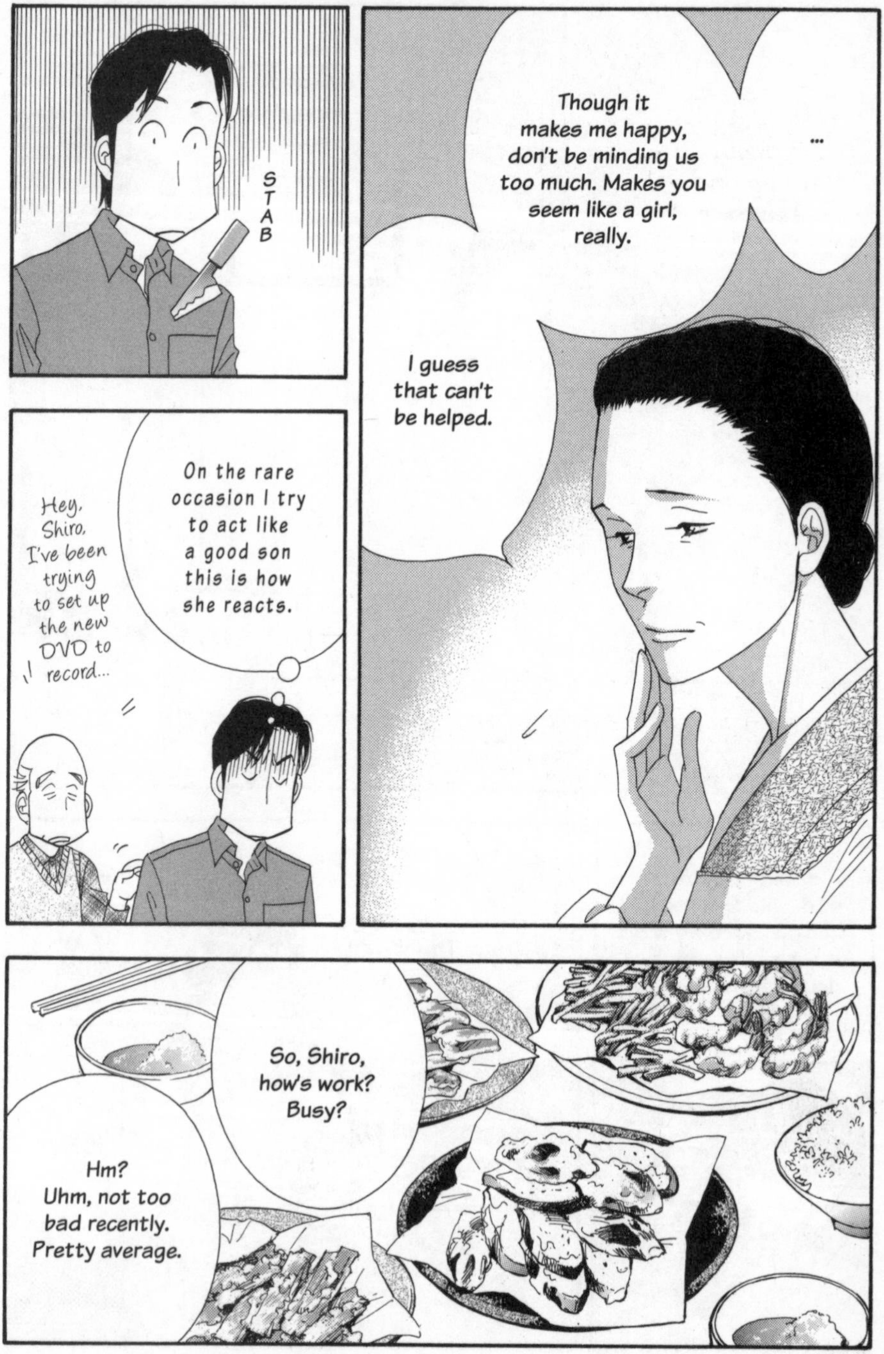
...
Though it makes me happy, don't be minding us too much. Makes you seem like a girl, really.
I guess that can't be helped.
STAB
On the rare occasion I try to act like a good son this is how she reacts.
Hey, Shiro, I've been trying to set up the new DVD to record...
So, Shiro, how's work? Busy?
Hm? Uhm, not too bad recently. Pretty average.

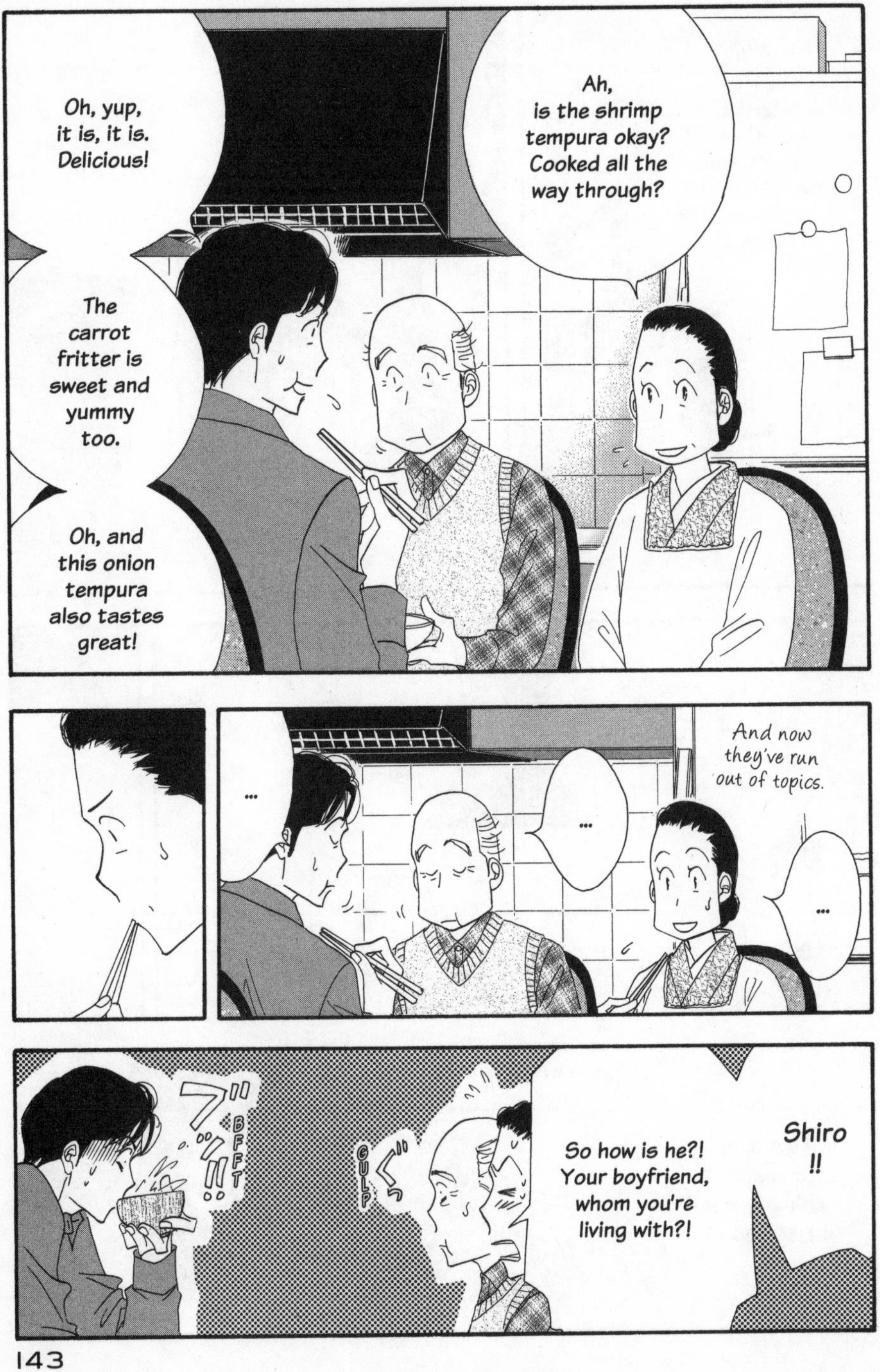
Ah, is the shrimp tempura okay? Cooked all the way through?
Oh, yup, it is, it is. Delicious!
The carrot fritter is sweet and yummy too.
Oh, and this onion tempura also tastes great!
And now they've run out of topics.
...
...
...
Shiro !!
So how is he?! Your boyfriend, whom you're living with?!
GULP
BFFT

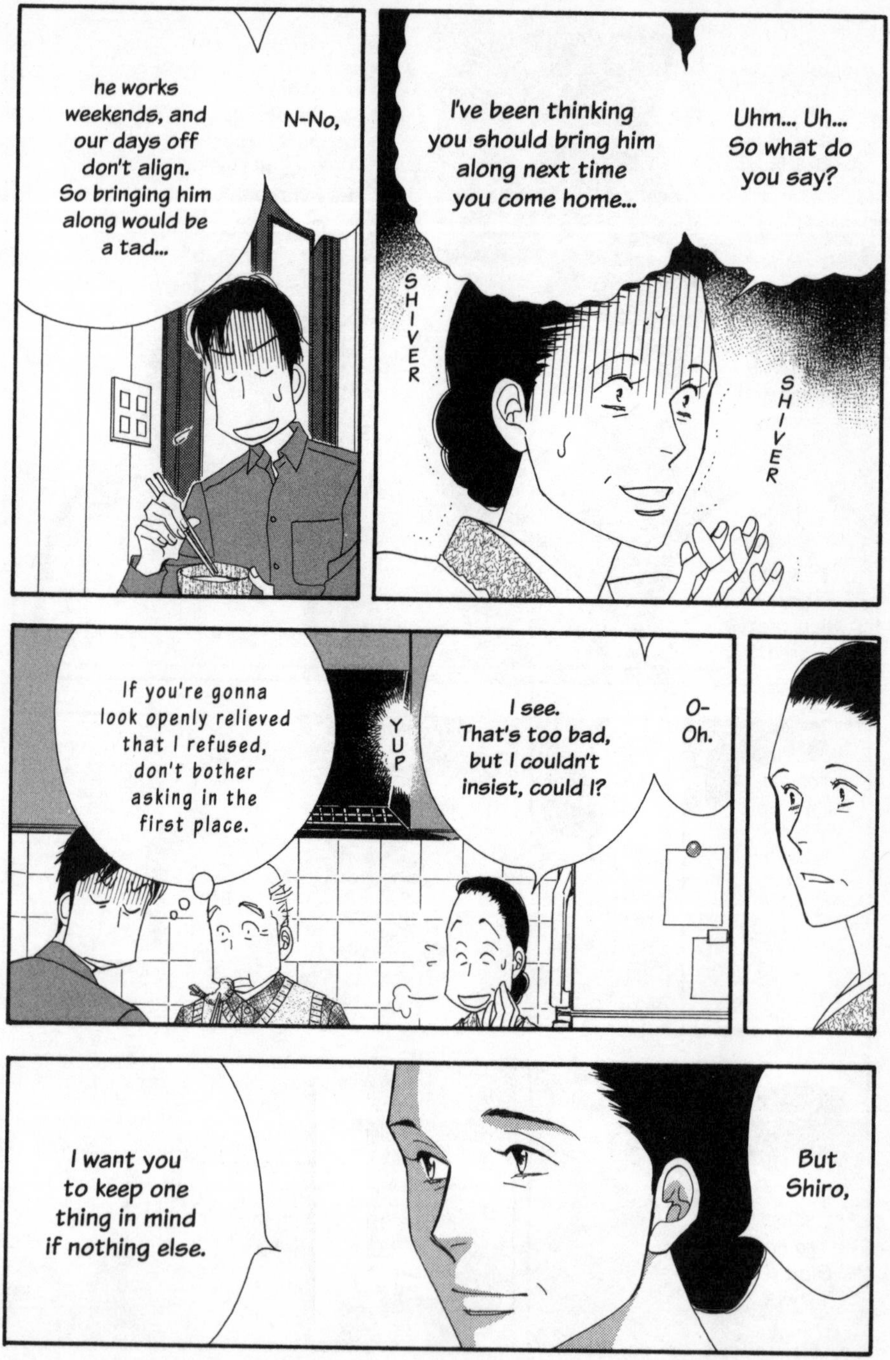
Uhm... Uh... So what do you say?
I've been thinking you should bring him along next time you come home...
SHIVER
SHIVER
N-No,
he works weekends, and our days off don't align. So bringing him along would be a tad...
O-Oh.
I see. That's too bad, but I couldn't insist, could I?
YUP
If you're gonna look openly relieved that I refused, don't bother asking in the first place.
But Shiro,
I want you to keep one thing in mind if nothing else.

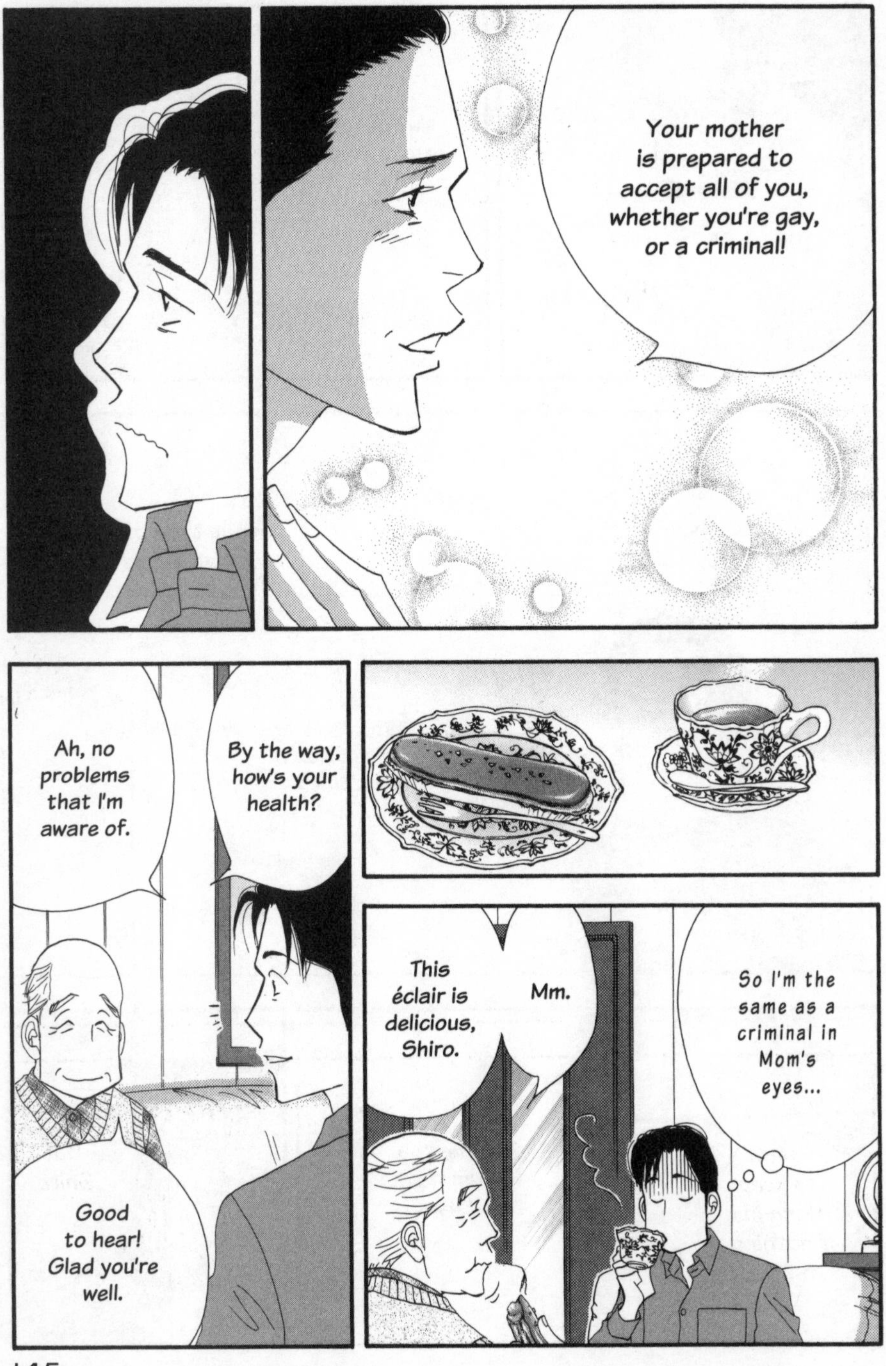
Your mother is prepared to accept all of you, whether you're gay, or a criminal!
So I'm the same as a criminal in Mom's eyes...
Mm.
This éclair is delicious, Shiro.
By the way, how's your health?
Ah, no problems that I'm aware of.
Good to hear! Glad you're well.

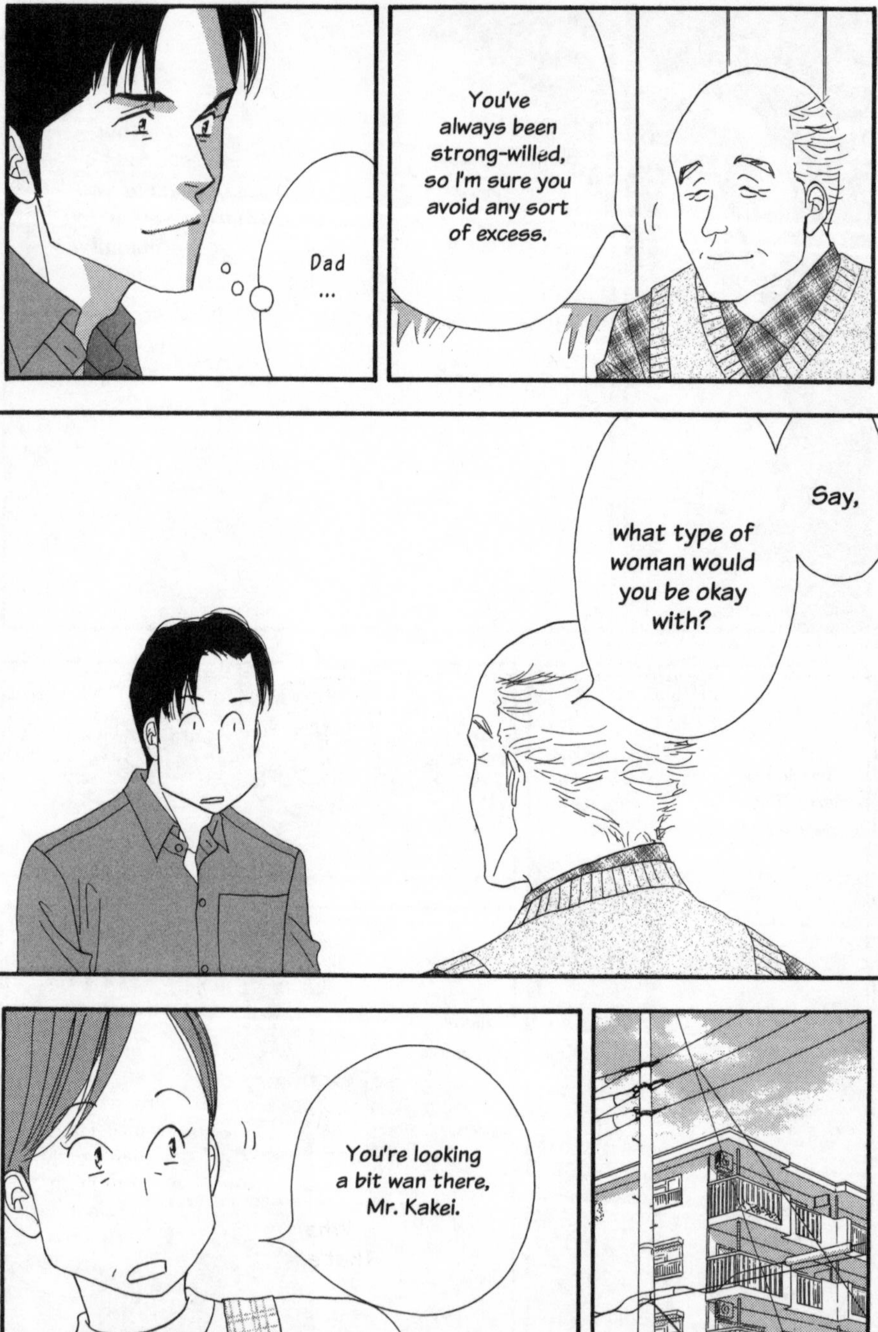
You've always been strong-willed, so I'm sure you avoid any sort of excess.
Dad ...
Say, what type of woman would you be okay with?
You're looking a bit wan there, Mr. Kakei.

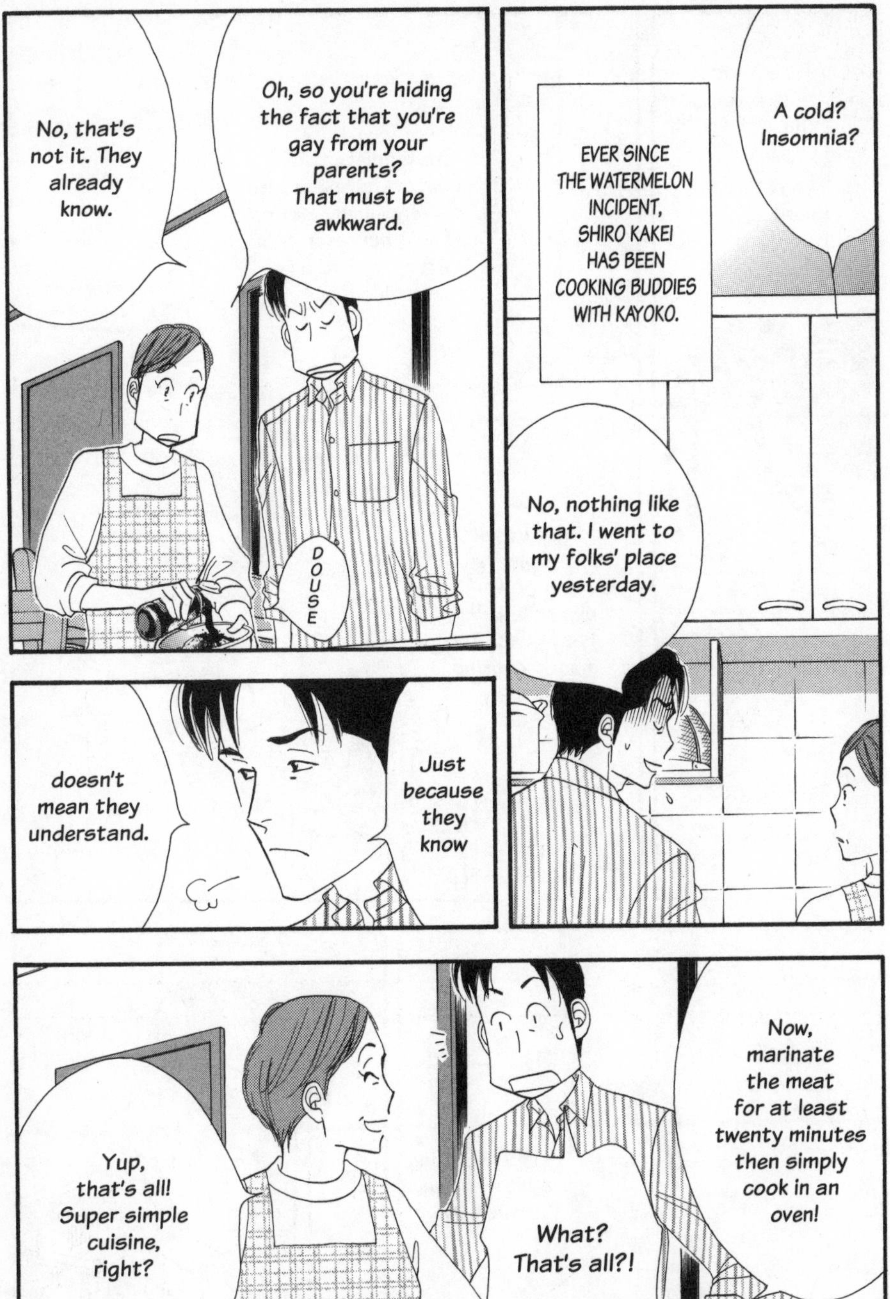
A cold? Insomnia?
EVER SINCE THE WATERMELON INCIDENT, SHIRO KAKEI HAS BEEN COOKING BUDDIES WITH KAYOKO.
No, nothing like that. I went to my folks' place yesterday.
Oh, so you're hiding the fact that you're gay from your parents? That must be awkward.
No, that's not it. They already know.
DOUSE
Just because they know
doesn't mean they understand.
Now, marinate the meat for at least twenty minutes then simply cook in an oven!
What? That's all?!
Yup, that's all! Super simple cuisine, right?

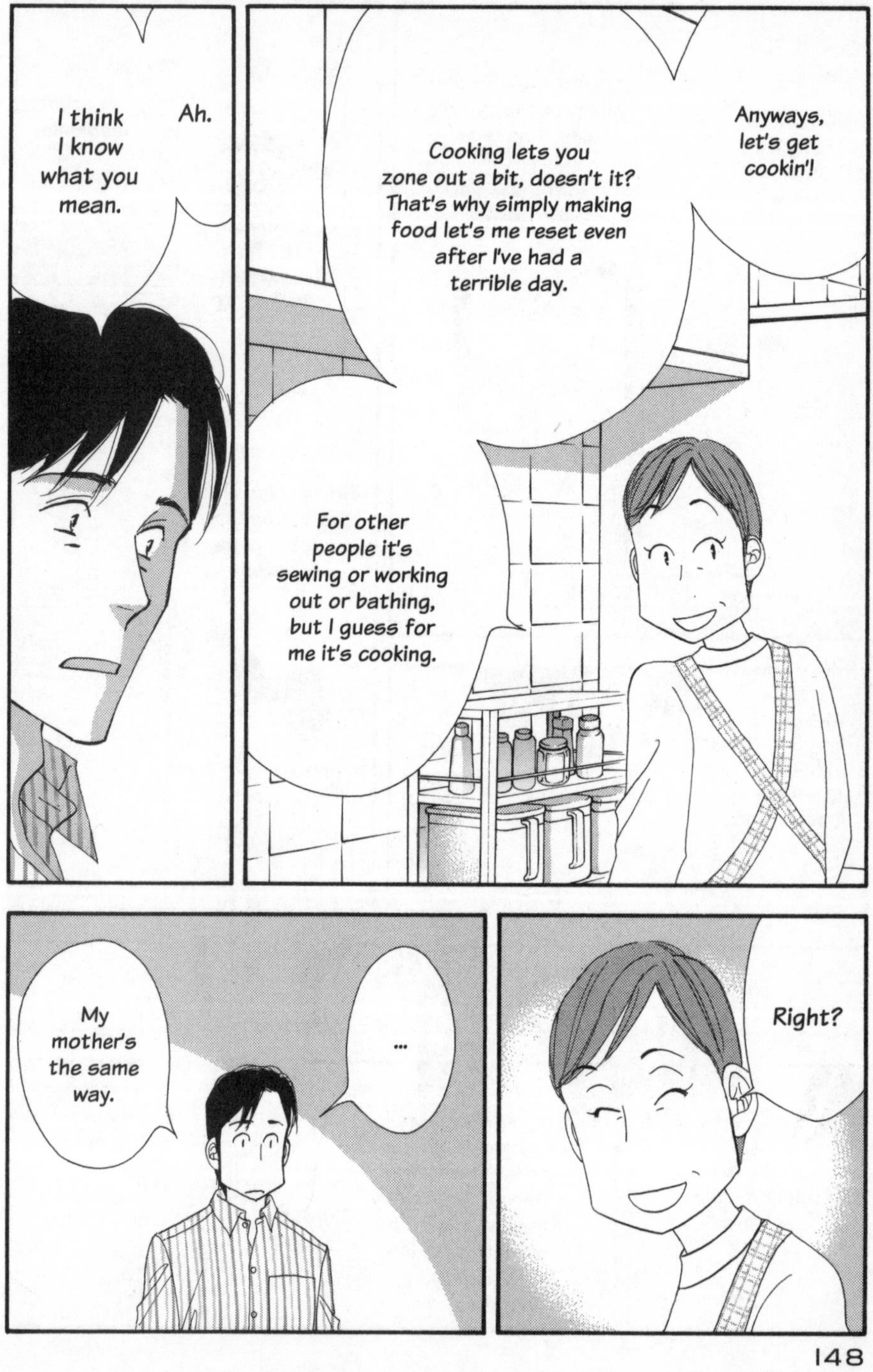

Anyways, let's get cookin'!
Cooking lets you zone out a bit, doesn't it? That's why simply making food let's me reset even after I've had a terrible day.
For other people it's sewing or working out or bathing, but I guess for me it's cooking.
Ah.
I think I know what you mean.
Right?
...
My mother's the same way.

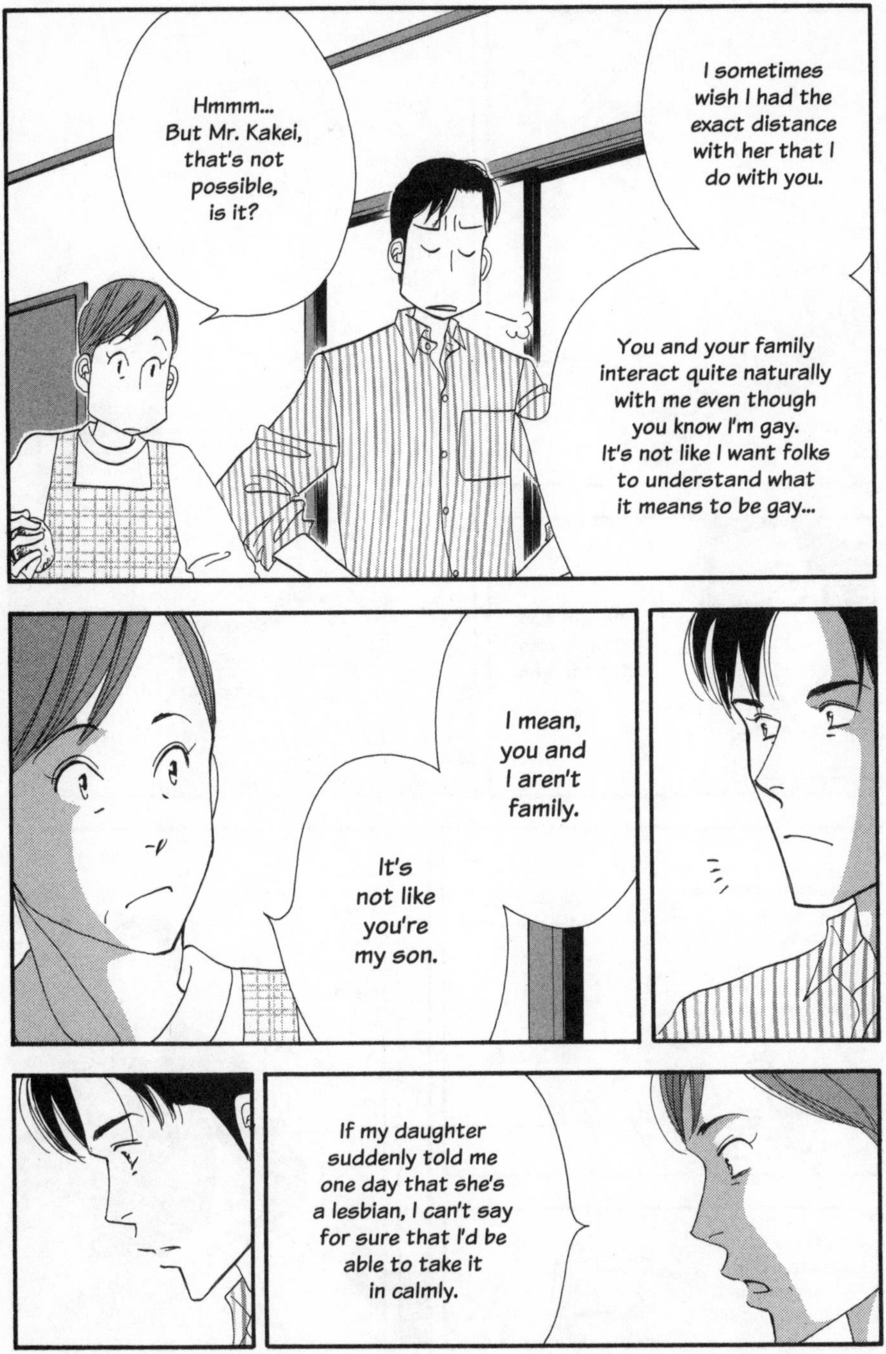
I sometimes wish I had the exact distance with her that I do with you.
You and your family interact quite naturally with me even though you know I'm gay. It's not like I want folks to understand what it means to be gay...
Hmmm... But Mr. Kakei, that's not possible, is it?
I mean, you and I aren't family.
It's not like you're my son.
If my daughter suddenly told me one day that she's a lesbian, I can't say for sure that I'd be able to take it in calmly.

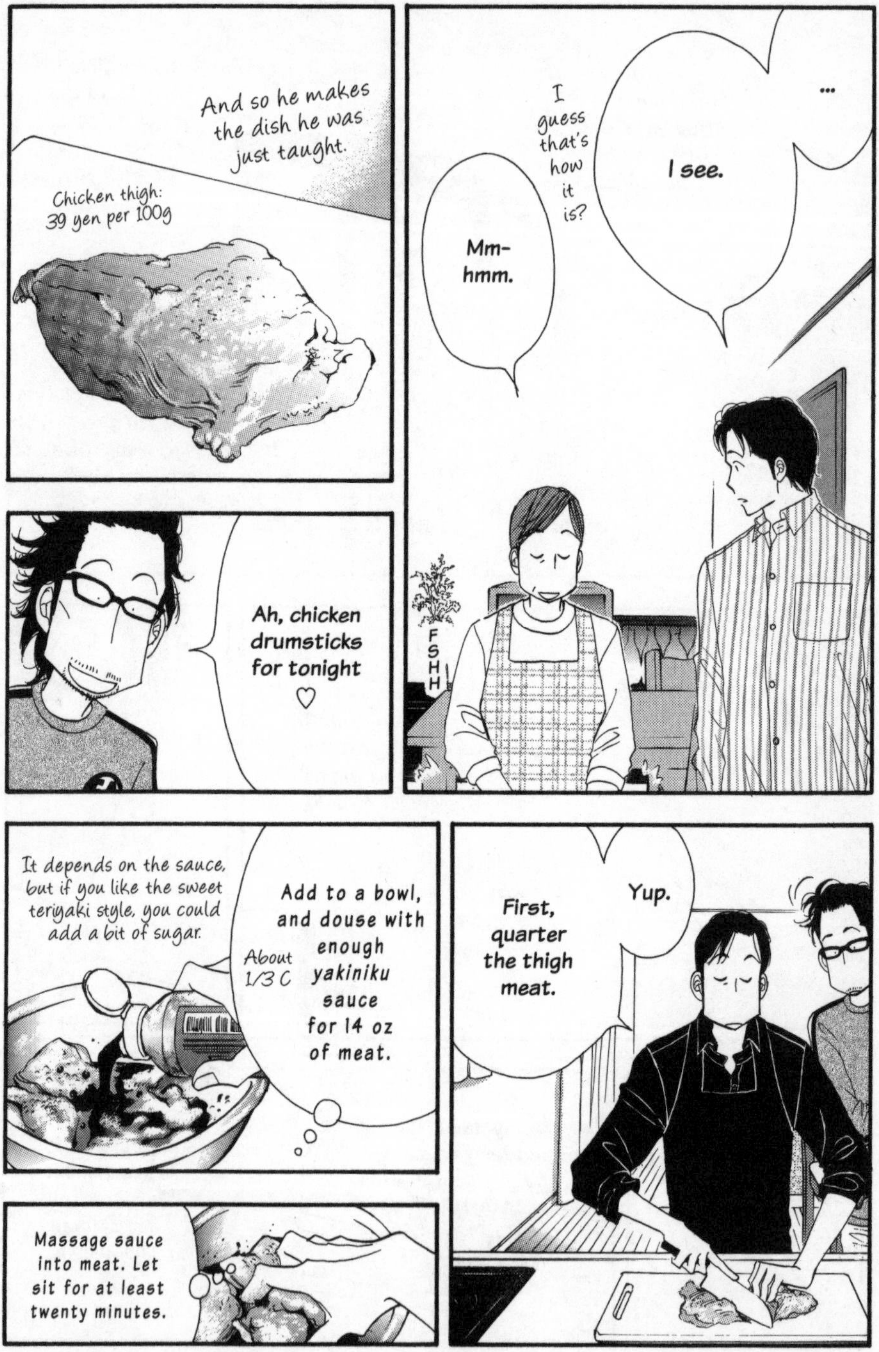
...
I see.
I guess that's how it is?
Mm-hmm.
FSHH
And so he makes the dish he was just taught.
Chicken thigh: 39 yen per 100g
Ah, chicken drumsticks for tonight ♡
Yup.
First, quarter the thigh meat.
Add to a bowl, and douse with enough yakiniku sauce for 14 oz of meat.
About 1/3 C
It depends on the sauce, but if you like the sweet teriyaki style, you could add a bit of sugar.
Massage sauce into meat. Let sit for at least twenty minutes.

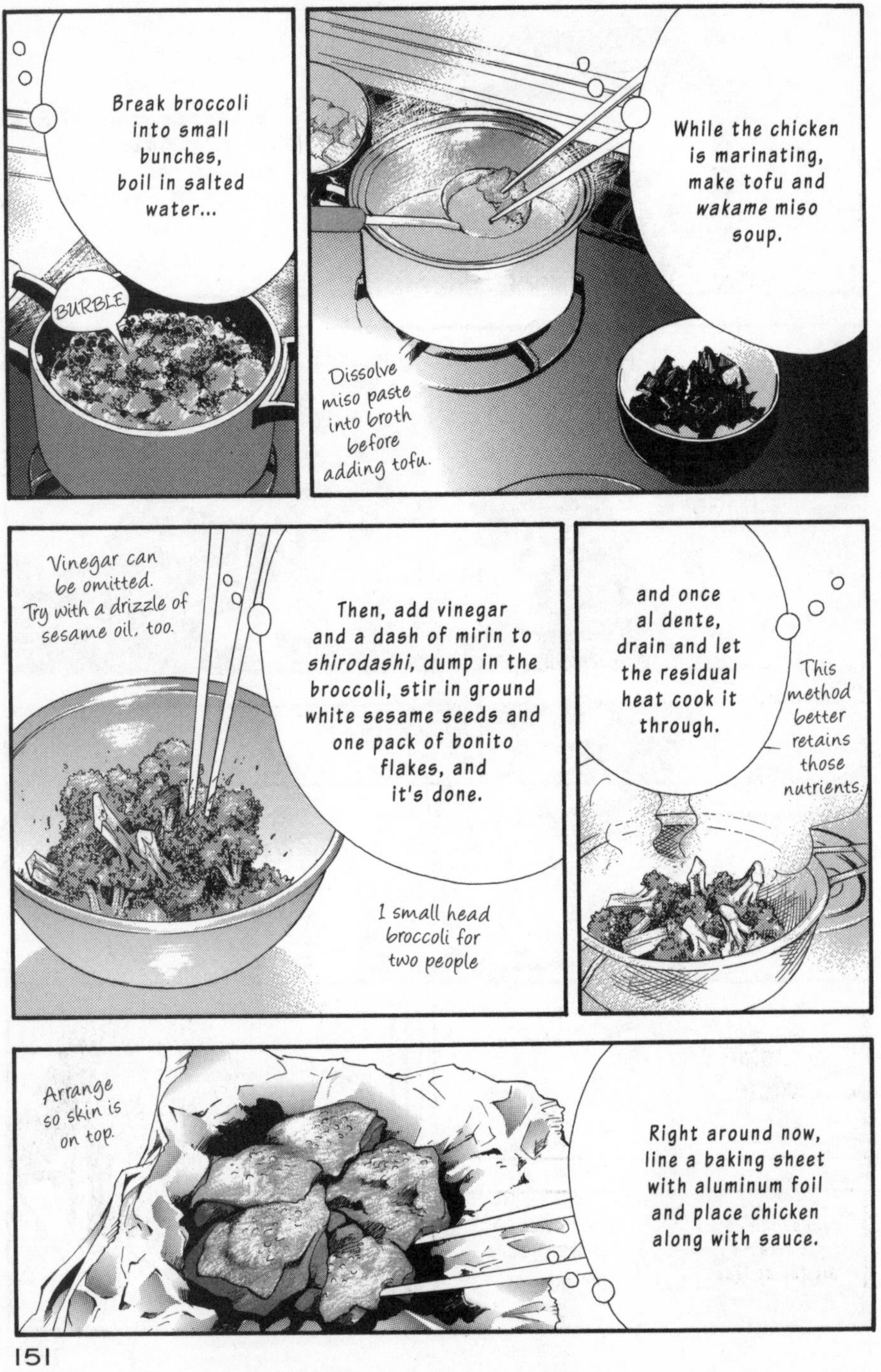
While the chicken is marinating, make tofu and *wakame* miso soup.
Dissolve miso paste into broth before adding tofu.
Break broccoli into small bunches, boil in salted water...
BURBLE
and once al dente, drain and let the residual heat cook it through.
This method better retains those nutrients.
Then, add vinegar and a dash of mirin to *shirodashi*, dump in the broccoli, stir in ground white sesame seeds and one pack of bonito flakes, and it's done.
Vinegar can be omitted. Try with a drizzle of sesame oil, too.
1 small head broccoli for two people
Right around now, line a baking sheet with aluminum foil and place chicken along with sauce.
Arrange so skin is on top.

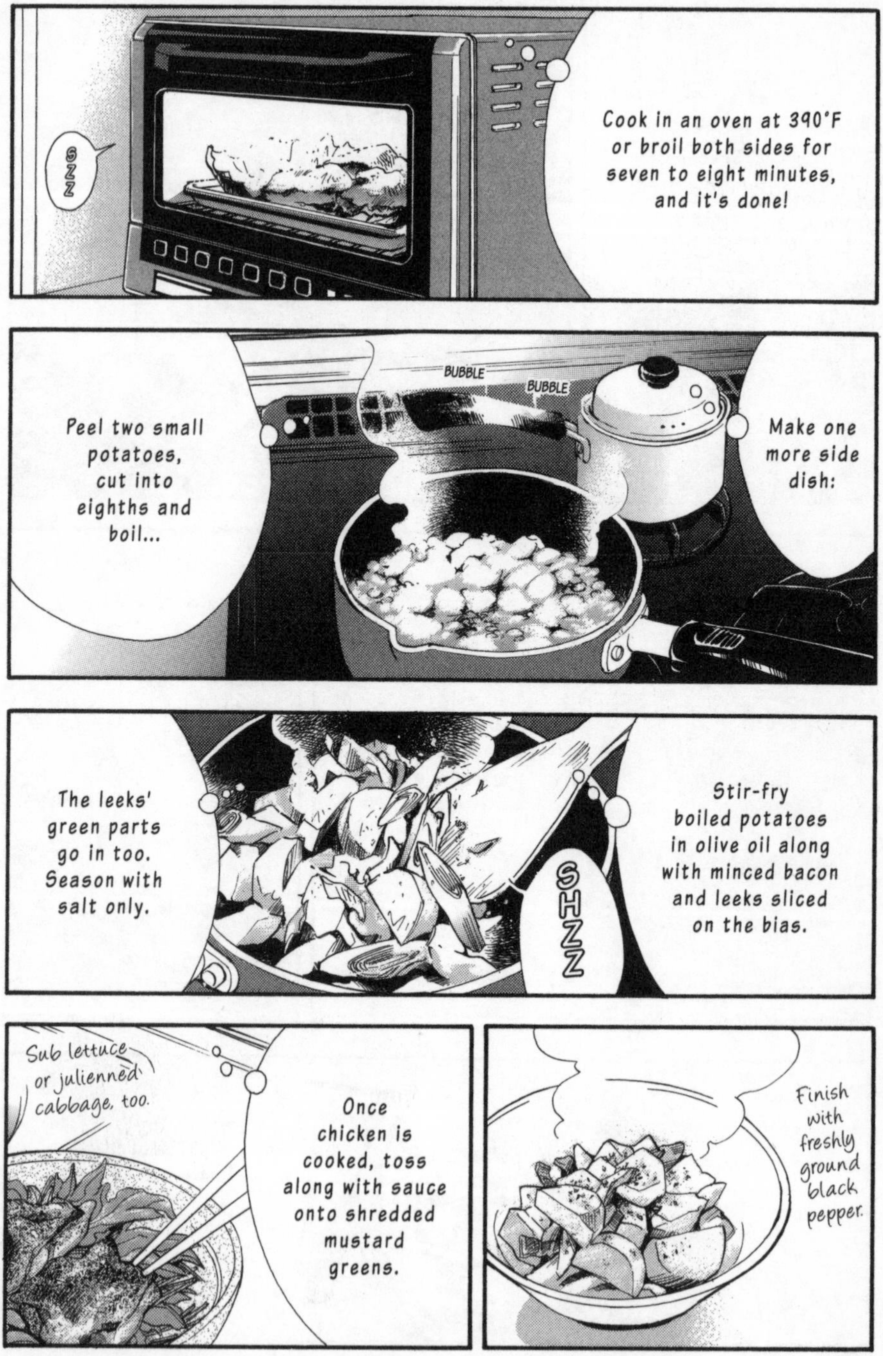
Cook in an oven at 390°F or broil both sides for seven to eight minutes, and it's done!
SZZ
Make one more side dish:
BUBBLE
BUBBLE
Peel two small potatoes, cut into eighths and boil...
Stir-fry boiled potatoes in olive oil along with minced bacon and leeks sliced on the bias.
SHZZ
The leeks' green parts go in too. Season with salt only.
Finish with freshly ground black pepper.
Once chicken is cooked, toss along with sauce onto shredded mustard greens.
Sub lettuce or julienned cabbage, too.

Done!

Today's Menu
- Oven-roasted chicken
- German potatoes with leeks
- Tosa-style sesame-dressed broccoli
- Tofu and wakame miso soup

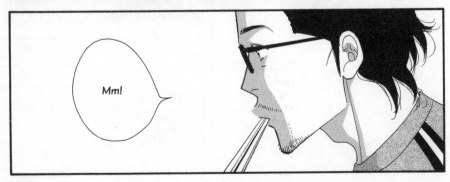

Mm!

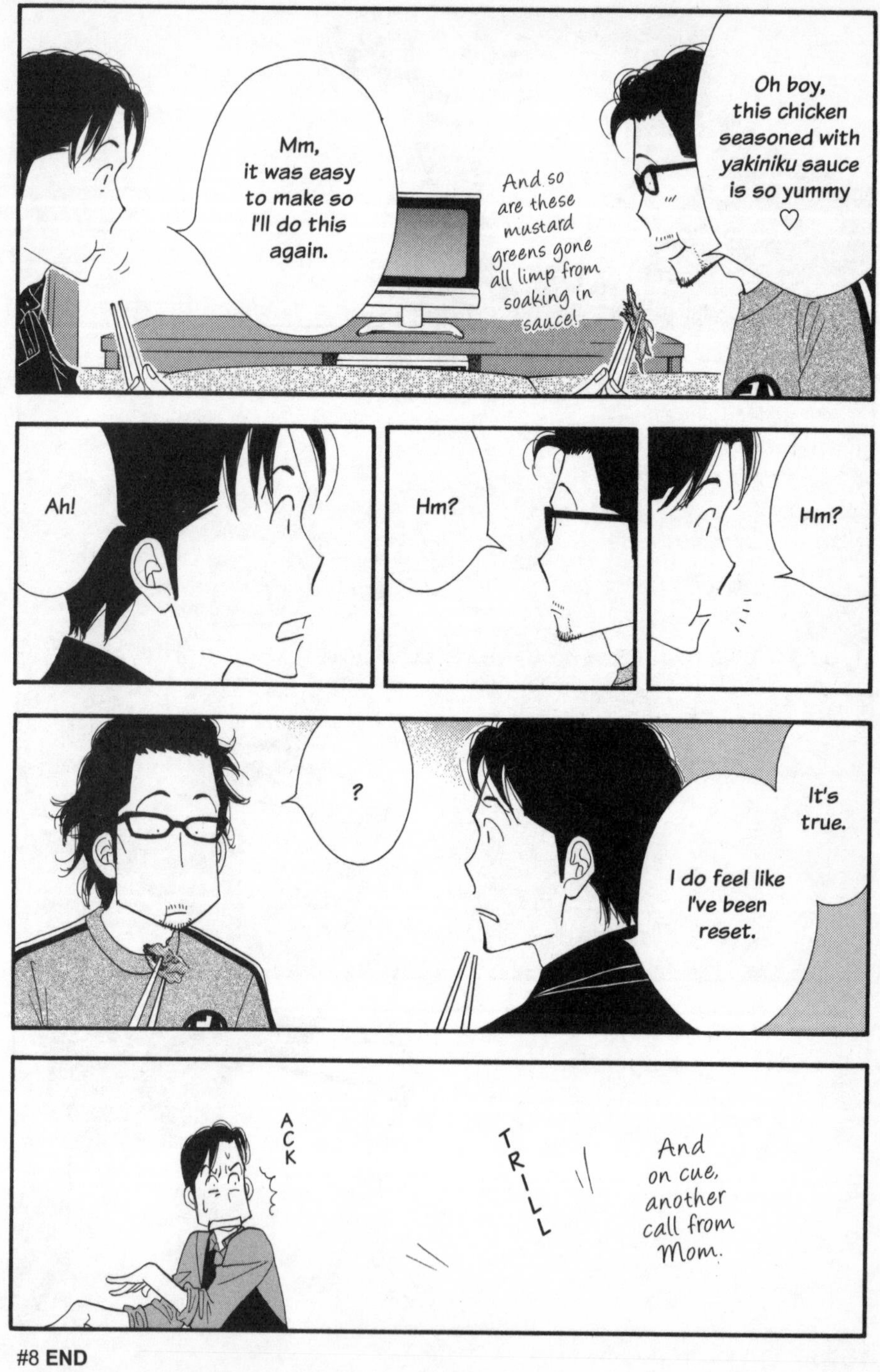
Oh boy, this chicken seasoned with yakiniku sauce is so yummy ♡
And so are these mustard greens gone all limp from soaking in sauce!
Mm, it was easy to make so I'll do this again.
Hm?
Hm?
Ah!
It's true.
I do feel like I've been reset.
?
And on cue, another call from Mom.
TRILL
ACK

#8 END

This episode featured broccoli prepared Tosa-style with sesame seeds, but you can use the same recipe with cabbage and onions:

Shred cabbage.
Slice 1/2 onion into 1/4" wedges.
Place vegetables in a heat-safe dish,
cover with plastic wrap and microwave for 4 to 5 minutes.
Stir in *shirodashi*, ground sesame seeds and
bonito flakes and it's done.
(Due to the onions' sweetness, you don't need mirin.)

what did you eat yesterday?, volume 1

translation: Maya Rosewood
production: Risa Cho
Tomoe Tsutsumi

Translation provided by Vertical, 2014
published by Kodansha USA publishing, LLC

originally published in Japanese as Kinou nani tabeta? 1 by Kodansha, Ltd.
Kinou nani tabeta? first serialized in Morning, Kodansha, Ltd., 2007-

This is a work of fiction.

ISBN: 978-1-939130-38-9

Manufactured in Canada

First edition

fifth printing

Kodansha USA publishing, LLC
451 park avenue south
7th floor
new york, ny 10016
www.kodansha.us

The Next volume Includes

spinach lasagne
Mentaiko sour cream dip & baguette
Herb-crusted grilled chicken
Tuna salad
Thick fried tofu, chives and cabbage
Miso pork stir-fry
citrus and soy sauce napa cabbage
wakame soup
Amberjack and daikon
Thick fried tofu grilled with miso
soy sauce-boiled chives
Egg soup with trefoil

etc...

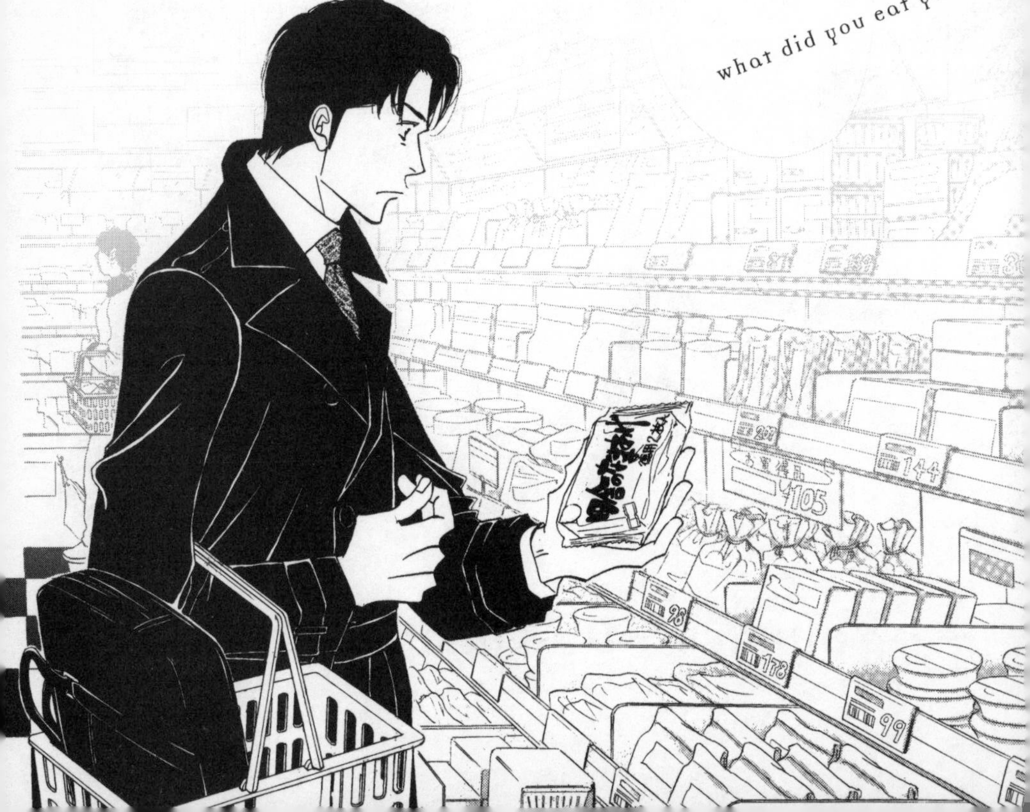
what did you eat yesterday

Prepare to be Bewitched!

Makoto Kowata, a novice witch, packs up her belongings (including a black cat familiar) and moves in with her distant cousins in rural Aomori to complete her training and become a full-fledged witch.

"*Flying Witch* emphasizes that while actual magic is nice, there is ultimately magic in everything." —Anime News Network

The Basis for the Hit Anime from Sentai Filmworks!

Volumes 1-9 Available Now!

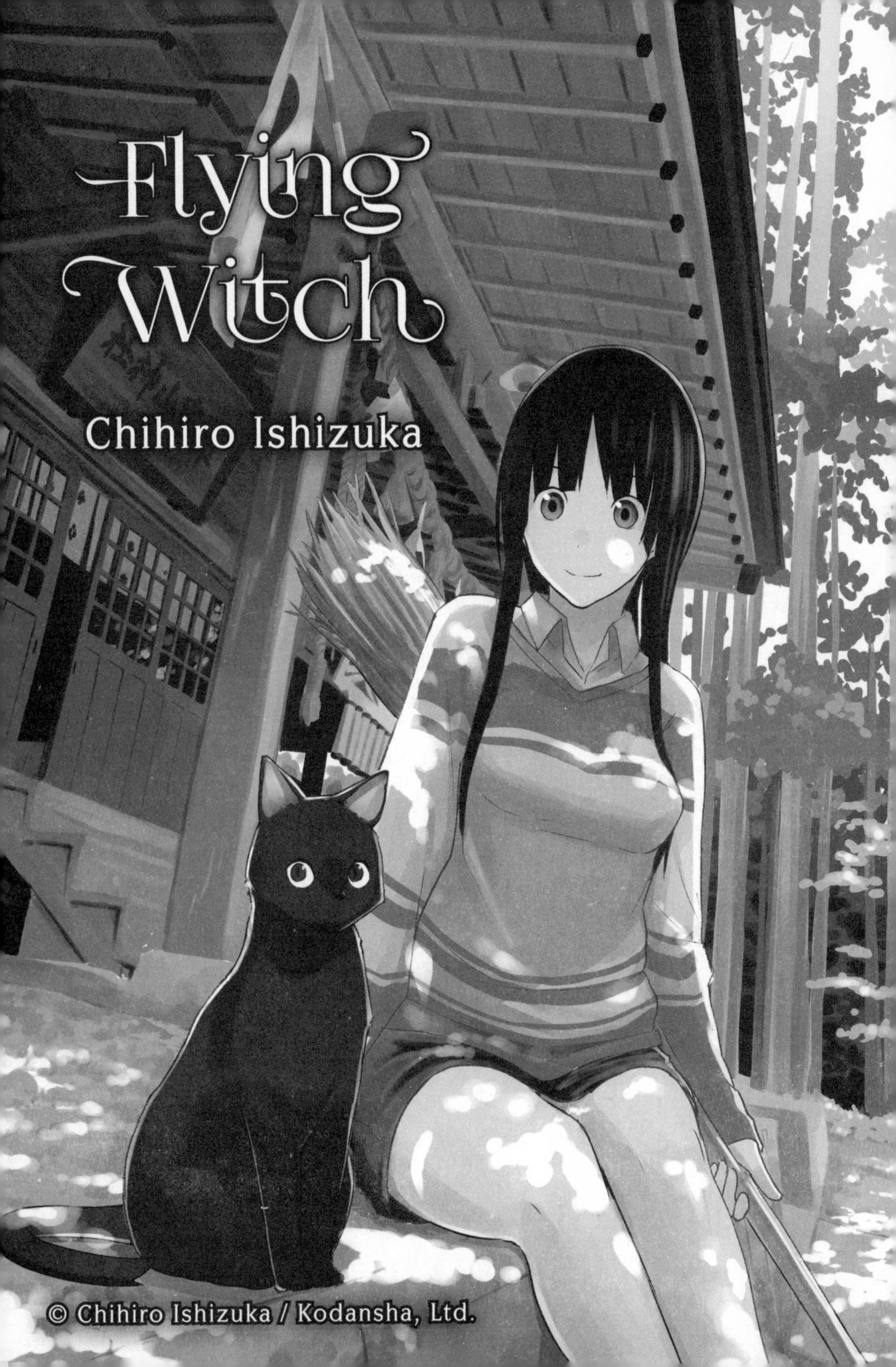
Flying Witch
Chihiro Ishizuka

WRONG WAY

japanese books, including manga like this one,
are meant to be read from right to left.
so the front cover is actually the back cover, and vice versa.
to read this book, please flip it over
and start in the top right-hand corner.
Read the panels, and the bubbles in the panels,
from right to left,
then drop down to the next row and repeat.
it may make you dizzy at first, but forcing your brain
to do things backwards makes you smarter in the long run.
we swear.